Regional and Interregional Intersectoral Flow Analysis

Regional and Interregional Intersectoral Flow Analysis

The Method and an Application to the Tennessee Economy

By Tong Hun Lee,
John R. Moore,
and David P. Lewis

THE UNIVERSITY
OF TENNESSEE PRESS
KNOXVILLE

Library of Congress Catalog Card Number 72-187360
International Standard Book Number 0-87049-139-3

Library of Congress Cataloging in Publication Data

Lee, Tong Hun.
Regional and interregional intersectoral flow analysis.

Includes bibliographical references.
1. Tennessee—Economic conditions. 2. Interindustry economics. I. Moore, John Robert, 1928- joint author. II. Lewis, David P., joint author. III. Title.
HC107.T3L42 330.9'768'05 72-187360
ISBN 0-87049-139-3

Preface

Interest in interindustry economics has broadened in recent years. In part this interest is manifested in the increasingly sophisticated models presented in the literature, and in part it is evidenced by the enthusiasm for interindustry data on the part of planners and others in business and government. Such an interest on the part of government planners and other state officials was, in fact, the motivation for the research underlying this monograph. Originally suggested by the Department of Research of the Tennessee State Planning Commission, the project soon engaged the joint interests of a number of departments of Tennessee state government. This interest extended to active participation in many of the basic decisions regarding the scope, objectives, and procedures of the study, which were further shaped in several conferences between representatives of these governmental departments and the research staff. An important aspect of the conduct of this research has been this close cooperation between academic researchers on the one hand and government officials as the consumers of this research on the other.

Originally we felt that the interest in our research would be entirely local and that our responsibilities could be discharged with a report directed to the sponsors of the research. Gradually we have felt that because of certain methodological and procedural innovations, the study might interest a wider audience. Our research has resulted in the production of a mass of significant data about interindustry and interregional linkages in the Tennessee economy with only a modest expenditure of money. Other states and regions might well wish to undertake research similar to that reported here since it involves securing many of the advantages of the "ideal" type of interregional input-output analysis but at far less expense. Outside of the United States there should also be an interest in the methodological and procedural innovations suggested here. In underdeveloped areas, in particular, where base multipliers can be important in development planning, the approach suggested can be very valuable since the cost, even in a multiregional application, would be much less than the traditional single-region input-output approach. The present models are also useful for economic planning of underdeveloped countries, which is demonstrated, for example, in evaluating the contribution of the Tennessee Valley Authority to regional economic development.

In presenting the models employed in the Tennessee study, it has been necessary to use basic matrix algebra, but this has been confined to Chapter 3. Those with some training in mathematics will find the discussion easy to follow, and even those with no background in matrices will find that the general features of the model can be followed. Those with limited mathematical background may find it helpful to review the essential concepts as presented in a few pages by Richard Stone in *Input-Output and National Accounts* (Paris: Organization for European Economic Co-operation, 1961; see especially pp. 74-82). In fact, the monograph has been organized so that it can be utilized by a number of different audiences. The general reader not interested in the details of model construction will probably wish to read Chapters 1 and 2, which constitute a survey and review of the literature, and Chapters 4 through 7, which describe the application of the regional and interregional models to Tennessee. Those interested in methodology alone will find Chapters 1 through 3 and perhaps Chapter 7 of interest. Readers primarily concerned with implementation of intersectoral flow analysis will want to concentrate on Chapters 1, 3, and 4, while those interested in the structural analysis of the Tennessee economy and its implications for recent structural hypotheses in interindustry analyses will want to read Chapters 5 and 6.

Individually and as a group, the authors owe a heavy debt of gratitude to many organizations and individuals who assisted at various stages in our work. We are grateful for the financial support received from various units of Tennessee state government, from the University of Tennessee, from the Graduate School of the University of Wisconsin-Milwaukee, from Valdosta State College, and in part from the National Science Foundation. We owe a particular debt of gratitude to Dr. David Grubbs, formerly Director of Research of the Tennessee State Planning Commission, who originally conceived the study and who served as our principal contact with the interested agencies of state government. Many individuals, too many to list, in various offices of state government gave of their time and knowledge to assist us in conferences and in response to requests for specific information.

Dean Arthur E. Warner of the University of Tennessee, College of Business Administration, has been a constant source of patient assistance in dealing with a number of problems relating to housing, staffing, and financing which otherwise would have become a real burden for the research staff. Dr. J. Fred Holly, then head of the Department of Economics, provided help and encouragement throughout the project. Additionally, we have benefited from the advice and counsel of Dr. John E. Lewis, formerly Director of the University of Tennessee Center for Business and Economic Research, and his successor, Dr. A. B. Biscoe, Jr. Ormond Corry of that center was a continual source of help in matters dealing with data sources. Associated with the project as graduate assistants and contributing heavily in the areas of data collection and processing have been Thomas Bieler, Charles Wiesner, Robert Ballance, and Lewis Siegal. Gerald McLaughlin was of invaluable assistance as our programmer. Finally, we note with gratitude our appreciation of the patient efforts of our efficient secretaries, Miss Marianne Greer, Miss Phyllis Jarboe, and Mrs. Edna Johnson.

Tong Hun Lee
The University of Wisconsin-Milwaukee

John R. Moore
The University of Tennessee, Knoxville

David P. Lewis
The University of Alabama, Birmingham

Contents

Preface *page v*

1. **Introduction** *1*

2. **Recent Developments in Interindustry Analysis** *6*

3. **The Models** *12*
   Regional Intersectoral Flow Model, *13*; Comparison with the Hansen-Tiebout Regional Model, *17*; Interregional Intersectoral Flow Model, *19*; Operational Advantages and Limitations, *25*

4. **Approach to Empirical Implementation** *30*
   Geographical Breakdown, *30*; Classification of Intermediate Sectors, *31*; Classification of Final-Demand Sectors, *33*; Unit of Analysis, *36*; Data on Employment, *36*; Sample Surveys on Sales Flows of Nonagricultural Sectors, *37*; Data on Sales Flows of Agricultural Sectors, *41*

5. **The Statewide Model: The Empirical Results** *43*
   Overall View of the Flow Table and the Multiplier Matrix, *44*; Intermediate-Sector Employment Multipliers, *47*; Final-Demand Multipliers, *55*; A Comparison of the Fundamental Structure of Production for the Tennessee and California Economies, *58*; Summary, *65*

6. **The Interregional Model: The Empirical Results** *69*
   Three-Region Intermediate-Sector Employment Multipliers, *71*; Interregional Final-Demand Multipliers, *87*; Interregional Feedback and Other Interregional Linkages, *94*; Summary, *97*

7. **Summary and Conclusions** *100*
   Some Contributions to Methodology, *100*; Empirical Findings and Their Implications, *102*; Pros and Cons of the Rows-Only Approach, *105*; Concluding Remarks, *107*

Appendix A: Tables of Basic Data *109*

Appendix B: The Form of Interview Questionnaires Used for Manufacturing Firms *147*

Bibliography *159*

Index *162*

List of Illustrations

Geographical Breakdown of Tennessee, As Adapted for Study of Its Economy *32*

Tables

Table 1. Intermediate Sector Numbers and Descriptions *34*
Table 2. Final-Demand Sector Symbols and Descriptions *35*
Table 3. Summary of Sectoral and Geographic Distribution of Usable Responses *38*
Table 4. Intermediate-Sector Employment Multipliers: Statewide Model *48*
Table 5. Final-Demand Multipliers: Statewide Model *57*
Table 6. Numbering and Description of Combined Sectors *60*
Table 7. The Fundamental Structure of Production—Tennessee *62*
Table 8. The Fundamental Structure of Production—California *63*
Table 9. Three-Region Employment Multipliers *72*
Table 10. Interregional Final-Demand Multipliers *88*
Table 11. Overall Percentage Errors *96*

Table A-1. Statewide Intersectoral Flow Table for Tennessee, 1964 *111*
Table A-2. Statewide Multiplier Matrix for Tennessee, 1964 *116*
Table A-3. Three-Region Multiplier Matrix for Tennessee, 1964 *120*

1. Introduction

Regional science or regional analysis is a field of inquiry which has expanded at a phenomenal pace during the last two decades. While one of the major characteristics of regional science is its interdisciplinary nature, the field has also drawn heavily upon the older methods in economic analyses. An example is the important contribution which interindustry (input-output, or intersectoral flow) analysis has made in regional studies.

Economists have been interested in interindustry types of relationships for many years. Most treatises trace this interest back to the Physiocrats in the latter portion of the eighteenth century. More important in the background of modern interindustry economics, however, is the work of Leon Walras in the field of general equilibrium economics. While Walras was able to specify in terms of a theoretical model the essential nature of economic interdependence, empirical implementation of his model was not considered at the time. The modern history of interindustry economics has its beginnings in the work of Wassily Leontief, who during the last few decades has modified and adapted the Walrasian framework for empirical implementation.[1]

Modern interindustry economics may mean different things to different people. To some, interindustry economics is simply a device for illustrating the underlying structure and logic of sectoral interdependence. For others interindustry economics provides the basis for one of the forms or systems of social accounts, occupying a place along with balance of payments accounts, national income accounts, and money flows accounts as a systematic way of presenting and summarizing the data which describe past and current economic activity.

Then there are those who regard this system as most useful as a device for planning. From a planning standpoint, interindustry analysis is useful as a means for generating forecasts of activity on a disaggregated, sectoral basis. Furthermore, it can be adapted or coupled with various side calculations to yield estimates of employment, housing and transportation requirements, educational needs, environmental control, and government revenue and expenditure requirements, all of which are necessary ingredients in the planning process. Certainly, the planning focus is of prime interest to economists in centrally directed economies working with interindustry studies, and the interest in these and other types of economies in the many multipliers which can be derived from interindustry studies is indicative of this planning focus. These types of concerns are, of course, interrelated, and no sharp distinction can be made among them. At the same time, it seems desirable to keep these somewhat divergent interests in mind in the empirical application of interindustry economics.

Until the 1950s, interest in interindustry studies was confined almost exclusively to applications to national economies. Since then, however, regional and interregional interindustry studies of increasing sophistication have appeared in ever-increasing volume. In the regional models an area smaller than the nation, say a state, county, or city, is studied. In interregional studies two or more areas are considered in the same or perhaps different detail. In such interregional studies the total area involved may be the nation, or a spatially less extensive area may compose the system. Ideally, the industrial structure of each region is specified in terms of both industrial output flows and the trade flows or linkages among regions. In other words, output is identified not only in terms of the industrial sector producing a given category of output and the sector buying it, but also in terms of the region of origin and of destination of that output.

Regional studies have been undertaken at the state level, for example, for Utah, California, and Mississippi.[2] On a local level, interindustry studies have dealt with the economies of Stockholm, the St. Louis area, and Kalamazoo County, Michigan.[3] Published interregional studies have been conducted, for instance, for California and the United States.[4]

In 1964 an interindustry study was undertaken for the state of Tennessee by the Tennessee Interindustry Study Group (TISG) in which both a regional and interregional model were implemented. The spatial extent of the regional model coincides with the boundaries of the state of Tennessee. For the interregional model, the state was divided into three regions corresponding generally to the three grand divisions of the state: East, Middle, and West Tennessee.

When a region, such as a state, is subdivided into such geographically distinct subregions that are connected through interindustry flows of goods and services, knowledge of the specific nature and magnitude of the economic interaction within and between subregions can be of considerable interest for regional economic planning. When an interregional study was first considered for the state of Tennessee, it was soon apparent that the data required for an interregional input-output analysis could not possibly be secured within the limitations of available resources. In an effort to circumvent this problem, we have explored an alternative method which can be implemented with data on only the sales distribution of each industry to other industries over the subregions.

This method is similar to the rows-only approach initiated by Hansen and Tiebout, but, unlike their application to a single-region model, it is utilized in the Tennessee interregional model to link interindustry sales flows both intraregionally and interregionally.[5] Thus while the regional model is similar to the Hansen-Tiebout model, the interregional model carries the methodology beyond the theoretical framework established by Hansen and Tiebout. Also, the method of treating a certain final-demand sector, viz., the household sector, as endogenous in both types of models differs from that utilized by Hansen and Tiebout in their model. The rationale for this treatment follows from a detailed examination of the fundamental properties of the Hansen-Tiebout model. This monograph, then, develops certain theoretical aspects of both the regional and interregional intersectoral flow models and presents the results of the application of these models to the Tennessee economy.

While the usefulness of the models for planning and policy-making will become apparent later, it is well to point out from the outset two important limitations of the approach adopted here. As in input-output models, it is assumed that there are no input substitutions or that the relative prices of all inputs remain constant. The realism of this assumption fades as the time period under consideration lengthens and relative input prices change significantly. If input substitutions occur, the analysis would result in unreliable forecasts or changes in the size of various multipliers. The second limitation is that our approach makes only the forward linkages of various processing sectors to final-demand changes while ignoring the backward linkages of final demand for outputs to changes in the supply of primary factors. While the traditional input-output approach is also based on forward linkages, it can be adapted to answer the questions concerning the requirements of primary factors or the effect on output of changes in the supply of primary factors. The supply of resources and the demand for final outputs are both important determinants of regional growth and the interrelationships between the two must be considered in a comprehensive policy for regional development. While we attempt to study the forward linkages, this effort should not be interpreted as a denial of the important role that resource development plays in regional economic planning.

By way of introducing the method employed in the present study, some recent theoretical developments pertaining to regional and interregional models are briefly outlined in Chapter 2. The purpose of this review is to provide a historical and analytical backdrop against which the models implemented by the TISG can be viewed.

In Chapter 3 of this monograph, the Tennessee models are presented so that the detailed structure of the study can be seen. Economists often regard model formulation as the most challenging and satisfying portion of their work. A more time-consuming activity, however, may involve the mundane activities associated with model implementation; this work is summarized in Chapter 4. Here we look at the problems of industrial and geographic sectoring, data collection, and so forth.

The results from the regional model are presented in Chapter 5, and the results from the interregional model are taken up in Chapter 6. These results show some important aspects of interindustry relationships in the Tennessee economy. Of specific interest is Chapter 5, which includes a comparison between the fundamental structures of production in the Tennessee and California economies, in which the recent hypothesis is tested concerning the similarity of production structures between seemingly different economies. Moreover, in Chapter 6 certain measures of interregional relationships are given in order to gauge the quantitative importance of interregional linkages in Tennessee. These measures yield some implications for the question of whether, in general, a multiregion model is more useful than a single-region model in studying interindustry relationships. The planning focus is also clear in the presentation of the various multipliers, both short run and long run, which show various types of economic interdependence.

In the final chapter, the contributions of this study on a conceptual and applied level are summarized. In addition, a possible agenda for further research is suggested.

Notes

1. Wassily Leontief and others, *Studies in the Structure of the American Economy* (New York: Oxford University Press, 1953); and Wassily Leontief, *The Structure of the American Economy, 1919-1939* (New York: Oxford University Press, 1951).

2. Frederick T. Moore and James W. Petersen, "Regional Analysis: An Interindustry Model of Utah," *Review of Economics and Statistics,* Nov. 1955, 37:368-380; W. Lee Hansen and Charles M. Tiebout, "An Intersectoral Flows Analysis of the California Economy," *Review of Economics and Statistics,* Nov. 1963, 45:409-418; W. Lee Hansen, R. Thayne Robson, and Charles M. Tiebout, *Markets for California Products* (Sacramento: State of California Development Agency, 1961); William E. Martin and Harold O. Carter, *A California Interindustry Analysis Emphasizing Agriculture, Part I: The Input-Output Models and Results,* Giannini Foundation of Agricultural Economics, Giannini Foundation Report no. 250 (Davis: California Agricultural Experiment Station, 1962); and John G. D. Carden and F. B. Whittington, Jr., *Studies in the Economic Structure of the State of Mississippi,* Vols. 1 and 2 (Jackson: Mississippi Industrial and Technological Research Commission, 1964).

3. Roland Artle, *Studies in the Structure of the Stockholm Economy* (Stockholm:

Business Research Institute, Stockholm School of Economics, 1959); Werner Z. Hirsch, "Interindustry Relations of a Metropolitan Area," *Review of Economics and Statistics,* Aug. 1959, 41:360-369; and Harold T. Smith, *The Kalamazoo County Economy* (Kalamazoo, Mich.: W. E. Upjohn Institute for Employment Research, 1960).

4. See the studies by Hansen and Tiebout and also Martin and Carter. See also: L. H. Moses, "Interregional Input-Output Analysis," *American Economic Review,* Dec. 1955, 45:803-832.

5. The expression "rows-only" was coined by Hansen, Tiebout, and their associates in indicating their method of analysis and data collection. Hansen and Tiebout, "An Intersectoral Flows Analysis"; Hansen, Robson, and Tiebout, *Markets for California Products;* and Richard S. Peterson and Charles M. Tiebout, "Measuring Regional Defense-Space Expenditures," *Review of Economics and Statistics,* Nov. 1964, 46:421-428.

2. Recent Developments in Interindustry Analysis

Recent substantive developments in interindustry analysis have involved two complementary areas of emphasis. One of these relates to the problem of data collection, a problem connected with both regional and interregional models. The other area of activity has involved, to a large extent, the extension of the interindustry technique to interregional models in an attempt to overcome some of the conceptual difficulties inherent in the regional models. Such interregional extensions, of course, tend to add to the already difficult problems of data collection.

Two conceptual deficiencies present in regional models have been pinpointed. First, ignoring interregional effects, we find that an increase in the final demand of a given region will increase the output of the industrial sectors of that region by a given amount. But when an interregional viewpoint is adopted, it is found that as output in the region in question increases, inputs are required from other regions, thus raising levels of production in those regions. Inputs in turn are required from the first region, thus increasing output in that region by more than would be the case if these interregional connections were absent or ignored. For instance, suppose that the output of the paper and allied products sector in East Tennessee increases because of an increase in final demand from the rest of the United States. In the process of increasing output, various inputs such as pulpwood and industrial chemicals would be required from producers in Middle and West Tennessee. Also, other intermediate sectors in East

Tennessee supplying inputs to the paper industry would require further inputs from other regions of the state. As the producers of these inputs in other regions increase their output, they would require additional inputs from East Tennessee, say, in the form of electricity generated by the Tennessee Valley Authority in East Tennessee. The additional demand for East Tennessee inputs is known as the interregional feedback effect. Such an effect is not captured in a strictly regional analysis.

A second drawback associated with regional models is that the effect on a given region of a change in the final demand of another region cannot be directly determined. In a single-region model of the state, with no identification of subregions, it would be impossible to determine, for example, the impact of changes in the final demand for paper and allied products in East Tennessee on the industrial activities of Middle or West Tennessee. Kuenne argues that interregional models were devised primarily to overcome one or both of these shortcomings.[1]

The data requirements in the regional application of the Leontief static model are substantial; the data requirements associated with interregional models are much more demanding. The recent innovations were, therefore, motivated in part by data problems, others had a conceptual focus, and in most, both the data and conceptual focus were prominent.

In the first regional studies, control totals for output and the values of inputs of a given region were applied to the national coefficients of the 1947 United States input-output table.[2] However, the assumption that the regional structure of production is a microcosm of that for the country as a whole is extremely artificial, and this technique for generating regional input-output tables is now considered to be unsatisfactory.

Significant departures from the use of national coefficients were first made in a study of the Utah economy undertaken by Moore and Petersen.[3] In their study, the national coefficients were modified for those sectors in which the structure of the Utah economy was thought to differ from that of the United States economy. Impact multipliers in terms of employment units were developed in the course of this investigation.

A more determined attempt to generate the basic row and column data was made by Hirsch in his study of the St. Louis Standard Metropolitan Statistical Area (SMSA).[4] Both output flows and estimates of inputs were obtained from extensive interviews with company officials. The sample data were blown up to correspond with the row and column control totals. Within the flow table in each cell a figure for input and one for output were obtained and, where they differed, a reconciliation was attempted based mainly on informed judgment. Hirsch's study marks a complete departure from the practice of using national coefficients. He follows Moore and Petersen in the calculation of output and employment multipliers. Most subsequent regional studies have been fashioned after the approaches of Hirsch, and Moore and Petersen.[5]

In the early 1950s, two interregional input-output models were developed, one by Leontief and the other by Isard.[6] In the balanced regional model devised by Leontief, the nation is divided into regions and within each region industrial sectors are placed in either a national or local category. The output of each local industrial sector is assumed to be absorbed within the region in which it is produced, either as an input or to satisfy regional final demand. The output of national industries is absorbed as an input in other regions or is absorbed as national final demand. In this model, the effect of a given level of national final demand upon the output of the national industries in a given region is first determined. Next, this change is translated into the total direct output required on the part of local industries supplying inputs to the national industries in the given region. Once the direct effect on local industries is known, the indirect and hence total impact on local industry can be calculated. To the local industry output so generated, the local industry output generated by regional final demand must also be added (the regional final demand is demand for the output of local industries in that region). This type of model may be applied, by way of example, to East Tennessee by treating the statewide economy as if it were the national economy. If such a model is applied and if the paper industry is classified as a statewide industry, the model could be used to determine the impact of a change in statewide final demand for the paper products on local industries in East Tennessee.

With the local-national dichotomy the model is designed primarily to answer the following question: what is the impact on local industry in a given region of a change in national final demand? Hence this model supplies an answer to the second criticism of regional models offered by Kuenne. The data requirements for this model, while severe, are not insurmountable. Most industries, however, sell their output both locally and nationally and, therefore, the local-national dichotomy is not too realistic. Furthermore, as an interregional model, this model does not deal with interregional feedback, thus not answering the first criticism of regional models offered by Kuenne. In other words, the change in regional final demand affects only the output of the local industries in the region in question.

In Isard's interregional model, a number of regions are designated and, within each region, a number of industrial sectors are determined. The number of industrial sectors can vary from region to region, but this is the exception rather than the rule. Once the geographic regions have been determined and the industrial sectors have been decided upon, the distribution of the output of each industrial sector in each region is determined. The distribution will be both intraregional and interregional in nature. Inputs purchased by a given sector in a given region may come from industries in that region or from industries in other regions. In the schema envisioned by Isard, both the industrial and spatial origin and destination of output are identified. This model has been described by some as the "ideal" interregional model in the sense that it successfully answers both of Kuenne's criticisms. While the model may be more general than Leontief's interregional model, it should be noted that the data requirements for implementing Isard's model are especially severe. Not only the equivalent of regional input-output tables must be constructed for each region in question, but tables describing interregional flows must be constructed sector by sector, by region of origin and destination. Such data requirements may easily be seen from an example of the paper and allied products industry in East Tennessee. While the paper product sales to various sectors in different regions should be enumerated, paper industry inputs must also be identified both by supplying industry and by supplying region. In other words, one must know from what parts of Tennessee the pulpwood and industrial chemicals come as the source of inputs to the paper industry in East Tennessee.

Since implementation of Isard's model is difficult, Moses and Chenery et al. have devised essentially similar methods for adapting the available data to Isard's framework.[7] First, the number of regions and industrial sectors within each region is determined. Next, the amount purchased from each industrial sector, regardless of region, by each sector in each region is determined. From these input flows, technical coefficients are formed showing the input of a given type required from all regions per unit of output of a given sector in a given region. The next step involves breaking down total per unit input requirements into per unit input requirements from the different areas. In order to achieve this result, trade coefficients are formed by determining the total use of each type of input by a given region and dividing this total into the amount obtained from each region, including the region in question. The resulting fractions are then used to break down the technical coefficients into regional technical coefficients showing inputs of a given type required from each region per unit of output in a given sector in a given region. While this approach does produce interregional technical coefficients identical in form to those required in Isard's model, the assumption of fixed trade patterns among regions is somewhat restrictive. Moreover, if this model is to be applied to the Tennessee economy comprising a number of subregions, input-output accounting data are required for each subregion. Thus for the paper industry in East Tennessee, for example, information on the sources of inputs and the destination of outputs within East Tennessee is required while for the paper industry in West Tennessee similar information is needed.

Another method of getting around the data problem inherent in Isard's model is simply to aggregate the sales of each industrial sector in each region up to the regional level. In this approach, developed by Henderson, the result is a table showing total interregional flows for each regional sector.[8] From the standpoint of implementation this approach has much to recommend it since neither intraregional nor interregional technical coefficients are required. At the same time, from the standpoint of an open region and its relationship to other regions, much information can be obtained concerning the effects of changes in final demand in other regions upon the output of the region or regions in question. A singular disadvantage of this approach may be the failure of this method to consider interindustrial linkages both intraregionally and interregionally.

An ingenious approach to the problem of estimating interregional flows has recently been advanced by Leontief and Strout.[9] For the multiregional case, their method amounts to combining the traditional input-output schema for the intraregional part of the model with a method for estimating interregional flows which is based on Isard's gravity flow or potential model. According to Leontief and Strout, industrial sectors in a given region buying an identical input are indifferent as to the regional origin of that input. By the same token, sellers of identical outputs are not concerned with the region in which their output is sold. On the basis of this pair of assumptions, regional demand and supply pools can be conceived of for each commodity. The flow of a given good from one region to another is then determined by a structural equation in which the flow is directly proportionate to its total output in the supplying region and to its total input in the region to which it is supplied and inversely proportionate to the total output of the good in all regions. Explicitly allowed for in this approach is the possibility of cross-hauling. Modifying the relationship just described is an empirical constant composed of factors relating to distance or transportation cost between supplying and demanding regions and to other parameters which capture the relationship of the supplying and demanding regions respectively relative to all other supplying and demanding regions. These last two parameters can be estimated statistically or can be solved for directly in a system of equations employing data which is generally available. Preliminary experiments with the approach have yielded encouraging results. The approach is highly imaginative and more exhaustive studies should be undertaken to determine the reliability of the estimates of interregional flows for a wide range of commodities for different combinations of regions.

The methods of interindustry analysis mentioned so far (except Henderson's method, which does not link interindustry relations) call for information on the input structure as well as output distribution of each industry. Such information, however, is not easy to come by in regional-scale research. In an attempt to overcome this difficulty, Hansen and Tiebout have formulated and implemented what has come to be known as the rows-only approach to interindustry analysis.[10] In this approach, only row or output information is needed; the input structure is assumed to be adequately represented by the row data. The approach can be used to approximate the data called for in regional models of the Leontief type.

Having developed a method for circumventing the data problem, Hansen and Tiebout have implemented a regional model for California as a whole and one for each of three subregions of that state. In both applications, the basic-flow tables were constructed from the sales distributions of a sample of firms. These distributions were then converted into employment distributions. Emphasizing final demand rather than the intermediate sectors, they develop a method of calculating final-demand multipliers that are analogous to base multipliers which, for example, measure the employment impact of changes in exports on the domestic economy in question.

The regional and interregional models implemented by the TISG build on both the conceptual and the data collection refinements outlined in this chapter which have evolved over the last two decades. Using the rows-only approach for the purpose of reducing the data requirements, the TISG regional flow model is fashioned after Leontief's static model and the interregional flow model is patterned along the lines of Isard's interregional model. The task of presenting these models in detail is taken up in the next chapter.

Notes

1. See Robert E. Kuenne, *The Theory of General Economic Equilibrium* (Princeton, N.J.: Princeton University Press, 1963), 420-428. In this context, Kuenne also notes the widely recognized problem of fixed supply areas inherent in regional models (see p. 423).

2. See, for example, Walter Isard and Robert E. Kuenne, "The Impact of Steel Upon the Greater New York-Philadelphia Industrial Region," *Review of Economics and Statistics,* Nov. 1953, 35:289-301.

3. Moore and Petersen, "Regional Analysis: An Interindustry Model of Utah." During the latter part of the 1960s there was a return to the use of modified national tables in regional and interregional input output analysis. This trend was due in large part, however, to the expense of generating the data using sample surveys. The rows-only approach elaborated in this study serves as a feasible alternative to the "modified national tables" approach. For recent examples of the approach see Roger Riefler and Charles M. Tiebout, "Interregional Input-Output: An Empirical California-Washington Model," *Journal of Regional Science,* Aug. 1970, 10:135-152; and Teddy T. Su, "A Note on Regional Input-Output Models," *Southern Economic Journal,* Jan. 1970, 36:325-327.

4. Hirsch, "Interindustry Relations of a Metropolitan Area."

5. See, for example, Carden and Whittington, *Economic Structure of Mississippi*; and Ronald E. Miller, "The Impact of the Aluminum Industry on the Pacific Northwest: A Regional Input-Output Analysis," *Review of Economics and Statistics,* May 1957, 39:200-209.

6. See Leontief and others, *Studies in the Structure of the American Economy,* 93-115, and Walter Isard, "Interregional and Regional Input-Output Analysis: A Model of Space Economy," *Review of Economics and Statistics,* Nov. 1951, 33:318-328.

7. See Moses, "Interregional Input-Output Analysis," 803-832, and Hollis B. Chenery, Paul G. Clark, and Vera Cao-Pinna, *The Structure and Growth of the Italian Economy* (Rome: United States Mutual Security Agency, 1953).

8. See the article by Henderson in James M. Henderson and others, *Four Papers on Methodology,* Technical Paper no. 1 (Minneapolis: University of Minnesota, 1961), 1-10.

9. Wassily Leontief and Alan Strout, "Multiregional Input-Output Analysis," in Tibor Barna, ed., *Structural Interdependence and Economic Development* (New York: St. Martin's Press, 1963), 119-150.

10. Hansen and Tiebout, "An Intersectoral Flows Analysis"; Hansen, Robson, and Tiebout, *Markets for California Products;* and Peterson and Tiebout, "Measuring Regional Defense."

3. The Models

Although the regional model used in this study can be shown to be formally identical to the intersectoral flow model initiated by Hansen and Tiebout, an operational difference does exist in the method of calculating multipliers by matrix inversion rather than by the Hansen-Tiebout iterative method of solution.[1] In fact, a systematic presentation of the model in terms of matrix notation renders both an insight into the basic characteristics of the model and the possibility of computing various multipliers, including the special case of the Hansen-Tiebout base multiplier. In particular, some characteristics of the model discussed in this chapter suggest a general way in which the flow model may be closed by treating some final-demand sectors as endogenous sectors. Although Hansen and Tiebout also attempted to close their model, their treatment in this respect is shown to be in error. Matrix formulation of the regional model in turn provides a basis for constructing a multiregion model which effectively incorporates both intraregional and interregional interindustry relationships. The present approach, therefore, may be seen as a generalization of the rows-only approach, which has hitherto been used for computing the base multiplier as a special case for a single region or for subregions not woven together in an interregional framework. In this chapter, the regional model is first presented and then compared with the Hansen-Tiebout model. The third section develops the interregional model, while the final section discusses the operational advantages of the models developed in this chapter.[2]

Regional Intersectoral Flow Model

For a formal presentation of the regional model first, define an interindustry sales-flow matrix X, a column vector of total sales q, a column final-demand vector y, and a column employment vector e as follows:

$$(1) \quad X = \begin{bmatrix} X_{11} & \cdots & X_{1n} \\ \cdot & & \cdot \\ \cdot & & \cdot \\ \cdot & & \cdot \\ X_{n1} & \cdots & X_{nn} \end{bmatrix}; \quad q = \begin{bmatrix} q_1 \\ \cdot \\ \cdot \\ \cdot \\ q_n \end{bmatrix}; \quad y = \begin{bmatrix} y_1 \\ \cdot \\ \cdot \\ \cdot \\ y_n \end{bmatrix}; \quad e = \begin{bmatrix} e_1 \\ \cdot \\ \cdot \\ \cdot \\ e_n \end{bmatrix}.$$

The typical element X_{ij} of the intermediate sales-flow matrix X indicates the sales flow of the ith industry to the jth industry to be absorbed in current production by the jth industry. Let q_i of the total sales vector q, y_i of the final-demand vector y, and e_i of the employment vector e denote the ith industry's total sales, sales to final demand, and total employment respectively. There are n industries in the region. Let us further define $\hat{q}$ and $\hat{e}$ as $(n \times n)$ diagonal matrices whose diagonal elements are the elements in the corresponding rows of q and e respectively.

In our empirical application of the model, the first and the second intermediate sectors are wholesale-retail trade and TVA respectively. Thus in an empirical context, X_{21} in the first entry of the second row [though not shown in (1)] of the sales-flow matrix would indicate the TVA sales absorbed by the wholesale retail trade sector for its use in producing the trading services. Similarly, X_{22} indicates intrasectoral sales among TVA facilities in Tennessee. The element q_2 represents the total sales of TVA and y_2 denotes TVA sales to a set of final-demand sectors such as the state and local government. Finally, the element e_2 stands for the full-time equivalent employment in the TVA sector.

As in the usual input-output approach, we assume throughout the chapter that the total sales of industrial sectors, excluding wholesale and retail trade industries, are directly assigned to the intermediate and final-demand sectors, thus bypassing the distributive system of the trading industries. But unlike the case in the input-output table, it is assumed that either the actual volumes of sales or the distribution charges of the trading industries may be distributed to the intermediate and final-demand sectors.[3]

Since the total supply of goods is equal to the total demand for goods consisting of intermediate and final demands, a basic-flow equation for sales becomes

$$(2) \quad q = Xi + y,$$

where i is an $(n \times 1)$ column vector of 1's. The total output of TVA, q_2, for example, is equated to the sum of its sales to intermediate sectors and its sales to final demand, that is,

$$\sum_{j=1}^{n} X_{2j} + y_2.$$

Since there are sales flows of other industries such as the wholesale-retail, equation (2) represents a set of simultaneous sales-flow relationships among industrial sectors.

Premultiplying through equation (2) by ($\hat{e}\hat{q}^{-1}$) gives an employment-flow equation:

$$(3) \quad e = \hat{e}\hat{q}^{-1} Xi + \hat{e}\hat{q}^{-1} y.$$

The total employment of each of the n industries is viewed as the sum of employees attributed to intermediate and final demand assigned according to the fractions of total sales of each sector sold to intermediate sectors and final-demand sectors. Taking up the example of TVA, the total employment by TVA, e_2, is expressed as the sum of employees working for various intermediate demands and employees working for final demand, viz.,

$$e_2(\sum_{j=1} X_{2j} / q_2) + e_2(y_2 / q_2).$$

In other words, the employment allocation is made by the percentage distribution of TVA sales to all intermediate sectors and to final demand.

We solve the system of simultaneous employment equations in (3) so that employment of each industry may be dependent upon a given final demand. While there are a number of ways to solve this problem, for simplicity we use the method of matrix inversion. Substituting ($\hat{e}^{-1} e$) for i in solving for e gives

$$(4) \quad e = (I - \hat{e}\hat{q}^{-1} X\hat{e}^{-1})^{-1} \hat{e}\hat{q}^{-1} y.$$

It can be shown that the solution for employment of each industry always exists and that positive changes in final demand will yield a non-negative value of employment of each industry.[4] Thus, if the expression in parentheses in (4) is known numerically, one can predict the employment impact on each industry for given changes in final demand in terms of employment.

The matrix $\hat{e}\hat{q}^{-1} X\hat{e}^{-1}$ in (4) above indicates a matrix of sales-flow coefficients in terms of employment. For instance, the element of $\hat{e}\hat{q}^{-1} X\hat{e}^{-1}$ in the ith row and the jth column, ($e_i X_{ij} / q_i e_j$), represents the employees required in the ith industry per employee in the jth industry in order to support production in the jth industry. The corresponding element of $(I - \hat{e}\hat{q}^{-1} X\hat{e}^{-1})^{-1}$ indicates the total demand for employment, direct and indirect, placed on the ith industry as a consequence of the jth industry's employing one man directly associated with final demand for the product of the jth industry. The inverted matrix, consisting of such direct and indirect effects, is the familiar matrix multiplier. For example, the sum of the second column (j=2) of this multiplier matrix designates the sum of all employment of Tennessee industries originating from one unit of employment by TVA for its final demand. Thus, an interpretation similar to that applied to input-output models can be applied to the model specified in equation (4) except that the present model is expressed in terms of employment rather than output.

The multiplier matrix in (4) may be estimated from employment figures and the sectoral percentage sales distributions as obtained from sample surveys for the base year. Assuming stability of the multiplier over time, one may predict the total employment impact on each industry from given changes in final-demand employment. It should be noted, however, that aside from an interest in employment multiplier, the use of employment figures in estimating the multiplier matrix is merely instrumental. The employment vector is used to transform the basic-flow equation (2) into the matrix equation with sales-flow coefficients rather than with input-output coefficients.[5] If there exists reliable data on the vector of total outputs, say q_r, which corresponds to that of total outputs in an input-output account, inserting $\hat{q}_r$ in place of $\hat{e}$ and using the sample estimates of $(\hat{q}^{-1}X)$ and $(\hat{q}^{-1}y)$ on the right-hand side of equation (4), one can obtain an estimate of the sales-flow multiplier equation in terms of the traditional input-output measurement unit. The present study utilizes employment figures rather than output figures owing to the availability of better data on employment for the year of the analysis.

To illustrate the several types of multipliers used in the study, we may rewrite equation (4) in convenient notation as

$$(5) \quad e = Mf,$$

where M is $(I - \hat{e}\hat{q}^{-1}X\hat{e}^{-1})^{-1}$ and f is $(\hat{e}\hat{q}^{-1}y)$ in equation (4). The element of the ith row and the jth column of the $(n \times n)$ matrix multiplier may be denoted by M_{ij}, and the element of the ith row of the $(n \times 1)$ final-demand vector in terms of employment may be designated by f_i. The multiplier most commonly associated with input-output theory is formed as the column sums of the multiplier matrix. Since in the present formulation the employment is the unit of measurement, the employment multiplier is calculated as the sums of the columns of the matrix M. The employment multiplier of the jth industry, for example, is

$$(6) \quad \sum_{i=1}^{n} M_{ij} \quad (j = 1, \cdots, n).$$

The sum of the jth column indicates the direct and indirect effect on employment in all n industrial sectors as a consequence of a change of one employee in the jth sector engaged in producing directly for final demand. For j=2 in our empirical application, the multiplier

$$\sum_{i=1}^{n} M_{i2}$$

would indicate the size of the impact on total employment to all Tennessee industries resulting from a change of one employee in TVA directly associated with final demand such as the government expenditures. This type of multiplier emphasizes the classification of intermediate sectors rather than final demand. Thus, this multiplier is useful in a policy context when the policy measures are deemed capable of altering the distribution of final demand for different industries. A comparison of the column sums indicates which intermediate sector produces the greatest total—direct and indirect—employment impact for a given equal change in the employment of each sector that is directly related to final demand.

The above employment multiplier can be weighted by a relative change in the final demand to take account of the importance of the distribution of final demand. The weighted employment multiplier for the jth industrial sector is defined as

$$(7) \quad \sum_{i=1}^{n} M_{ij}(\triangle f_j / \sum_{i=1}^{n} \triangle f_i) \qquad (j=1, \cdots, n),$$

where

$$\triangle f_j \,/\, \sum_{i=1}^{n} \triangle f_i$$

is the weight indicating the relative change in the final demand for the jth product in employment units. Since the weight reflects a given pattern of final-demand distribution, the weighted multiplier measures the impact of the jth intermediate sector on total employment reflecting the relative importance of the final demand for the jth among other products. If changes in final demand are assumed to be proportional to the final demand of the base year, the weighted multipliers so computed can be compared to determine which sector would generate the greatest change in total employment. Thus, in contrast to the unweighted multiplier in (6) the weighted multipliers are useful for explaining observed economic growth rather than for policy purposes.

The base multiplier, which is shown below as the Hansen-Tiebout multiplier, emphasizes the classification of final demand into different categories and the importance of each final-demand category as a generator of employment. In the present notation, when only one final-demand category is used, the base multiplier for a given final demand is defined as

$$(8) \quad \sum_{i=1}^{n} \sum_{j=1}^{n} M_{ij} f_j \,/\, \sum_{i=1}^{n} f_i .$$

Since a matrix of more than one final-demand category could have been introduced in the basic model without altering the matrix multiplier, the base multiplier in (8) may conveniently be regarded as one of several base multipliers that can be computed for various categories of final demand. For a given type of final demand, the base multiplier indicates the total employment generated by the given type of final demand per employee directly assigned to the final-demand category. For example, the final-demand multiplier for the state and local government is the ratio between the total, direct plus indirect, employment traceable to government expenditures and the employment directly assigned from all the intermediate sectors to this final-demand category. A comparison of the base multipliers for different final-demand categories should indicate the comparative importance of each final-demand category as an employment-creating source.[6]

The methods of computing various multipliers are twofold: one by direct inversion of the relevant matrix and the other by an iterative method of computation subject to certain conditions of the matrix. To examine the condition of the matrix for iterative computation, the matrix multiplier $(I - \hat{e}\hat{q}^{-1} X\hat{e}^{-1})^{-1}$ is rewritten as $\hat{e}(I - \hat{q}^{-1} X)^{-1}\hat{e}^{-1}$. The rows-only information with some nonzero elements in the final-demand vector provides a set of measurement units in the matrix $(I - \hat{q}^{-1} X)$ such that no row sum may be greater than unity and at least one row sum may be less than unity. Under this condition it is possible to write $(I - \hat{q}^{-1} X)^{-1} = [I + (\hat{q}^{-1} X) + (\hat{q}^{-1} X)^2 + \cdots]$.[7] Hence, equation (4) with the iterative method of computing the matrix multiplier can be expressed as

$$(9) \quad e = [I + \hat{e}(\hat{q}^{-1} X)\hat{e}^{-1} + \hat{e}(\hat{q}^{-1} X)^2 \hat{e}^{-1} + \cdots]\,\hat{e}\hat{q}^{-1} y.$$

In this study, we define the first term in the bracket of the above equation, I, as the direct multiplier effect of final demand and the sum of the remaining terms, $[\hat{e}(\hat{q}^{-1} X)\hat{e}^{-1} + \cdots]$, as the indirect multiplier effect of final demand.

The induced multiplier effect of final demand can also be defined in the present framework. As in the input-output model, certain final-demand categories can be transferred to the inside of the intermediate sector matrix by creating the relevant rows and columns of the corresponding sectors within the matrix. The induced multiplier effect is then defined as the magnitude obtained by subtracting the direct and indirect effects from the total multiplier effect generated as a consequence of incorporating new endogenous sectors in the model. In this study, the household noncapital sector is first treated as a final-demand category and later transmitted into the intermediate sector matrix as an endogenous sector in order to obtain the induced employment effect due to household spending.

Comparison with the Hansen-Tiebout Regional Model

At this point, it is instructive to compare the Hansen-Tiebout model and its solution method with the approach developed in this monograph.[8] Hansen and Tiebout express their basic-flow table as the sales distributions in fractions of total sales of industrial sectors. Expressing their table in terms of our symbols in (1), we define $\| X_{ij} / q_i \|$ as an $(n \times n)$ matrix for the intermediate sales distributions in fractions of total sales of individual sectors and $\| y_i / q_i \|$ represents an $(n \times 1)$ column vector for the sales to final demand in fractions of total sales of individual sectors.[9] In their first round of computation, the employment of the ith industry is allocated by the sales fractions of the ith industry, (y_i / q_i) and (X_{ij} / q_i), where the subscript j runs from the 1st to the nth intermediate sector. The resulting $e_i(y_i / q_i)$ and $e_i(X_{ij} / q_i)$ are respectively the employment of the ith industry assigned directly to the final-demand sector and to the intermediate-demand sectors. The employment assigned to the jth intermediate-demand sector that runs through n intermediate sectors can be assigned indirectly to the final-demand sector of the jth industry by using the sales fractions of the jth industry. This, according to Hansen and Tiebout, is the second round of iteration. After the second round there remains some residual employment not assigned indirectly to the final-demand sector of the jth industry. These residuals are summed over industries for each column of intermediate-demand sectors, and the sum of each of the residuals is again distributed to intermediate sectors and the final-demand sector by using the sales fractions of that intermediate industrial sector. This gives the third round of iteration. This iterative procedure can be continued until no residual employment remains in the intermediate-demand sectors. The employments of all industries other than the ith industry can similarly be assigned to the final-demand sector through the first, the second, and the third rounds, and so forth.

Noting the direct and indirect assignments of employment to the final-demand sector, we can define the Hansen-Tiebout base multiplier as the ratio of the sum over all industries of the total demand for employment, direct and indirect, to the sum over all industries of direct final demand for employment. It can easily be seen that the column sums of the first and the second product terms on the right-hand side of equation (9) are respectively the first and the second rounds of the Hansen-Tiebout iterative computations that are summed for all the industries. It therefore is shown that the regional model used in this study is identical to the model of Hansen and Tiebout and also yields the Hansen-Tiebout base multiplier by direct inversion of the matrix in equation (4).

Despite the identity of the two models, the matrix formulation brings to light some interesting characteristics of the model not intuitively clear from the Hansen-Tiebout formulation. First, whereas the Hansen-Tiebout iterative method of computation yields only the base multiplier, the matrix inverse provides bases for computing not only the base multiplier but also other types of multipliers common in input-output analysis. Although Hansen and Tiebout appear to visualize the possibility of solving the model by matrix inversion, they do not present a formal proof of the identity between their iterative method and the matrix-inversion method.

Second, since the iterative method is only a computational aspect of the model, the method is not related to the question of whether some final-demand sectors may be removed by iteration as endogenous sectors. Hansen and Tiebout choose certain final-demand sectors as endogenous and allocate the employments in these final-demand sectors to the ultimate final-demand sectors by iteratively using the sales fractions of each industry's ultimate final-demand sectors.[10] Since the model is an extension of the input-output model as seen in the present formulation, it is an error to treat certain final-demand sectors as endogenous without introducing the corresponding rows into the basic-flow equation.

Third, because the column of an endogenous sector has to be matched by a row of the corresponding sector, an intersectoral flow table for intermediate sectors must be a square matrix. One should not, therefore, confuse this principle with an incorrect view that rows-only information can be used by rows-only operation. Hansen and Tiebout form a rectangular matrix for intermediate sectors of their California flow model even before they consider endogenous treatment of some final-demand sectors. Peterson and Tiebout go still further and use a single column against about three dozens of rows of intermediate sectors in their intersectoral flow analysis.[11] The use of a non-square matrix for the endogenous part of flow analysis may have been due to lack of the information necessary to square the matrix. In any case, when intersectoral relationships between rows and columns are ignored, the multipliers derived from such a model do not reflect the impact of final-demand changes through the appropriate interindustry sales network.

Fourth, the intersectoral flow model is seen to be an extension of the traditional input-output model, utilizing an instrumental variable such as employment and output.[12] The reason for this device is to simplify the data requirements to rows-only information. The usefulness of the model in empirical application, therefore, depends on the reliability of available estimates of the instrumental variables and the rows-only information on sales distributions. Finally, since intersectoral flow analysis is a variation on input-output analysis, it indicates the possibility of extending the regional model to a multiregional model with a framework similar to that of Isard's interregional input-output model.[13]

Interregional Intersectoral Flow Model

In order to construct the interregional intersectoral flow model with particular reference to Tennessee, let us first define the East, Middle, and West Tennessee regions as E, M, and W respectively, each with n industrial sectors. Let X^{EE} denote a $(n \times n)$ matrix of intraregional sales flows from each industrial sector to each intermediate-demand sector in region E and X^{EM} denote a $(n \times n)$ matrix of interregional sales flows from each industrial sector in region E to each intermediate-demand sector in region M. When a pair of superscripts on X are labeled in this manner, a partitioned matrix $\underset{\cdot}{X}$ for interregional and intersectoral sales flows for intermediate demand is defined as in (10). Also defined in (10) are the partitioned column vectors of total sales q, final demand y, and total employment e, in which the elements q^E, y^E, and e^E, for example, are $(n \times 1)$ vectors indicating total sales, final demand, and total employment in region E respectively:

$$(10)\quad X = \begin{bmatrix} X^{EE} & X^{EM} & X^{EW} \\ X^{ME} & X^{MM} & X^{MW} \\ X^{WE} & X^{WM} & X^{WW} \end{bmatrix};\ q = \begin{bmatrix} q^E \\ q^M \\ q^W \end{bmatrix};\ y = \begin{bmatrix} y^E \\ y^M \\ y^W \end{bmatrix};\ e = \begin{bmatrix} e^E \\ e^M \\ e^W \end{bmatrix}.$$

By equating the flows of total sales to the total demand, intermediate and final, we write the basic three-region flow equation for sales as

$$(11)\quad q = Xi + y,$$

where i is assumed to be a $(3n \times 1)$ column vector of 1's. The second row of (11), for example, is

$$q_2^E = \sum_{j=1}^{n} (X_{2j}^{EE} + X_{2j}^{EM} + X_{2j}^{EW}) + y_2^E$$

where sector 2 indicates TVA in our empirical application. The supply of outputs by TVA in East Tennessee is seen as the sum of the sales to intermediate sectors in its own, Middle, and West Tennessee regions and sales to a set of final-demand sectors. Thus, the simultaneous equation system in (11) is identical in form except for dimensionality to the equation set in (2) for the single-region model. Therefore, the algebraic procedure used earlier can similarly be adopted here to solve equation (11) for an employment-multiplier equation.

By premultiplying $(\hat{e}\hat{q}^{-1})$ and inserting $(\hat{e}^{-1}e)$ for i, one can solve equation (11) as

$$(12)\quad e = (I - \hat{e}\hat{q}^{-1}X\hat{e}^{-1})^{-1}\hat{e}\hat{q}^{-1}y,$$

where $\hat{e}$ and $\hat{q}$ are $(3n \times 3n)$ diagonal matrices whose diagonal elements are the same as those in the corresponding rows of e and q respectively.

The elements of $\hat{e}\hat{q}^{-1}X\hat{e}^{-1}$ in the ith row of region E and the jth column of region M is

$$(e_i^E X_{ij}^{EM} / q_i^E e_j^M).$$

It indicates employees directly required in the ith industry of region E per employee in the jth industry of region M. Hence, the corresponding element of the interregional matrix multiplier $(I - \hat{e}\hat{q}^{-1}X\hat{e}^{-1})^{-1}$ shows the direct plus indirect employment generated by the ith industry in region E as a result of adding one employee to the jth industry in region M who is directly assigned to final demand for the product of the jth industry in region M. In our empirical model, for example, the second column of the above inverted matrix may be identified as the employment-multiplier effect on various industries in East, Middle, and West Tennessee in that order, resulting from the employment of one man by TVA in East Tennessee to meet final demand. Equation (12), therefore, is equivalent to the framework of Isard's interregional input-output model except that it is expressed in terms of employment rather than output.[14]

The relevant estimates of sales distributions and employment, may be utilized to compute various multipliers for the interregional intersectoral flow model. To define various multipliers, one may rewrite equation (12) in convenient notation as:

$$(13)\quad \dot{e} = \begin{bmatrix} M^{EE} & M^{EM} & M^{EW} \\ M^{ME} & M^{MM} & M^{MW} \\ M^{WE} & M^{WM} & M^{WW} \end{bmatrix} \begin{bmatrix} f^{E} \\ f^{M} \\ f^{W} \end{bmatrix}.$$

On the right-hand side of the equation, the partitioned matrix is the matrix multiplier $(I - \hat{\dot{e}}\hat{\dot{q}}^{-1} X \hat{\dot{e}}^{-1})^{-1}$ that is partitioned corresponding to the intermediate sales-flow matrix in (10). The partitioned final-demand vector above corresponds to $\hat{\dot{e}}\hat{\dot{q}}^{-1}\dot{y}$ in (12), where the partition is carried out according to the partitioned vectors in (10). The typical elements of submatrices and subvectors may similarly be defined as before by using subscripts. For example,

$$M_{ij}^{EM}$$

is the element of the ith row in region E and the jth column in region M of the $(n \times n)$ matrix M^{EM}; and f_i^E is the element of the ith row in region E of the $(n \times 1)$ column vector f^E.

The intermediate-sector multipliers for the interregional case are calculated by summing the columns of the matrix multiplier given in equation (13). The employment multiplier of the jth industry in region E, for example, is written as:

$$(14)\quad \sum_{i=1}^{n} (M_{ij}^{EE} + M_{ij}^{ME} + M_{ij}^{WE}) \quad (j=1, \cdots, n) \text{ and (the second superscript, } E = E, M, \text{ and } W).$$

This sum indicates the total employment generated in the intermediate sector in all three regions for a change of one employee in the jth industrial sector in region E directly engaged in producing output for final demand. The sum of the last two terms in (14) indicates the direct plus indirect impact on employment in regions M and W of a change of one employee directly related to final demand in the jth industrial sector in region E. Therefore, the partial sum as such tends to indicate the degree of regional interdependence, viewed from the standpoint of the jth intermediate sector in region E. To give an example, suppose that TVA in East Tennessee employs one man for meeting the final demand for its products and denote this industry as the second sector (j=2) in region E. Then, the total employment impact on all intermediate sectors in East Tennessee would be given by the partial column sum

$$\sum_{i=1}^{n} M_{i2}^{EE} .$$

The total interregional employment effects on all intermediate sectors in Middle and West Tennessee are given by

$$\sum_{i=1}^{n} M_{i2}^{ME} \quad \text{and} \quad \sum_{i=1}^{n} M_{i2}^{WE}$$

respectively.

The column sums of all intermediate sectors in all regions can be ranked by the magnitude of overall potential employment effect per employee directly assigned to final demand. Additionally, the column sums for any given intermediate sector can be compared on a regional basis, yielding information as to which region, for a given intermediate sector, has the greatest impact multiplier. From a policy standpoint, information such as this has potential usefulness for determining the regional location of industries. It should be pointed out, however, that from the firm's viewpoint many other factors enter into the process of choosing a location. Nevertheless, considering the differential employment effects according to different locations, policy-makers can initiate such programs as creation of industrial parks and road construction in order to attract industries to the preferable sites.

Weighted employment multipliers can also be constructed for the interregional model by summing the products of a column of the multiplier matrix in (13) and the percentage change of its corresponding final-demand output to all other final-demand outputs. The weighted employment multiplier of the jth industry in region E, for example, is written as:

$$(15) \quad \sum_{i=1}^{n} (M_{ij}^{EE} + M_{ij}^{ME} + M_{ij}^{WE}) \frac{\triangle f_j^E}{\sum_{i=1}^{n} (\triangle f_i^E + \triangle f_i^M + \triangle f_i^W)}$$

(j=1, · · · , n) and (the second superscript of M_{ij} and the superscript of f; in the numerator, E = E, M, and W),

where

$$\triangle f_j^E / \sum_{i=1}^{n} (\triangle f_i^E + \triangle f_i^M + \triangle f_i^W)$$

indicates a relative change in the final demand for the jth product of region E to changes in final demand for all other products in all regions. If changes in final demand are proportional to the final demand of the base year, the weighted multipliers calculated from the base year may be ranked, in order to examine which sector in which region produces the greatest effect on total employment for a relative change in final demand. Also, the total employment effects for the same sectors in different regions can similarly be compared. As previously pointed out, while unweighted multipliers are useful for policy purposes, the weighted multipliers are useful for explaining observed growth of industries or subregions.

Following the format previously set out for the regional model, one can develop an interregional base multiplier which utilizes the regional identity of final-demand categories and also relates the effect of changes in direct final-demand employment in one region on total employment in all regions. Using the notation with only one final-demand sector in equation (13), the interregional base multiplier for region E, for example, can be defined as:

$$(16)\quad \sum_{i=1}^{n} \sum_{j=1}^{n} [(M_{ij}^{EE} + M_{ij}^{ME} + M_{ij}^{WE}) f_j^E] \; / \; \sum_{i=1}^{n} f_i^E .$$

Since in general several final-demand categories can be introduced in the basic multiplier equation, the above interregional base multiplier may be regarded as one exemplary of the many that can be calculated for different final-demand categories. Different final-demand categories can consist of the given final-demand category generated from three different regions. In this case, one may attach a second superscript to

$$f_j^E, \text{ namely } f_j^{EE}, f_j^{EM}, \text{ or } f_j^{EW},$$

indicating the final demand for region E generated from region E, M, or W respectively. For convenience of notation, however, we will omit the first superscript in presenting the empirical results later, with a clear indication that the demand generated from region E, M, or W is for region E.

At this juncture, it should be noted that although the Hansen-Tiebout iterative method of computation can be modified to obtain the base multiplier in (16), a straightforward use of the method does not yield this multiplier. Moreover, when their iterative method is applied to the multiregion model, it is not so obvious how to identify other types of interregional multipliers specified above and also the effects of interregional relationships to be defined below. It may be for this reason that Hansen and Tiebout did not extend their single-region intersectoral flow model to a multiregion model. When they attempted to study the interregional aspects of the subregions of the California economy, they treated each subregion within the framework of a single-region model and failed to mention the possibility of linking the subregions of the state by an interregional intersectoral flow analysis.[15]

Within the present framework of the interregional model, it is possible to identify the two types of effects of interregional relationships that are ignored in the regional model. One is the interregional feedback effect that Miller defines in the context of the Isard interregional model and the other is the effect on a given region of the final demand of other regions.[16] Since the present model is similar to Isard's model, it is not too difficult to apply Miller's analytical method to identify the interregional feedback effect. It is, however, rather lengthy and tedious to follow this method. An intuitive approach, though not rigorous, is used here to demonstrate the method of isolating the interregional feedback effect.

Given a change in a region's employment directly related to final demand, the effect of interregional feedback is measured by the expanded employment in that region of an interregionally connected economy over the employment that would be achieved if interregional connections were absent. The expanded employment results from the additional employment generated in the region in question in order to supply inputs to other regions whose intermediate products are needed as inputs in the region in question to satisfy the final-demand change. The overall percentage error, in region E for example, that measures an extent of the expanded employment in the interregional model can be defined as:

$$(17) \quad \frac{\sum_{i=1}^{n} \sum_{j=1}^{n} \left| M_{ij} - M_{ij}^{EE} \right| \triangle f_j^E}{\sum_{i=1}^{n} \sum_{j=1}^{n} M_{ij}^{EE} \triangle f_j^E} \times 100 \text{ for region } E,$$

where M_{ij} of the first term in the numerator is the element of M in equation (5) of the single-region model which is applied to region E, and the symbol $\triangle$ indicates changes in the relevant variable. The overall percentage error in region M can similarly be defined by substituting M for E as superscripts in (17) and interpreting the first term in the numerator of (17) as a single-region multiplier now applied to region M. This definition is the same as that used by Miller in his empirical measurement of the interregional feedback effects.

The other type of interregional effects that Miller does not consider should also be included in measuring the extent of interregional linkages. In planning for a subregion from the vantage point of a set of subregions composing a political area such as a state, not only is a knowledge of feedback effects useful, but also a knowledge of the effect on employment in a given subregion of changes in final-demand employment in other regions becomes important. Inability to obtain the two types of knowledge within the framework of a regional model has been pointed out by Kuenne as two conceptual deficiencies inherent in regional model.[17] In this study, the quantitative importance of both types of interregional effects for region E is defined as:

$$(18) \quad \frac{\sum_{i=1}^{n} \sum_{j=1}^{n} \left| M_{ij} \triangle f_j^E - (M_{ij}^{EE} \triangle f_j^E + M_{ij}^{EM} \triangle f_j^M + M_{ij}^{EW} \triangle f_j^W) \right|}{\sum_{i=1}^{n} \sum_{j=1}^{n} (M_{ij}^{EE} \triangle f_j^E + M_{ij}^{EM} \triangle f_j^M + M_{ij}^{EW} \triangle f_j^W)} \times 100,$$

where M_{ij} of the first term in the numerator is the typical element of M in equation (5) of the single-region model which is applied to region E. Similar expressions for region M can readily be defined as:

$$(19)\quad \frac{\left| \sum_{i=1}^{n} \sum_{j=1}^{n} M_{ij} \triangle f_j^M - (M_{ij}^{ME} \triangle f_j^E + M_{ij}^{MM} \triangle f_j^M + M_{ij}^{MW} \triangle f_j^W) \right|}{\sum_{i=1}^{n} \sum_{j=1}^{n} (M_{ij}^{ME} \triangle f_j^E + M_{ij}^{MM} \triangle f_j^M + M_{ij}^{MW} \triangle f_j^W)} \times 100,$$

and for region W as:

$$(20)\quad \frac{\left| \sum_{i=1}^{n} \sum_{j=1}^{n} M_{ij} \triangle f_j^W - (M_{ij}^{WE} \triangle f_j^E + M_{ij}^{WM} \triangle f_j^M + M_{ij}^{WW} \triangle f_j^W) \right|}{\sum_{i=1}^{n} \sum_{j=1}^{n} (M_{ij}^{WE} \triangle f_j^E + M_{ij}^{WM} \triangle f_j^M + M_{ij}^{WW} \triangle f_j^W)} \times 100.$$

Now, M_{ij} of the first term in the numerator in (19) indicates the typical element of M for the single-region model of region M. Similarly, M_{ij} in (20) is the element of M for the single-region model of region W. In general, they measure the percentage of total employment in a given region that cannot be accounted for by the single-region model.

As in the case of the regional model in a preceding section, the above multipliers for the interregional model can similarly be obtained from an iterative method of computation. As a result, the direct and indirect multiplier effects are defined the same as before in the case of the regional model. In implementing the interregional model for the Tennessee economy, we shall also treat household noncapital as an endogenous sector, so that it is possible to measure the induced multiplier effect of final demand generated from household noncapital expenditures.

Operational Advantages and Limitations

The single-region and multiregion models developed in this chapter may be regarded as substitutes for the regional and interregional input-output models. The necessary information for both types of analyses is mostly obtained from extensive sample surveys of individual firms. However, firms usually do have better information as suppliers about the destination of their products to intermediate sectors as compared to the information they possess as producers about the source of their inputs from different industries. In addition, the column information or the input structure of a given intermediate sector would be most difficult to obtain if the Isard type interregional input-output analysis were to be implemented, because most firms have little, if any, idea of the geographical origin of their inputs.[18] Although for a multiregional interindustry analysis on a regional scale the type of interregional model developed by Leontief and Strout or Moses may be implemented, it requires the column as well as the row information for intraregions rather than the rows-only information.[19]

In a small-scale regional study usually characterized by a modest budget, the additional costs of obtaining column information are often prohibitive. Also, from a pragmatic viewpoint, the costs incurred in securing column information have to be weighed against the resulting improvements in the accuracy of the estimates for cells in each row of the input-output table. In view of these considerations, the intersectoral flow analysis has an operational advantage of using only the row information and bypassing the need for column information in both the regional and interregional applications.

The second advantage is that even when intersectoral sales flows among regions are not available, they may be estimated within the framework of the rows-only approach. Suppose that the sectoral flow of each industry is obtainable without interregional classifications and also that information on the percentage sales of one region to another for each industry may be obtained. Then, each row of intersectoral sales (with no regional classification) can be broken down into an interregional intersectoral sales flow. For three regions, each with n industries, $(3 \times 3)\, n$ observations are needed for the percentage interregional sales for industries. If the interregional intersectoral sales flows are directly obtained from the sample surveys, $(3 \times 3) n^2$ observations are required to fill the cells in the sales matrix defined in (10). Thus, the data requirement becomes less if we estimate the interregional sales pattern instead of collecting the basic data. In the TISG study, we used the basic data for the interregional intersectoral sales flows, since such data were obtainable. Nevertheless, the availability of a method of estimating the interregional intersectoral sales flows makes the rows-only approach more operational for multiregion interindustry analysis.

Third, as noted earlier, the rows-only approach makes it possible to fill the rows of the trading industries with the actual sales flows rather than with the distribution charges by the trading industries. In a similar manner, the rows of the communication and transportation sectors, etc., in the present models may be filled with the actual volumes of sales in some physical units rather than with the charges in dollars made by the communication and transportation industries. These procedures, if adopted, will further reduce the difficulty and the cost of obtaining the necessary data for implementing the present models.

Despite such operational advantages, there are a number of limitations worth mentioning. First, it should be borne in mind that the rows-only approach sacrifices the data discipline which an input-output account requires in balancing the row and column information. That, in fact, is the main criticism of intersectoral flow analysis aired by such writers as Miernyk and Bramhall.[20]

The rows-only approach, therefore, calls for careful sample surveys on the sales distribution of industrial sectors, since there will be no check provided by independently derived column information. Particular problems connected with the Tennessee study in this respect are dealt with in the next chapter.

Second, the use of rows-only information implies that there is no information available on imports to an overall region defined by the regional or interregional analysis. The models developed in this chapter implicitly treat imports as an external sector in a sense that the sales coefficients are not affected by the imports. While this treatment is similar to that of the input-output analysis which avoids the use of input coefficients for imports, the flow analysis does not incorporate imports as a part of final demand. In the absence of adequate data on imports, the empirical analysis that follows in this monograph ignores the role of imports. From a methodological viewpoint, however, it is worth pointing out that the intersectoral models, like input-output models, can be adapted to treat imports within the models.[21]

The third limitation is that the intersectoral sales-flow coefficients may not be stable over the period of time for which the model is used in forecasting and planning. However, while the question of stability is an empirical issue, the assumed stability in the empirical application of these models may not be unrealistic when the analysis refers to a modest period of time. Also, since the rows-only approach can be carried out within a small budget and hence on a repeated basis, changes in the interindustry relationships may readily be studied rather than assumed away.

Finally, the flow analysis used in this monograph is designed to make the forward link from the domestic intermediate sectors to changes in final-demand sectors but not the backward linkage. While input-output models are constructed on a similar foundation in principle, input-output analysis can be adapted to answer the questions concerning the requirements of primary factors or the effect on final demand of changes in the supply of primary factors. The intersectoral flow analysis cannot, of course, answer such questions. The rows-only approach, therefore, places emphasis on the operational aspect of the interindustry analysis on a regional scale rather than on the rigorousness of its theoretical construction in comparison with the traditional input-output approach.

Having developed regional and interregional flow models in this chapter, in the following chapters we will deal with the application of these models to the Tennessee economy. Empirical formulations of each model take two forms: one with the household noncapital sector as one of the final-demand sectors and the other with the household noncapital sector as an endogenous intermediate-demand sector. The latter case for the regional model is formulated by incorporating the row and the column of the household noncapital sector into the statewide intermediate sales-flow matrix. Similarly, for the interregional model, the endogenous treatment of the household noncapital sector is carried out by incorporating the relevant row and column into each submatrix of the three-region intermediate sales-flow matrix. Thus, the empirical models in this monograph allow for possible long-run effects on total employment of changes in employment associated with final demand other than household income.

Notes

1. Hansen and Tiebout, "An Intersectoral Flows Analysis"; and Hansen, Robson, and Tiebout, *Markets for California Products,* ch. 2.

2. The major part of the third section on interregional models consists of material taken from the authors' article, "Multiregion Intersectoral Flow Analysis," *Journal of Regional Science,* April 1971, 11:49-56.

3. In an input-output model, the distribution charges by the trading industries are treated as an element of cost borne directly by an industry buying goods and hence as an input directly to the purchasing industry. The volumes of sales, therefore, cannot be used as an input directly to the purchasing industry in the input-output account.

4. That this proposition holds true can be shown as follows. By writing $(I-\hat{e}\hat{q}^{-1}X\hat{e}^{-1})^{-1}$ as $\hat{e}(I-\hat{q}^{-1}X)^{-1}\hat{e}^{-1}$ and noting $\hat{e}$ as a non-negative and nonsingular diagonal matrix, the proof is complete if the matrix $(I-\hat{q}^{-1}X)$ has the necessary condition for the above conclusion. But the condition of the matrix is the same as that of the Leontief matrix except that the former refers to rows rather than columns. Since in a formal presentation of the proof the necessary condition could be stated in terms of either rows or columns, the existence of a solution for a non-negative output vector in an input-output model immediately implies the conclusion stated above about equation (4). For the proof in case of input-output models, see, for example, Richard Stone, *Input-Output and National Accounts* (Paris: Organization for European Economic Co-operation, 1961), 92-93.

5. By substituting $(\hat{q}^{-1}q)$ for i in equation (2) and solving for q, we can express equation (2) as: $q=(I-X\hat{q}^{-1})^{-1}y$. If we interpret sales flows in X as the output flows directly required by the absorbing industry and also define y and q in such measurement units, we can identify the latter equation as the traditional static Leontief input-output model. By premultiplying $(\hat{e}\hat{q}^{-1})$ through the equation and inserting $(\hat{e}\hat{q}^{-1})^{-1}(\hat{e}\hat{q}^{-1})$ in front of y on the right-hand side of the equation, the Leontief model can be transformed into the sales-flow matrix equation in terms of employment shown in (4). Thus, with this transformation, we convert the input-output coefficients into sales-flow coefficients in order to utilize the rows-only information. For the Leontief model, see Leontief, *The Structure of the American Economy, 1919-1939.*

6. The other results reported by Hansen and Tiebout concern the direct plus indirect employment of each intermediate sector assigned to final demand as compared with that directly assigned. The total employment, direct plus indirect, assigned to final demand can be calculated by not summing over rows in the numerator of (8). See Hansen and Tiebout, "An Intersectoral Flows Analysis."

Because of the extensiveness of the resulting tables, they are not reported in this monograph, although they were derived. Some reference, however, will be made to these tables in chs. 5 and 6. For a more elaborate explanation of this standard type of structural analysis see, for example, A. Gosh, *Experiments With Input-Output Models, An Application to the Economy of the United Kingdom, 1948-1955* (Cambridge: Cambridge University Press, 1964), 17-19.

7. Robert Dorfman, Paul A. Samuelson, and Robert M. Solow, *Linear Programming and Economic Analysis* (New York: McGraw-Hill, 1960), 255-256.

8. Hansen and Tiebout, "An Intersectoral Flows Analysis"; and Hansen, Robson, and Tiebout, *Markets for California Products,* 12-14. For their numerical illustration of the first, the second, and the third round of iterations, and so forth, see the latter reference.

9. Without a great loss of generality and for simplicity in exposition, it is assumed that

there is one final-demand sector. One may conveniently treat the final-demand sector as a given one among several final-demand sectors in the model.

10. For their treatment of certain final-demand sectors as endogenous, see Hansen and Tiebout, "An Intersectoral Flows Analysis"; and Hansen, Robson, and Tiebout, *Markets for California Products,* ch. 2.

11. Peterson and Tiebout, "Measuring Regional Defense."

12. When an extraneous estimate of the total output vector is used as an instrumental variable, the intersectoral flows analysis may be regarded as an attempt to study the input-output structures of the given economy by resorting to indirect information. In this sense, one may make an analogy of this approach to the instrumental variable method of estimating statistical equations in econometrics.

13. Isard, "Interregional and Regional Input-Output Analysis."

14. Ibid.

15. Hansen and Tiebout, "An Intersectoral Flows Analysis"; and Hansen, Robson, and Tiebout, *Markets for California Products,* ch. 2.

16. For Miller's analytical method of isolating the interregional feedback effects, see Ronald E. Miller, "Interregional Feedback Effects in Input-Output Models: Some Preliminary Results," *Papers and Proceedings of the Regional Science Association,* 1966, 17:105-125.

17. Kuenne, *The Theory of General Economic Equilibrium,* 420-428.

18. Isard, "Interregional and Regional Input-Output Analysis."

19. Leontief and Strout, "Multiregional Input-Output Analysis"; Moses, "Interregional Input-Output Analysis."

20. William H. Miernyk, *The Elements of Input-Output Analysis* (New York: Random House, 1965), 72-75, and David F. Bramhall, "Markets for California's Products: Analysis of the Sources of Demand," *Journal of Regional Science,* Sept. 1962, 4:102-104.

21. When data on imports are available by industrial sectors, there are two methods of incorporating the data in the model. One method is to subtract imports from the industry's final bill of sales. This is analogous to a method of treating imports as an exogenous sector in input-output models. The other method is to treat imports as being determined endogenously within the model. To present this, let m_i denote the ith industry's import coefficient, which is defined as the ratio of imported commodity to the total supply of that commodity produced by the ith domestic industry. For n domestic industries, a $(n \times 1)$ column vector, m, of the import coefficients may be formed in which each element of the vector is ordered column-wise in terms of the natural order of subscripts. Also, designate $\hat{m}$ as a $(n \times n)$ diagonal matrix whose diagonal elements are the elements in the corresponding rows of m. Since the vector of imports is $\hat{m}q$, the basic-flow equation that is equivalent to equation (2) above may be written as follows:

$$q = Xi + y - \hat{m}q.$$

When this equation is premultiplied by $\hat{e}\hat{q}^{-1}$ and $(\hat{e}^{-1}e)$ is substituted for i, the solution for e becomes

$$e = [I - \hat{e}(\hat{q}^{-1}X - \hat{m})\hat{e}^{-1}]^{-1}\hat{e}\hat{q}^{-1}y.$$

If for the base year import figures by industrial sectors are available together with the rows-only information, the relevant matrix multiplier can readily be computed. The corresponding extension of the interregional model can easily be carried out along the above lines. For an example of this treatment of imports in an input-output model, see Leontief, *The Structure of the American Economy, 1919-1939,* 173-178.

4. Approach to Empirical Implementation

In Chapter 3 of this monograph, the theoretical construction of the models used by the TISG is presented in detail. The results of empirical implementation of the single-region model are presented in Chapter 5, and in Chapter 6 the results for the multiregion model are considered. Some understanding of the basic procedures involved in implementing these models is needed in order to evaluate the results obtained for the Tennessee economy as well as to appreciate the models' applicability to regional studies in general. In this chapter, we discuss these basic procedural considerations with respect to: geographical breakdown, the classification of intermediate and final-demand sectors, the unit of analysis, and the use of a direct interview sample survey and other available data in constructing the basic-flow tables for the Tennessee economy.

Geographical Breakdown

The purpose of the study was to illustrate the nature of interindustry relationships for Tennessee as a whole and to similarly illustrate these relationships among subregions of the state. Concerning geographical divisions for interregional analysis, Meyer points out that traditionally three bases for drawing such boundaries have been used: homogeneity, polarization, and policy orientation.[1] As noted by Meyer, the boundaries employed in practice often show a compromise among these pure types. Such was the case in defining the regions in this study.

Tennessee is long, narrow, and

rhomboidal in shape, with an east-west dimension of approximately 430 miles and a north-south dimension of about 110 miles. Traditionally the state has been divided into political subdivisions known as the three "grand divisions": East, Middle, and West.[2] In terms of policy orientation, polarization, and homogeneity respectively, these divisions make a great deal of sense. In this study we have adhered to this threeway geographical classification scheme but have deviated somewhat from the traditional divisions in drawing the boundary lines.[3] This threeway regional breakdown of Tennessee using such boundary lines is shown in the map below.

Our eastern region is composed of forty-nine counties with the Appalachian Mountains to the east separated from the Cumberland Plateau to the west by the valley of the Tennessee River and its tributaries. This valley, running in a generally northeast-southwest direction, represents a fairly continuous band of industrial activity and relative urbanization. For the most part, a policy or program focus led to the establishment of this area as a subregion since it comprises the portion of Tennessee incorporated in the Federal Appalachian Regional Program.

Physiographically, the middle region consisting of twenty-five counties is characterized by rolling hills. Industry in this region is concentrated in Nashville and surrounding counties, with a scattering of activity in the smaller cities and towns in the region. This region may be most easily characterized in terms of polarization.

Consisting of twenty-one counties, the western region is demarcated on the east by the Tennessee River as it flows north and on the west by the Mississippi River. Here the land slopes gently to the Mississippi and traditionally is cotton country. Memphis in the southwestern corner of this region is the industrial and commercial hub of West Tennessee, as it is for economic activity in adjoining areas of the states of Arkansas and Mississippi. There is a scattering of light manufacturing activities in the small urban areas. Thus, the third region for the most part can best be defined in terms of homogeneity and polarization.

Classification of Intermediate Sectors

A number of factors influenced the intermediate sectoring of economic activity utilized in this study, and the final breakdown is the result of an evolutionary process. Some of the factors which influenced the final selection of sectors include: policy emphasis on particular sectors, data availability, disclosure problems, and similarity of sales patterns between sectors. In the final formulation of the model, twenty-five intermediate sectors are identified. In the interregional model, the same sectors are identified in each of the three regions. A listing and description of sectors is found in Table 1.

For the most part, the intermediate sectors consist of two-digit standard industrial classifications (SIC) categories or, in some cases, combinations of

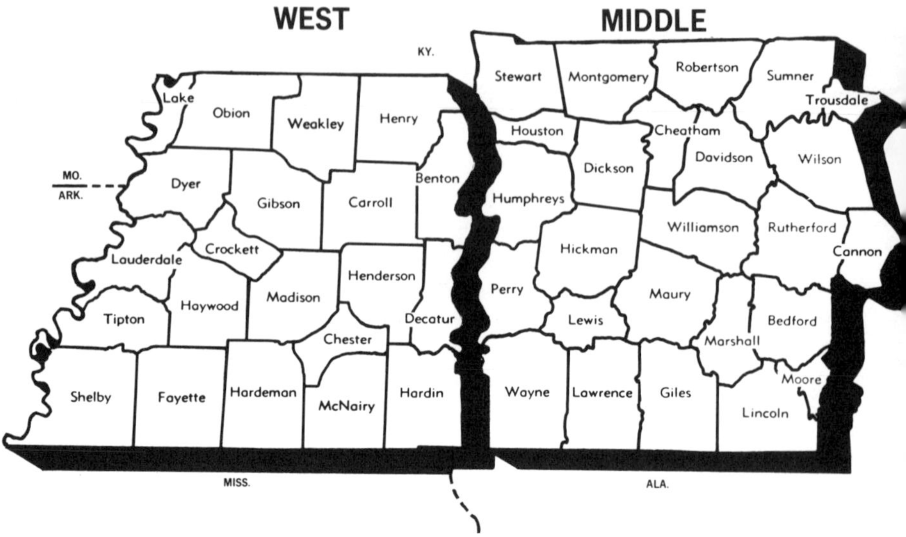

GEOGRAPHICAL BREAKDOWN OF TENNESSEE,

two-digit categories. One of the basic decisions underlying this study was that emphasis would be placed on manufacturing activity, and this emphasis is reflected from the fact that sixteen of the twenty-five intermediate sectors (sectors 7 through 22) are so classified. By and large, the manufacturing sectors follow a two-digit SIC breakdown, with a few exceptions. Sector 7 (food and tobacco products) is a combination of two SIC groupings. Likewise, sector 22 (transportation, instruments, and miscellaneous manufacturing) is a combination of SIC groups 29, 37, 38, 39, and 19. Each of these SIC groups involves relatively little employment in Tennessee and little detail is lost in combining them. Furthermore, in some cases, disclosure problems alone would have prevented their separation into distinct sectors. A further exception to the two-digit SIC classification scheme should be noted. Sector 13 (industrial inorganic and organic chemicals) is the three-digit SIC category 281, and sector 14 (plastics and synthetics) is associated with the three-digit SIC categories 282 through 289. The large total employment in Tennessee generated by industrial inorganic and organic chemicals along with the belief that the sales distributions for sectors 13 and 14 would differ substantially were the main reasons for this separation.

In agriculture only two sectors were identified: sector 3 (livestock) and sector 4 (crops). This, of course, represents a substantial consolidation of

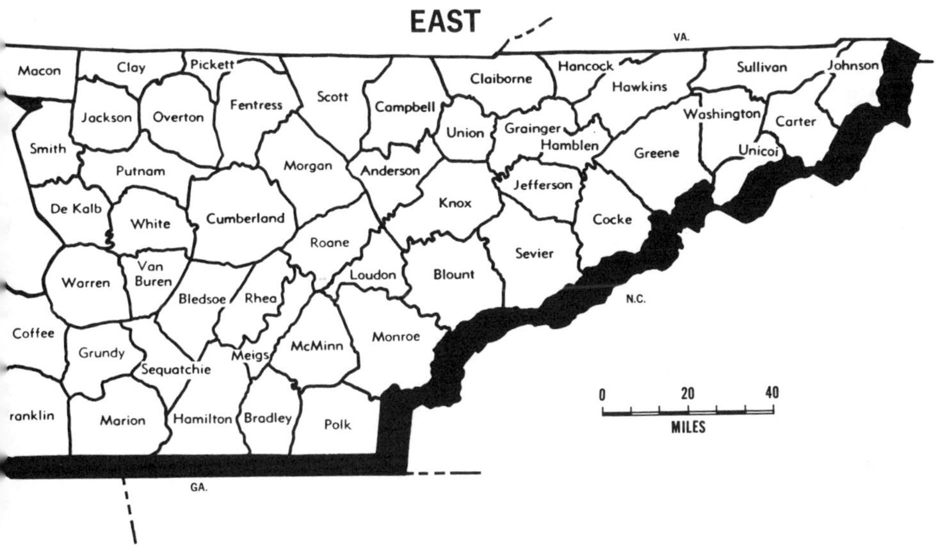

AS ADAPTED FOR STUDY OF ITS ECONOMY

product categories in the agricultural sectors. In addition, consolidation of SIC categories 10 through 14 into sector 5 (mining) and SIC categories 15 through 17 into our sector 6 (construction) was made necessary by the low number of observations and the similarity of sales patterns revealed in the recorded observations. Also, the consolidations associated with sectors 23 (transportation and communications), 24 (finance, insurance, and real estate), and 25 (miscellaneous services) were similarly motivated. For simplicity, wholesale and retail trade (SIC 50 through 59) are combined into sector 1.

One major departure from the SIC scheme of classification is found in the establishment of a separate sector, sector 2, to reflect the activities of the Tennessee Valley Authority. This departure was thought justified by the uniqueness and relative importance of this agency in the economic structure of Tennessee.

Classification of Final-Demand Sectors

In the statewide model there are seven final-demand sectors. The three-region model contains thirteen final-demand sectors which consist of the same four final-demand categories in the statewide study and the three-way regional breakdowns of the three final-demand categories in the statewide study. The

TABLE 1

INTERMEDIATE SECTOR NUMBERS AND DESCRIPTIONS

Sector No.	*SIC*	*Description*
1	50-59	Retail and wholesale trade
2		Tennessee Valley Authority
3		Livestock and livestock products
4		Crops
5	10; 12; 13 and 14	Metal mining; bituminous coal; crude petroleum and natural gas, mining and quarrying of nonmetallic minerals
6	15; 16	Building construction, general contractor and construction other than building construction general contractors;
	17	Construction, special trade contractors
7	20; 21	Food and tobacco products
8	22; 23	Textile mill products; apparel and other finished products made from fabrics and knit goods
9	24	Lumber and other products, except furniture
10	25	Furniture and fixtures
11	26	Paper and allied products
12	27	Printing and publishing and allied industries
13	281	Industrial inorganic and organic chemicals
14	282; 283-289	Plastic materials and synthetic resins, synthetic rubber, synthetic man-made fibers except glass
15	30	Rubber and miscellaneous plastic products
16	31	Leather and leather products
17	32	Stone, clay, and glass products
18	33	Primary metal industries
19	34	Fabricated metal products, except ordnance, machinery, and transportation equipment
20	35	Machinery, except electrical
21	36	Electrical machinery equipment and supplies
22	37; 38	Transportation equipment; professional science and control instruments, photographic and optical goods—watches and clocks
	29, 39, 19	Miscellaneous manufacturing
23	40-47, 48	Transportation; communications
24	60-67	Finance and insurance and real estate
25	49; 70-89	Agricultural services; electric, gas and sanitary services; business and personal services
26		Household noncapital expenditure when used as an intermediate sector

TABLE 2

FINAL-DEMAND SECTOR SYMBOLS AND DESCRIPTIONS

Symbols				*Descriptions*
Statewide	*Regions*			
	East	*Middle*	*West*	
HC	HC^E	HC^M	HC^W	Household noncapital expenditure*
HI	HI^E	HI^M	HI^W	Household capital expenditure*
BI	BI^E	BI^M	BI^W	Business investment expenditure*
GSL				State and local government expenditure
GF				Federal government expenditure
EUS				Exports to the rest of the United States
EW				Exports to the rest of the world

*Superscripts indicate geographical origins of the corresponding final-demand category.

classification of the final demand sectors and symbols for their abbreviations are given in Table 2.

One feature of this classification of final demand is the distinction made between household capital and household noncapital expenditures. The distinction is a useful one because the determinants of both types of expenditure differ. Also, by making this distinction, one can close the model by bringing the household noncapital sector into the intermediate part of the regional and interregional models. The distinction between the two types of expenditures was made on the basis of the durability of the products purchased. In general, those products lasting more than one year were classified as durable and those that may be completely consumed in a year were classified nondurable.

Business investment expenditures include outlays incurred for inventory build-ups of finished goods. Also, business investment expenditures include the purchase of products whose services, but not substance, are consumed in the course of current production. Products that were purchased and directly used by the industries for current production were not, of course, allocated to business investment expenditures but rather to the appropriate intermediate sectors. For convenience in obtaining data, the expenditures of state and local governments were combined into one final-demand sector. Federal government expenditures were identified separately because of their importance as a potentially volatile component of final demand. Exports to the rest of the United States from Tennessee and exports to the rest of the world make the last two final-demand sectors.

Unit of Analysis

Following the procedures adopted by Hansen and Tiebout in their California study, we used employment as the unit of analysis in this study. The main reason for this is that fairly reliable employment figures by industrial sectors as well as by geographical breakdowns can be obtained from a number of published and unpublished data sources. Another reason is that while measurement in terms of output or income would perhaps be preferable on conceptual grounds, an employment measure per se is also useful. As Hansen and Tiebout point out, "Basically this amounts to a kind of value-added approach, in contrast to the gross sales flows in an input-output table."[4] From the standpoint of regional planning, too, it is useful to be able to gauge the impact of new industry or changes in the output of existing industries directly upon the employment of that region. Employment figures are probably more directly relevant than output or income figures in gauging such impacts on labor markets, housing, municipal services, and so forth.

Data on Employment

For the most part, the statewide employment control totals utilized in this study consisted of the latest available Bureau of Labor Statistics employment estimates for 1964, classified according to the intermediate sectors identified in the TISG models. The statewide employment estimates for each sector were then broken down on a regional basis by multiplying the Bureau of Labor Statistics estimate for each sector by the ratio of the Tennessee Department of Employment Security (TDES) estimates of sectoral employment in each region to the related total TDES employment.[5]

For those sectors whose employment was not identifiable from the Bureau of Labor Statistics estimates, independent estimates were obtained. For example, the total Tennessee employment figures for the TVA, sector 2, in each region as well as in the entire state, were obtained directly from the TVA. Employment in the agricultural sectors was estimated in large part from preliminary 1964 census of agriculture information. The agricultural wage bill was adjusted by means of the average wage for hired labor (reported by the Tennessee Crop Reporting Service) to get a measure of full-time equivalent employment. Similarly, the number of farm operators was adjusted to secure a measure of full-time equivalent operators. Employment was then divided between the two agricultural sectors on the basis of data by type of farm contained in the preliminary 1964 Census of Agriculture report for Tennessee. For each sector, estimates of agricultural employment by region were obtained by applying the ratio between regional and total Tennessee agricultural output to the total employment estimate. Alternative methods of computing and allocating employment were attempted, and they yielded substantially similar results.

In introducing the household noncapital sector into the endogenous part of the model, estimates of household employment are required in order to make the household row in terms of household employment figures. The estimates of household employment were developed in the following manner. First, an estimate of 1964 wages and salaries paid to private household workers in Tennessee was obtained as explained in the next section. This estimate was then divided by an estimated annual wage of $1,250 to arrive at an approximation to private household full-time equivalent employment in the state. Finally, the employment estimate for the state was apportioned among the three regions according to the relative amount of total 1964 employment in each region. Admittedly, the household employment figure thus estimated is rough and is likely to be underestimated; its effect on the analysis will be discussed later.[6]

Sample Surveys on Sales Flows of Nonagricultural Sectors

The basic sales-flow data for nonagricultural sectors employed in this study were drawn from direct interview surveys of individual firms. The year chosen for study was 1964. Since field interviewing was scheduled for the first half of 1965, it was decided that the memory estimates required for some questionnaire items would be most valid if requested for the calendar year just concluded.

The sampling frame from which the survey sample was drawn was obtained from a state agency. The sampling frame consisted of some 4,000 manufacturing establishments and 21,000 nonmanufacturing establishments located throughout the state, covering nearly all the establishments operated in 1964. These establishments in the universe were stratified by our three-region breakdown and also by the four-digit or, in some cases, the three-digit SIC code for different lines of business establishments within each one of our intermediate sectors. Within each stratum, a sample of establishments was drawn with probabilities proportional to the size of establishments. The sample sizes within the strata were determined by considering a number of factors. They include the size distributions of establishments, an anticipated variation on geographical and sectoral sales distributions of establishments, and even a likelihood of nonresponse from some lines of business establishments. Preliminary contacts with a number of prospective interviewees and initial experiments with pilot interviews had greatly facilitated some of the above considerations. From the sample frame, a sample of about 1,000 manufacturing and 1,500 nonmanufacturing establishments was drawn. In all, 1,799 usable responses were elicited,

TABLE 3

SUMMARY OF SECTORAL AND GEOGRAPHIC DISTRIBUTION OF USABLE RESPONSES

Industrial Sector	*Regions*			*State-wide*
	East	*Middle*	*West*	
Manufacturing (Sectors 7-22)	258	204	227	719*
Nonmanufacturing (Sectors 1, 5, 6, 23-25)	560	270	250	1,080
Total	818	474	477	1,799

* Row totals for East, Middle, and West regions do not equal statewide figure for the manufacturing sector since some responses were not usable at the regional level due to disclosure and similar problems.

which covered over 25 per cent of the total employment in nonagricultural sectors of Tennessee economy. The sectoral and geographical distribution of these responses is summarized in Table 3.

By directly interviewing firm executives with specific questionnaires, the researchers obtained sample data on 1964 total sales, sectoral sales distribution, wages, salaries, rent, and noncorporate profits. A basic form of the questionnaire was first designed to apply to manufacturing establishments. In addition, to accommodate differences in the nature of various nonmanufacturing activities, six main adaptations of the basic questionnaire form were used in the intermediate categories of finance, transportation, communications, wholesale and retail, and business and personal services.

The basic questionnaire itself was designed around the idea that firms have a clear understanding of who their ultimate customers are, even when their goods pass through middlemen, and of where their customers are located. Furthermore, it was supposed that, with the aid of a trained interviewer, a representative of the firm could classify its customers according to the sectors used in this study.

A representative of each firm was asked to indicate total sales in 1964 and to break down the total sales on a percentage basis between sales within Tennessee and sales outside the state, including sales to the federal government. Sales outside the state were then allocated on a percentage basis among exports, sales to the rest of the United States, and sales to the federal government. Next, the percentage of sales made inside the state to each of the intermediate sectors was determined. Utilizing carefully worded instructions, the interviewer asked the interviewee to break down sales to each sector between capital and noncapital on a percentage basis.[7] Finally, the interviewee was requested to determine on a percentage basis the sales to each sector, capital and noncapital, going to each region of the state. In addition to sales information, the respondents were requested to indicate inventory changes over the year. These inventory changes were then entered to adjust the total sales figure. Since inventory additions generate current employment, they were added into business investment in the region in which the firm in question was located.

Preliminary forms of the questionnaire were pretested at the beginning of 1965, and at each step some improvements in the form of the questionnaires were introduced. The final questionnaire so prepared was found to yield satisfactory responses to the requested information. The form of this interview questionnaire for manufacturing firms and its accompanying instructions are given in Appendix B.

In order to solicit cooperation from the establishment to be interviewed, a letter explaining the purposes and objectives of the interview was sent to all the establishments in the sample in advance of actual interviewing. An effort had also been made to make the prospective respondents aware of the general purpose of the TISG study through announcements and reports in a number of business publications in Tennessee.

At an initial stage, it was suspected that the interviewee might often find it difficult to provide the geographic breakdown of sectoral sales distributions. For this reason, at the time of interviewing, a handy Tennessee map demarcated by the regional breakdown was presented to the interviewee. Also, the fact that the regional divisions of the state nearly coincide with the popularly known three grand divisions undoubtedly helped the interviewee identify each region. The field interviews showed that a surprisingly large number of respondents had a good idea as to the regional distribution of their sales within Tennessee. In cases where the respondents did not have a clear notion of the nature of their sales distribution passing through middlemen, the respondents were encouraged to complete some questionnaire items by requesting the relevant information from their middlemen and returning the questionnaire form later. All in all, the cooperation of respondents was excellent and the overall response rate of over 70 per cent of the total sample interviewed was quite encouraging. This, we feel, indicates the feasibility of conducting this type of survey in implementing regional and interregional flow analyses at the regional level.

Because of the nature of the information sought and the memory estimates required, a certain amount of response error was unavoidable, and no attempt was made to gauge the extent of these errors. It is significant to note, however, that for the most part the respondents occupied key positions that were mainly connected with sales functions.

After the sample data on sales and their distribution over sectors and regions were obtained, it was necessary to inflate the sample data to arrive at an estimate of the distribution of total sales for each sector in each region. This was accomplished by weighing the sample results for each line of business within a given sector by firm sizes (indicated by the sales volume) and by aggregating over lines of business to the level of our intermediate sectors. Finally, multiplying the fractional sales distribution by the corresponding sector employment estimates provides a basis for computing the basic-flow table in employment units, corresponding to equation (3) in the preceding chapter. The procedures outlined above were followed in determining the rows of the transactions table for sectors 1, 5-22, 24, and 25 in the statewide model and their counterparts in each of the three regions.

For sector 2 (TVA) sufficient information was provided by TVA to allow for estimation of the initial allocation of employment both for the statewide and the interregional models. Sector 23 (transportation and communications) was originally intended to be two separate sectors, one for transportation and the other embracing communications. Disappointing returns on the transportation questionnaire forced a merging of the two types of economic activity into one sector. Data provided by Southern Bell Telephone Company on the sectoral and geographic distribution of their receipts along with that obtained by questionnaire from other communications and transportation firms provided the basis for an estimate of the sales distribution of this combined sector.

In bringing the household noncapital sector into the endogenous part of the model, it was necessary to develop a household row, corresponding to the sales flows of other sectors, for the statewide model and for each region of the three-region model. For both models the relevant entries consisted of wages, salaries, rent, and noncorporate profits paid to Tennessee residents by each sector in 1964. Estimates of these amounts were obtained from the sample survey and were inflated and aggregated to the sector level as previously described concerning the sample sales flows. In the case of the three-region model, the reasonably plausible assumption was made, for lack of better information, that wages, salaries, and the like, paid by sectors in a given region were received entirely by the household sector in that region. Interest and dividends paid to Tennessee residents on a sector basis were not included because of the difficulty of obtaining the data. The omission of these items, however, is not uncommon in regional interindustry analysis. Due to its relative unimportance, such omission is not expected to affect the present analysis to any significant extent.

An estimate of wages and salaries paid by the household sector to itself for both models was made in the following manner. From the 1960 census data, the ratio of wages and salaries received by private household workers to the total paid to private household and personal service workers was obtained. An estimate of wages and salaries paid in 1964 to private household and personal service employees was obtained from the unpublished detail of the Tennessee personal income estimates made by the Office of Business Economics, Regional Economics Division, United States Department of Commerce. The ratio computed from the 1960 census data was then applied to this total to form an estimate of wages and salaries paid to private household workers in Tennessee in 1964. This total was then allocated among the regions according to the relative amount of total employment in each region in 1964.

Dividing the household rows so developed by the relevant total wages and salaries produced the fractional distribution of wages and salaries. To this the estimates of private household employment were multiplied in order to obtain the household rows in the basic-flow tables in employment units.

Data on Sales Flows of Agricultural Sectors

Data on the sectoral and geographic allocation of sales of agricultural products came from a number of sources: personal interviews with agricultural economists knowledgeable about specific products, published reports from the United States Department of Agriculture, annual and weekly reports of the Tennessee Crop Reporting Service, bulletins of the Agricultural Experiment Station at the University of Tennessee, and the 1959 Census of Agriculture. It had originally been hoped that the 1964 Census of Agriculture would be an important data source, but unfortunately most of the relevant figures were not available in time for use in this study.

It is difficult to describe in detail the way in which the entries for the two agricultural sectors, sectors 3 (livestock) and 4 (crops), were prepared since each of some thirty products was handled separately and differently depending upon available data sources. A few general remarks may be indicative of the methods typically used, however. Control totals for the value of production were taken from the annual report of the Tennessee Crop Reporting Service for 1964.[8] These figures were then allocated regionally using the crop reporting data when available on a county basis or using the 1959 distribution of production by county from the Census of Agriculture. Sales of each region were then distributed to the intermediate and final-demand sectors and geographically on the basis of information elicited from a variety of sources.

For example, for cotton the basic distribution of sales was made from published and unpublished information provided by the cotton-marketing expert in the University of Tennessee Department of Agricultural Economics, who was able to distribute output on the basis of government loans, sales to Tennessee spinning mills, and sales to spinners outside Tennessee. On the basis of his knowledge of the industry, this expert allocated sales regionally to these spinners. Sales outside Tennessee were divided between domestic and foreign sales based on the 1961-1962 breakdown of Tennessee export sales reported by the United States Department of Agriculture.

For the major grain crops, a breakdown of variations in utilization between food and feed by region was provided by a grain expert in the Department of Agricultural Economics along with figures on the movement of these grains out of state. This information supplemented information on grain markets published by the Agricultural Experiment Station.[9] Similar expert assistance was employed in estimating the distribution of livestock output as required in rounding out and updating the picture furnished by two other experiment station bulletins.[10]

Notes

1. John R. Meyer, "Regional Economics: A Survey," *American Economic Review,* March 1963, 53:19-54.

2. Tennessee Grand Divisions are defined in *Tennessee Code Annotated* (Indianapolis: Bobbs Merrill, 1955), vol. 2, sections 4, 109, and 112.

3. The counties included in region E are: Macon, Clay, Pickett, Claiborne, Hancock, Sullivan, Jackson, Overton, Fentress, Scott, Campbell, Hawkins, Johnson, Smith, Union, Grainger, Hamblen, Greene, Washington, Carter, Unicoi, Putnam, Morgan, Hamilton, Anderson, Jefferson, De Kalb, White, Cumberland, Knox, Cocke, Roane, Warren, Van Buren, Loudon, Blount, Sevier, Bledsoe, Rhea, Coffee, Grundy, Sequatchie, Meigs, McMinn, Monroe, Franklin, Marion, Bradley, and Polk. Region M includes the following counties: Stewart, Montgomery, Sumner, Robertson, Trousdale, Houston, Cheatham, Dickson, Davidson, Wilson, Humphreys, Hickman, Williamson, Rutherford, Cannon, Perry, Maury, Lewis, Bedford, Marshall, Moore, Wayne, Giles, Lawrence, and Lincoln. The counties included in region W are: Obion, Weakley, Henry, Dyer, Benton, Gibson, Carroll, Lauderdale, Crockett, Haywood, Madison, Henderson, Decatur, Chester, Tipton, Shelby, Fayette, Hardeman, McNairy, Hardin, and Lake.

4. Hansen and Tiebout, "An Intersectoral Flows Analysis," 411.

5. The aggregated TDES employment estimates, classified according to the sectors and regions used by the TISG, were supplied by the Bureau of Business Research, University of Tennessee, Knoxville. The Bureau of Labor Statistics employment estimates were provided directly by the TDES. The principal difference between the two estimates lies in the fact that the TDES estimates are for firms or payroll reporting units employing four or more workers, whereas the Bureau of Labor Statistics estimates are for all establishments regardless of number employed. Hence, the Bureau of Labor Statistics estimates are more inclusive and, therefore, more appropriate for our analysis.

6. Even if the figure is correct, the household employment figure does not reflect the service generated by housewives, among other things. Since the relevant income concept for the household column should include the income imputed from household services of wives, the exclusion of this item seriously understates the relevant household employment.

7. Interviewers made it clear to the interviewee that noncapital goods were defined as goods which are ordinarily completely used up during the year to produce other goods by buying firms or goods completely consumed during the year by households. The respondents were also told that in determining the noncapital sales, the possible use of products by buyers is more important than the nature of the product. In addition, a number of examples were given by the interviewer and in the questionnaire to help illustrate this principle.

8. Tennessee Crop Reporting Service, *Annual Report* (Nashville: Tennessee Crop Reporting Service, 1964).

9. C. E. Fuller and J. K. Robertson, *The Sources and Disposition of Grain in Tennessee* (Knoxville: The University of Tennessee Agricultural Experiment Station, April 1964).

10. W. L. Fishel, Irving Dubov, D. D. Rohdy, and R. G. Stout, *Hog and Pork Movements in the Southeast,* Southern Cooperative Series Bulletin No. 83 (Jan. 1963). Roy G. Stout, J. C. Purcell, and W. L. Fishel, *Marketing, Slaughter, and Consumption of Livestock and Meats in the South,* Southern Cooperative Series Bulletin No. 66 (Aug. 1961).

5. The Statewide Model

The Empirical Results

Having described the models and the data employed in their implementation, we can report in this chapter the empirical results as they apply to Tennessee taken as a single economic entity. In the next chapter, the results obtained from the implementation of the three-region model will be considered.

Specifically, this chapter analyzes the sectoral interdependence of the Tennessee economy by examining various multipliers computed from the multiplier matrices and the final-demand categories of the regional intersectoral flow model. Of particular interest are the induced final-demand effects computed from both the present method and the Hansen-Tiebout method. These results differ significantly as expected on the basis of the developments presented in Chapter 3 and bring out again the importance of correctly treating a final-demand category as an endogenous sector. In addition to multiplier analyses, this chapter investigates the fundamental structure of production in the Tennessee economy by utilizing the method of Simpson and Tsukui.[1] Although Simpson and Tsukui initiated the method with an input-output model, a similar method can also be applied to the intersectoral flow model. For a regional comparison, the same method is applied to the California intersectoral flow model which originated with the work of Hansen and Tiebout.[2] While the regional comparison is interesting per se, it provides a basis for testing the general hypothesis of Simpson and Tsukui concerning the similarity of basic production structures among different countries or regions.

In the first section of this chapter, the nature of the intersectoral flow table and of the relevant multiplier matrices is briefly discussed. Intermediate-sector multipliers and final-demand multipliers are analyzed in the second and third sections respectively.[3] A comparison between the fundamental structures of production for Tennessee and California is taken up in the fourth section. A brief summary composes the last section.

Overall View of the Flow Table and the Multiplier Matrix

The intersectoral flow table in employment units may be regarded as a convenient form in which the total employment of each industrial sector is assigned according to the destinations of its output of a given period or alternatively according to the sources of costs associated with the outputs of other sectors. Such a table for the state of Tennessee is given in Table A-1 in Appendix A. Two basic models are incorporated within this table. In the first model—termed model A for the sake of brevity—the household noncapital sector, HC, is treated as exogenous; hence, the HC column becomes part of the final-demand sector while the HC row can be disregarded. In the second model—hereafter referred to as model B—household noncapital is treated as endogenous by bringing the HC column and row into the part of intermediate sectors.

Viewing the table from the standpoint of model A, two observations are worth noting concerning the manufacturing industries (sectors 7 through 22), which provide about 35 per cent of the total employment in Tennessee. The first concerns the large percentage of employment directly assigned to final demand. In the manufacturing division, at least 90 per cent of the total employment of most sectors is directly assigned to final demand. In only three manufacturing sectors is the percentage directly assigned to final demand less than 90 per cent. The sectors in which this is the case are: sector 11, paper, sector 12, printing and publishing, and sector 17, stone, clay, and glass. The percentage assigned directly to final demand in sector 11 is 84.6; that of sector 12 is 61.7; and that of sector 17 is 57.6. Owing to the nature of the products of these sectors, one would have expected that the fraction of sales made endogenously is relatively large in comparison with other manufacturing sectors. As a result, a comparatively smaller percentage of employment is assigned directly to final demand. If the manufacturing division is looked at from the standpoint of model B, the same conclusions hold in general. Additionally, less than 90 per cent of the employment of sector 7, food and tobacco, is directly assigned to final demand. This change comes as no surprise since a large portion of the sales and hence employment of this sector is directly assigned to HC.

Second, from the standpoint of both models for the manufacturing division (sectors 7-22), most of the employment is directly assigned to a single final-demand category: expenditure by the rest of the United States. Total manufacturing employment amounts to 362,000 employees and of this total, 287,041 employees, or 79.3 per cent, are directly assigned to expenditures by the rest of the United States. These two observations indicate that the manufacturing division of the Tennessee economy is extremely open in nature with its sectoral growth connected to changes in final demand outside the state. Since exports outside the United States account for less than 2 per cent of the total employment of manufacturing division, this division's growth is mainly linked to changes in out-of-state domestic final demand.

The nonmanufacturing industries (sectors 1, 3-6, 23-26), which account for approximately 63 per cent of employment in Tennessee, are more closely tied to the domestic economy of the state. Only 33 per cent of total employment of these sectors is attributable to final demand outside the state. With model B in particular, more than 50 per cent of total employment of nonmanufacturing sectors are accounted for by intermediate sectors in Tennessee. Such intersectoral connections within Tennessee are not surprising, since the nonmanufacturing sectors include many essentially local activities such as various business services, transportation and communications, and wholesale and retail trade.

It is important to note the contribution in the Tennessee economy of the TVA (sector 2) which was left out in the above discussion. Although the TVA contributes about 2 per cent of total employment of Tennessee, the absolute size of employment is fairly large, at 10,900. Moreover, 75 per cent of the TVA employment is generated by the Tennessee economy while 49 per cent of the employment is associated with intermediate sectors of the statewide model B. Thus, the importance of this sector together with its unique sales distribution again justifies the treatment of the TVA as a separate sector in this monograph.

Another overall measure of direct intersectoral dependence in the Tennessee economy can be observed from the number of entries in the statewide flow table. Out of a total of 625 cells in the (25×25) table related to model A, there are 381 entries. For model B with the dimension of (26×26), entries are found in 428 cells out of a total 676 cells. When the entries in each row of Table A-1 in Appendix A are divided by the total employment of the sector given in each row, the flow table is transformed into the statewide sales-flow coefficient matrix (not reported). Either one of these tables for either model can be used to glean some insight into the degree of direct dependence. While the extent of direct dependence as measured by the number of entries is fairly extensive, many of the cell entries are quite small relative to the total employment of each sector, thereby resulting in rather small sales-flow coefficients in general. Thus, the degree of direct intersectoral dependence is not so strong as it might first appear to be from the extensive number of entries in the flow table in employment units.

The direct plus indirect interdependence of the Tennessee industries can be observed from the relevant multiplier matrix of model A that is computed with the formula (4) of Chapter 3. Each entry in a given column shows the direct plus indirect employment generated in the industry identified on a row basis, as a consequence of a change of one employee directly assigned to final demand from the sector identified by its column number. Although this matrix multiplier is not reported because of space limitation, all but one of the cells in the matrix were filled. With the direct connections filling 381 cells, it can be said that indirect employment is extensively generated through the existing patterns of sectoral interdependence. While this observation appears sound, it is also true that many of the entries in the multiplier matrix were extremely small.

The multiplier matrix associated with model B is given in Appendix A as Table A-2. Each entry in a column captures either the sum of the direct, indirect, and induced employment impacts or the sum of the indirect and induced employment impacts on the corresponding row sector due to a change of one employee in a column sector directly assigned to final demand. Referring to the first page of Table A-2, we see that the total impact on each sector of a one-employee change in employment directly from sector 1, retail and wholesale trade, is given in the first column. The first entry in this column, 1.0756, indicates the total employment impact on sector 1 of such a final-demand change. The "1" is the employee directly assigned. As a result of indirect and induced effects, employment in this sector changes by an additional 0.0756 employees. The indirect and induced impact of a final-demand change in retail and wholesale trade on some other sectors—say sector 2, TVA—can be found by reading 0.0034 in the second entry of the first column. Examining Table A-2 in this way, we can observe the pattern of sectoral interdependence when the household sector is treated endogenously. While most of the entries in this matrix multiplier are somewhat larger than the corresponding entries in the matrix multiplier of model A, the sectoral interdependence appears again to be weak.

In general it can be said that although the manufacturing division of the Tennessee economy is open, the Tennessee economy as a whole is largely confined to local economic activities. This follows from the fact that the employment share of the nonmanufacturing division in the Tennessee economy is relatively large. The sectoral interdependence among industries in Tennessee is modest even when the household consumption sector is brought into the endogenous part of the model. Such interdependence as exists, however, is woven mainly through connections with the nonmanufacturing division and TVA, directly or indirectly.

Before turning to the next section, one should note the implication of ignoring imports into Tennessee for the analysis in this study. Although data on imports were not collected, the bulk of the inputs of Tennessee industries were probably imported from outside the state, as is implied by the low percentage of sales by Tennessee's manufacturing sectors to the local industries. If this is the case, changes in relative price between inputs produced inside and outside the state could alter the composition of the basic-flow table and thus the matrix multiplier. In this study, however, it is assumed that drastic changes in the geographical price structure do not take place for the time period under consideration. Granting that input prices are more or less competitively determined and therefore that regional price differences are largely accounted for by transportation and distribution charges, the geographical price structure may not change drastically in a time period of modest length.

Intermediate-Sector Employment Multipliers

In this section, employment multipliers are reported for each intermediate sector. As presented in formula (6) of Chapter 3, these multipliers are simply the column sums of the relevant multiplier matrix. An examination of these multipliers yields insight into which sectors are likely to be most important, assuming a given final-demand structure.

Two sets of multipliers are calculated, the first set corresponding to model A and the second set to model B. In the first set in which HC is treated as exogenous, each multiplier shows the direct and indirect effect on the employment in all sectors in response to a change of one employee in each intermediate sector required to produce directly for final demand. For example, the sum of the second column of this matrix multiplier indicates the direct and indirect impacts on employments of all Tennessee industries as a result of the hiring of one employee by TVA (the second sector) to meet a direct final demand for its output. Such a multiplier captures a relatively short-run impact on employment and ignores the prolonged induced impact on employment of household spending. The multipliers of all intermediate sectors are reported in Table 4. In this table, the first column identifies the intermediate sector number, the second column contains the multipliers, and the third column gives the rank of ordering each multiplier.

A second set of multipliers corresponding to model B is also reported in Table 4. As an intermediate sector expands its output and employment due to a change in its final demand, output and employment in other sectors are affected, directly and indirectly. This expansion is also reflected by the increased wages and salaries paid by the sector in question which in turn provides additional demand for the output of the various intermediate sectors. The additional demand in turn generates further increase in the employment of the local economy. Such an increase in employment generated by household spending is called induced employment and is captured in the second set of multipliers. Column 4 of Table 4 gives the multiplier of each sector which represents the total (direct plus indirect plus induced) changes in employment in all sectors due to a change of one employee in the given sector directly

TABLE 4

INTERMEDIATE-SECTOR EMPLOYMENT MULTIPLIERS: STATEWIDE MODEL

(1) *Sector Name and No.*	*(2) Multiplier* HC *Exogenous*	*(3) Rank*	*(4) Multiplier* HC *Endogenous*	*(5) Rank*	*(6) Induced Effect from Treating* HC *as Endogenous*	*(7) Weighted* HC *Exogenous Rank*	*(8) Weighted* HC *Endogenous Rank*
1 Retail and wholesale	1.120	14	1.363	13	0.242	1	1
2 TVA	1.408	5	1.893	4	0.484	19	21
3 Livestock	1.458	4	1.617	7	0.159	10	24
4 Crops	1.025	25	1.137	25	0.112	8	9
5 Mining	1.188	9	1.516	10	0.328	25	25
6 Construction	1.786	2	2.111	2	0.325	5	4
7 Food and tobacco	2.906	1	3.358	1	0.451	3	3
8 Textiles and apparel	1.088	19	1.234	22	0.147	4	2
9 Lumber	1.047	23	1.241	21	0.194	18	17
10 Furniture	1.050	22	1.262	20	0.212	13	13
11 Paper	1.172	10	1.476	11	0.304	23	20
12 Printing and publishing	1.128	13	1.366	14	0.237	21	22
13 Ind. inorganic and org. chem.	1.158	12	1.539	9	0.380	14	11
14 Plastics and synthetics	1.095	17	1.379	12	0.285	9	8
15 Rubber and misc. plastics	1.036	24	1.190	24	0.155	24	23
16 Leather	1.101	16	1.302	19	0.201	15	15
17 Stone, clay, and glass	1.255	7	1.581	8	0.326	22	19
18 Primary metals	1.076	20	1.335	15	0.259	17	16
19 Fabricated metals (not elsewhere classified)	1.102	15	1.329	16	0.226	16	14
20 Nonelectrical machinery	1.161	11	1.747	5	0.586	19	18
21 Electrical machinery and equip.	1.089	18	1.304	18	0.215	12	12
22 Transp., instrument, and misc. mfg.	1.641	3	1.960	3	0.318	11	10
23 Transportation and communications	1.073	21	1.232	23	0.159	7	7
24 Finance, ins., and real estate	1.313	6	1.711	6	0.399	6	6
25 Misc. services	1.201	8	1.319	17	0.118	2	5

Note: Due to rounding errors, column 4 minus column 2 may not provide column 6 exactly. The sectors are fully defined in Table 1 of ch. 4.

related to final demand. The multipliers presented in this column are computed as the column sums of the multiplier matrix reported in Table A-2 of Appendix A, which includes a HC row and column for the endogenous treatment of the household sector.[4] Column 5 of Table 4 shows the ranking of the multipliers with HC treated as endogenous. Column 6 identifies the size of the induced employment effect for each intermediate sector and is obtained by subtracting column 2 from column 4 of Table 4. Since it would take additional time to achieve the induced effects, the total employment effects implied by the multipliers in column 4 take longer to work themselves out. Hence, the multipliers in column 4 can be interpreted as being somewhat longer-run in nature than those shown in column 2.

An overview of the multipliers of both models reveals that the multipliers generated from model B are consistently larger than their counterparts in model A. Including HC in the endogenous part of the model produces induced demand for output, thus stimulating larger employment changes than those realized when only direct and indirect employment effects are considered. The multipliers in model A range from a low of 1.025 in sector 4, crops, to a high of 2.906 for sector 7, food and tobacco. In model B the smallest multiplier is also associated with sector 4, but its magnitude is 1.137. Likewise, the largest multiplier for model B is associated with sector 7 and is 3.358. The induced employment effects generated by including HC as endogenous are in general quite large. In all but five sectors the induced impact on employment generated by model B is larger than the indirect employment impact of final-demand changes in model A. The large size of the induced effect in general indicates the strong impact of consumer spending in Tennessee on the output and employment of Tennessee intermediate sectors. A comparison of the rankings of the multipliers between models A and B reveals that the importance of the multipliers change, sometimes dramatically.

Comparing multipliers in each model, one sees that the largest multiplier in each case is associated with food and tobacco products, sector 7. When one examines in detail the multiplier matrix of model A (not reported), however, the total impact on employment arising from final-demand change in sector 7 is heavily concentrated in a few sectors. The bulk of the employment change is confined to the two agricultural sectors, 3 and 4. The sum of the employment effects on the two agricultural sectors is 1.726 employees. When the one employee directly assigned to final demand is added to this figure, the resulting 2.726 employees are already accounted for out of the total employees of 2.906 reported in column 2 for the sector 7 of Table 4. This leaves only 0.180 employees to be accounted for indirectly by the remaining intermediate sectors, including sector 7. Apparently in model A final-demand changes in food and tobacco products have their main impact on that sector and on the agricultural sectors with little effect on the employment in the remaining sectors.

Reflecting the induced employment generated by the explicit inclusion of

HC in the endogenous part of the model, the multiplier for sector 7 in model B is higher than it is in model A. Again, however, a major portion of the total employment change can be traced to the direct final-demand change in sector 7 of one employee and the indirect plus induced effects on agricultural sectors 3 and 4. The effects on the agricultural sectors amounting to 1.812 employees can readily be obtained by summing the entries for sectors 3 and 4 in column 7 of Table A-2 reported in Appendix A. Adding one direct employee to this figure gives 2.812 employees. Out of the total employment impact of 3.358 employees in column 4 for the sector 7 of Table 4, there remains only 0.546 employees that are generated indirectly in nonagricultural sectors, including sector 7. Hence, in both models a rather self-contained interdependence is exhibited between final-demand changes in agricultural processing and the two agricultural sectors.

Sector 6, construction, ranks second in model A with a multiplier of 1.786. In contrast to the self-contained interdependence that exists between agricultural processing and the agricultural sectors, the effect on total employment due to a change of one employee directly assigned to final demand from the construction sector is rather widespread. With a multiplier of 2.111, the same is true of construction in model B. While the employment impacts affect several sectors in both models, sizable employment effects on sector 1, wholesale-retail, and sector 25, miscellaneous services, are recorded. In model A a one-employee change in final-demand employment in the construction sector results in an employment change of 0.240 in sector 1 and one of 0.111 in sector 25. Reflecting the induced employment impact of the HC sector, in model B the employment change in sector 1 increases to 0.328 and in sector 25 it is 0.225.

As required by the model, the construction row for intermediate-demand sectors in the intersectoral flow table contains only employment related to maintenance and repair construction. Thus, the entries are rather small relative to total employment in construction. On the input side in construction, employment is directly assigned from several sectors to the construction sector and the size of some of the entries is large relative to total employment in construction. Thus the input structure for the construction sector and the accompanying indirect and induced employment effects are responsible for the large multipliers and the relatively widespread employment effects of this sector. The finding, therefore, implies that if the government final-demand categories in the form of public works increase, the public works program would have a large impact on total employment over all sectors in Tennessee. This conclusion is, in general, consistent with the traditional view concerning the efficacy of public construction programs in stimulating a regional economy. This conclusion must, of course, be interpreted in light of the model, which does not consider the possible adverse effect on growth of the financing of government expenditures via taxation or debt creation. If the expenditure is locally financed through local taxation, the net growth effect of state and local government expenditures may be substantially smaller than the gross effects described in a multiplier developed by the present study. On the other hand, given local expenditures financed by means of some program of revenue-sharing, the net and gross effects may be almost the same.

The third-ranked employment multiplier in both models is associated with sector 22, transportation, instruments, and miscellaneous manufacturing. In model A the multiplier is 1.641, and in model B it is 1.960. In model A a large part of the total impact on employment is located in the transportation and communication sector and in the service sector. The total change in employment in these sectors is 0.382, which is slightly larger than half the total change in employment in all sectors due to a change of one employee directly related to final demand in sector 22. This sector is composed of transportation equipment, professional science and control instruments, photographic and optical goods, watches and clocks, and miscellaneous manufacturing. The makeup of this sector clearly indicates why the input sectors just mentioned would be important sources of inputs. In model B employment in these same sectors is affected importantly by directly assigned final-demand changes from sector 22. In addition, in model B sector 22 generates a sizable employment impact on wholesale and retail, sector 1. This reflects the circular effects of final-demand changes in sector 22 on wages and salaries and, hence, upon sales and employment in the wholesale-retail trade sector. Altogether, the three aforementioned sectors in model B account for 0.647 of the total (direct, indirect, plus induced) changes in employment in sector 22 due to a one-employee increase in final-demand employment in that sector.

The fourth- and fifth-ranked multipliers in model A are sector 3, livestock, and sector 2, TVA, respectively. In model B TVA ranks fourth and sector 20, nonelectrical machinery, which ranked eleventh in model A, now ranks fifth. Livestock, the fourth-ranked sector in model A, ranks seventh in model B.

Regarding the livestock sector in model A, the respectable size of its multiplier, 1.458, stems mainly from its large total employment impact on sector 4, crops. A one-employee change in the livestock sector which is directly related to final demand will bring about an indirect increase in employment of the sector for crops by 0.351, which is almost three-fourths of the total employment impact of livestock sector on all industries. This again shows between the two agricultural sectors a self-contained interdependence similar to that between the agricultural processing sector and the two agricultural sectors. These observations, therefore, indicate that while the Tennessee agricultural sectors are closely interrelated, they are not so closely tied to the remaining manufacturing sectors. In other words, an increase in agricultural products has only a small effect on output and employment elsewhere in the manufacturing division of the Tennessee economy.

TVA, the fifth-ranked sector in model A, has a multiplier of 1.408. Although it is not reported, a glance at the relevant multiplier matrix would indicate that the sectors whose total employment is importantly affected are sectors 1 (retail and wholesale), 5 (mining), 23 (transportation and communications), 24 (finance, insurance, and real estate), and 25 (miscellaneous services). In model B, TVA is ranked fourth with its employment multiplier of 1.893, which is much larger than the corresponding multiplier for model A. The induced employment impact of 0.489 is larger than the indirect employment impact of 0.408 and is spread among many sectors. This is due to the fact that TVA has a large direct input absorbed from and a large output sold to the household sector, coupled with its input-output link with a relatively large number of other sectors in Tennessee. Like TVA in model A, the employment impact of final-demand changes in TVA is concentrated in the same sectors but with a particularly heavy employment impact of 0.525 evidenced in the wholesale-retail and service sectors together. Many of the activities engaged in by the TVA are specifically directed toward regional economic development and growth. It is, therefore, significant to find that in the process of supplying power to Tennessee intermediate sectors TVA appears as a relatively important link in the structure of the Tennessee economy.

The rise to prominence in model B of sector 20, nonelectrical machinery, is due to the large induced employment effect generated by this sector. Sector 20 has an induced employment effect of 0.586, which is the largest one recorded in column 5 of Table 4.

As seen in the above analysis, for the majority of the sectors, a goodly portion of the employment impact of directly assigned final-demand changes is frequently concentrated in a few sectors. The remainder of the impact is spread over many sectors, with the result that none of these sectors registers really significant changes in employment. In many instances, the sector whose employment is importantly affected by final-demand changes in other sectors is classified in the nonmanufacturing division (sectors 1-6 and 23-25). This same tendency seems to hold for many of the remaining sectors. The reason for this tendency in both models stems from the fact that employment in most nonmanufacturing sectors is relatively large, and in most cases a large percentage of this employment is directly assigned to intermediate sectors. Additionally, in model B the induced employment effect of household spending has a particularly strong impact on retail and wholesale trade, sector 1, and on miscellaneous services, sector 25. Despite some obvious exceptions, therefore, changes in directly assigned final-demand employment have their main impact on the sector in which the change occurs and upon the sectors in the nonmanufacturing division. For the reason given above, this tendency is more pronounced in model B than in model A. It appears that encouraging a higher degree of development in the manufacturing division could result in a closer interdependence among Tennessee manufacturing sectors and would thus increase employment impacts within the manufacturing division.

So far, the analysis of multipliers has been confined to the unweighted multipliers. An implicit assumption in this analysis is that some final-demand items can be influenced by regional economic planners so that one could bring about desirable income and employment changes in a given region.

Another way of analyzing the multipliers is to weigh the multipliers in accordance with the relative importance of final demand for a given sector to final demand for all intermediate sectors. In other words, the relative importance of different industries in a given regional economy is being looked upon without specific regional planning in mind. Such relative importance in terms of the rankings of each sector is reported in columns 7 and 8 of Table 4. The rankings in column 7 were generated from model A and those in column 8 were derived from model B. The method of determining the change in total employment is given in formula (7) of Chapter 3. It amounts to the following: first, multiply each of the unweighted multipliers in columns 2 and 4 of Table 4 by the relative change in final demand for each sector to total change in final demand for all sectors and then rank the products according to their sizes. Since employment changes for each sector could not be ascertained from available data, it was assumed that each element in the final-demand vector changes in the same proportion. Weighting the unweighted multipliers by these changes will indicate which sectors may contribute most importantly to overall employment changes. Such an interpretation must be applied with caution, however, since the assumption of equal percentage changes in all final-demand elements is at best a rough first approximation to reality. Nevertheless, given this assumption, the employment changes and the rankings are probably more relevant for model B than for model A. Support for this assertion lies in the fact that changes in final demand most certainly will produce changes in wages and salaries, which will in turn be used to contribute additionally to the demand and hence output and employment of the several intermediate sectors, assuming an infinitely elastic supply of labor. This effect is, of course, captured in model B but not in model A. From the standpoint of analyzing the observed growth process the weighted multipliers are most useful, while the unweighted multipliers are most useful in a policy context.

Moving HC into the endogenous part of the model affects not only the absolute and relative size of the resulting final-demand elements, but also the size and ranking of the unweighted employment multipliers. This being the case, one would expect the ranking of the change in total employment to differ substantially between columns 7 and 8. Surprisingly, the five leading sectors are the same in both models, although their rankings do differ somewhat. In model A the five leading sectors are 1 (retail and wholesale trade), 25 (miscellaneous services), 7 (food and tobacco), 8 (textiles and apparel), and 6 (construction), in that order, and in model B the leading sectors listed in descending order of importance are 1, 8, 7, 6, and 25.

The preeminence of sector 1 in both models is explained by the large total employment in retail and wholesale trade coupled with the fact that much of this employment is assigned to final demand. Even when HC is treated endogenously, the amount of wholesale-retail employment remaining in final demand is impressive. This is the case because a relatively large portion of the employment in retail and wholesale trade was assigned to HI due to the fact that most household semidurables have a useful life in excess of one year and were thus treated as durable goods. Since the unweighted multipliers for the retail and wholesale trade sector in both models were fairly low, the importance of this sector in the present analysis can be explained by the large size of its final-demand employment. In model A, sector 1 accounts for 20.8 per cent of the total employment, while in model B it accounts for 19.1 per cent. Thus, the relative change is less in model B than in model A.

Sector 25, the miscellaneous service sector, ranks second in model A and fifth in model B. Its high rank in model A is explained by the large total employment in the sector, the major portion of which is allocated to final demand. The reason for the drop in the rank of sector 25 in model B is rather straightforward and revolves around the effect on employment in sector 25 directly assigned to final demand as a result of treating HC as endogenous. As expected, the majority of employment in sector 25 directly assigned to final demand is assigned to HC. In all, of the 99,629 employees directly assigned to final demand, 59,070 are assigned to HC, and moving HC into the endogenous part of the model reduces final-demand employment by that amount. Even though the unweighted employment multipliers for sector 25 in Table 4 increase from 1.201 in model A to 1.319 in model B, the increase is not enough to offset the decline in final-demand employment.

Sector 8, textiles and apparel, ranks second in model B. The high rank is due to the large total employment in sector 8, a large portion of which is assigned to final-demand categories other than HC. The same sector in model A ranks fourth, and the reason for its high rank is substantially the same. In both models the relatively small unweighted employment multipliers are counterbalanced by the impressive size of the employment directly assigned to final demand.

Sectors 7 and 6, food and construction, maintain an important standing when their multipliers are weighted by final-demand employment. As indicated above, sector 7 ranks third in both models and sector 6 ranks fifth in model A and fourth in model B. The importance of the weighted employment multipliers of these sectors is explained by their large unweighted multipliers, which occupy the first or the second rank among the unweighted multipliers of both models.

As shown in detail above, weighting the intermediate employment multipliers by a given structure of final demand results in a considerable change in the rankings of the sectors in comparison with the previous rankings of the sectors among the unweighted multipliers. Such rankings constitute a rough forecast of likely leading sectors in the Tennessee economy in the absence of a shift in the given structure of final demand. The importance of these sectors is also characterized by the fact that in both models employment changes are heavily concentrated in these sectors. Of the total employment in Tennessee, 54 per cent is contained in the leading five sectors of model B and about 59 per cent is generated in the same sectors of model A.

In summary, the analysis in this section indicates that dominant sectors for explaining observed growth of the Tennessee economy are mostly locally oriented and nonmanufacturing industries such as service, construction, and wholesale-retail (the exceptions being food and textile industries). From a regional planning viewpoint, if policy measures can influence the magnitude of final demand for specific industries, the important industries to be considered are such sectors as food, construction, TVA, miscellaneous manufacturing, and nonelectrical machinery. The analysis in this section, therefore, suggests that a higher employment impact on the Tennessee economy can be achieved by changing the existing pattern of final demand. Given the influence of final-demand changes, however, the existence of weak interindustry connections, particularly among manufacturing sectors, indicates the desirability of encouraging entry of new firms or expansion of existing firms.

To put this another way, given a change in final demand, a stimulus in the nonmanufacturing segments of the economy tends to be captured within the boundaries of the region, whereas in general a stimulus in the manufacturing area tends to leak away into other regions as a result of the sparseness of the entries in the manufacturing portion of the matrix and of the smallness of many of the entries which do exist. This is the classical problem of the relatively underdeveloped area, which tends to lack forward and backward domestic linkages, particularly in the area of secondary activity.

Final-Demand Multipliers

The preceding multiplier analysis viewed the economy from the standpoint of the intermediate sectors and considered the impact on total employment over all sectors resulting from final-demand changes for each intermediate sector. On the other hand, it is also instructive to view the economy from the standpoint of the final-demand sectors and to compare the total employment effect of equal percentage changes in the employment directly assigned to each of the various final-demand categories. For this purpose final-demand multipliers for both models A and B are calculated according to the method given in formula (8) of Chapter 3. In this approach the total employment assigned to each final-demand sector is determined by premultiplying the multiplier matrix to the final-demand matrix and summing the columns of the product matrix.[5] The employment directly assigned to each final-demand sector is simply the column sum of the final-demand matrix. Dividing the total employment assigned to each final-demand category by that directly assigned results in the final-demand multipliers.[6]

The final-demand multipliers so calculated are presented in Table 5. In the first column, the final-demand categories are represented by their symbols as defined previously in Table 2 of Chapter 4. The final-demand multipliers with household noncapital, HC, as exogenous are presented in the second column and the rank of each multiplier is given in column 3. In the fourth column the final-demand multipliers presented therein were calculated by moving the HC column and row into the endogenous part of the model and forming a new multiplier matrix. Their rank is presented in column 5.

The final-demand multipliers corresponding to model A range from a low of 1.109 for exports to the rest of the world, EW, to a high of 1.412 for the state and local governments, GSL. With a multiplier of 1.399, the final-demand sector for business investment, BI, ranked second. When only direct and indirect employment effects are allowed for, the size in general of these multipliers is, however, relatively low as expected, and the multipliers for BI and GSL are large relative to the other multipliers. Since direct expenditures on the state and local level and, hence, changes in directly assignable final-demand employment are controlled by state and local governments, the size of this multiplier is noteworthy from a policy standpoint.

In addition to the direct plus indirect impact, the multipliers in column 4 corresponding to model B capture the induced impact on employment of the HC sector. A comparison of these multipliers with their counterparts in column 2 indicates that not only are the multipliers in column 4 larger but their ranking differs to some extent. With HC endogenous, BI now ranks first with a multiplier of 1.678, whereas GSL ranks second with a multiplier of 1.636. Although the numerical difference between the two multipliers is small, in the long run the business investment apparently has a stronger impact on Tennessee economy than do the expenditures of state and local governments. One can also conclude that irrespective of time span involved, the expenditures of state and local governments have a stronger effect on Tennessee employment than do federal government expenditures. This observation supports the general view that the expenditures of state and local governments are more tied to their local economies than are federal government expenditures in general. Finally, the Tennessee economy appears to be modestly influenced by the expenditures of the rest of the United States, EUS, but it is least affected by sales outside the United States.

At this point, it is interesting to examine empirically to what extent our final-demand multipliers differ from the multipliers obtained from the method suggested by Hansen and Tiebout. The resulting difference will demonstrate the methodological differences discussed in Chapter 3.

The method employed by Hansen and Tiebout amounts to forming a local consumption multiplier by calculating the ratio of HC direct plus indirect

TABLE 5

FINAL-DEMAND MULTIPLIERS: STATEWIDE MODEL

(1) *Final-Demand Sector Symbols*	(2) *Final-Demand Multiplier* HC *Exogenous*	(3) *Rank*	(4) *Final-Demand Multiplier Calculated with* HC *Row and Column Endogenous*	(5) *Rank*	(6) *Final-Demand Multiplier* HC *Endogenous as Calculated by* H-T *Method*	(7) *Rank*
HC	1.266	3				
HI	1.158	6	1.398	5	1.449	5
BI	1.399	2	1.678	1	1.750	2
GSL	1.412	1	1.636	2	1.766	1
GF	1.209	5	1.462	4	1.512	4
EUS	1.261	4	1.505	3	1.578	3
EW	1.109	7	1.317	6	1.387	6

Note: The symbols for the final demand sectors are defined in Table 2 of ch. 4.

employment to employment of the other final-demand sectors. The ratio calculated from model A is 0.251.[7] This ratio is then multiplied to each multiplier in column 2 of Table 5 that indicates direct and indirect employment impact of each final-demand employment. According to Hansen and Tiebout, such a product indicates the induced employment impact per unit of final-demand employment. Adding this product to the corresponding multiplier in column 2 gives the Hansen-Tiebout final-demand multipliers reported in column 6 of Table 5. Since this procedure amounts to changing each multiplier in column 2 by adding the same multiple, the ranking of the Hansen-Tiebout multiplier incorporating induced employment is not affected, though the absolute size of their multiplier is increased. Inherent in this approach, therefore, is the assumption that the induced employment effect of household consumption on other final-demand sectors is just a simple multiple calculated from an arbitrary ratio. This assumption is not correct in view of the traditional method in input-output analysis of closing a model by moving relevant sectors into the endogenous part of the model.

With the intersectoral flow models as developed in this monograph, the household noncapital sector, HC, is treated as endogenous by inserting a HC row and column into the intermediate part of the model. Following this procedure allows the induced effects of consumer spending to play themselves out on the basis of the established network of interdependence. This interplay is, of course, not captured in an exact manner in the local consumption multiplier approach employed by Hansen and Tiebout. As Table 5 shows, not only are the Hansen-Tiebout multipliers different from the correct multipliers derived by our method, but also the ranking of the former differs from the ranking of the latter. Moreover, when the model is closed by treating household spendings as endogenous in the manner suggested by Hansen and Tiebout, the ranking of the final-demand multipliers is not changed as compared to the case when the model was not closed. Thus, it is important to specify correctly the induced impact of household spending in the intersectoral flow analysis.

A Comparison of the Fundamental Structure of Production for the Tennessee and California Economies

In an article Simpson and Tsukui have formulated a method for identifying the fundamental structure of production on the basis of an input-output model.[8] Since, as seen in Chapter 3, the intersectoral flow model is similar to the input-output model, the method of Simpson and Tsukui can be applied to the regional model discussed in this chapter. The result of such an application yields some insight into the fundamental structure of production in Tennessee. Since it is interesting to compare the structures of production in different regions, the same method is applied to the California intersectoral flow table originally prepared by Hansen and Tiebout.[9] Comparison of the application to Tennessee and California will in fact provide a basis for testing the general hypothesis advanced by Simpson and Tsukui that production structures in seemingly different economies are essentially the same.

It should be pointed out at the outset that the flow coefficients computed in the Tennessee and the California studies are not strictly the technical coefficients of production. To a lesser extent this is also true of the input-output coefficients used by Simpson and Tsukui for those countries with substantial imports. Simpson and Tsukui approximated the production structure by eliminating the small coefficients and looking only at large coefficients. Since we will examine the rough order of large flow coefficients, it would be possible to glean the nature of the production structures for the two regional economies.

Briefly, the method employed by Simpson and Tsukui involves aggregating the intermediate sectors of the national tables of different countries to make for comparability among sectors. The smaller coefficients in a given technical coefficient table are cleared away by ignoring all coefficients whose size is smaller than one divided by the numbers of sectors.[10] The remaining larger coefficients are said to represent the fundamental structure of production. The sectors are then classified into four blocs: metals, nonmetals, energy, and services. Each bloc of intermediate sectors is then triangularized, and in the principal experiment conducted by Simpson and Tsukui—a comparison between Japan and the United States—the result exhibited a tendency toward bloc-triangularity, i.e., triangularity within each bloc and little or no connection between blocs.[11] A principal theoretical implication is that technological advance over the decades has not resulted in an appreciable increase in substitutability between metals and nonmetals.

While this procedure is applied to only a limited number of countries by Simpson and Tsukui, they argue that their findings should hold for any such comparison between industrialized countries. A comparison of Tennessee and California based on this method should add to the empirical evidence as to the generality of their findings and, it is hoped, provide some insight into the basic structural differences in the two regional economies.

While the economies of both states can be termed industrial, California is certainly more advanced than Tennessee in this respect. Differences, if any, within or between blocs then may be subject to rationalization on the basis of the relative degree of industrial advancement. Such a comparison on a regional level is useful because important structural relationships peculiar to the economic structure of a given region may well be washed out in the compilation of a national table. Also, from the viewpoint of data collection, since both tables were constructed on the basis of questionnaire data on sales flows, at least some confidence can be generated in the size and distribution of coefficients showing direct connection between sectors.

In order to make the intermediate sectoring of Tennessee and California comparable, we aggregated initial sectors into nineteen sectors for each state and formed a matrix of sales-flow coefficients in terms of employment again for each state. Such tables are constructed by following the matrix formula of sales-flow coefficients in terms of employment in equation (4) of Chapter 3. In other words, the tables indicate the number of employees required in the row industry per employee in the column industry to support the production of the column industry. The number and identification of each sector newly created for the comparison in this section is given in Table 6. Sectors 1 through 5 compose the metal bloc, the nonmetal bloc is made up of sectors 6 through 15, and energy and services have been combined into a single bloc and are represented by sectors 16 through 19.[12] The results of the triangularization process are presented in Table 7 for Tennessee and in Table 8 for California. Whenever an arrangement of sectors produces a perfectly triangular order within a bloc, following Simpson and Tsukui, we have imposed that same arrangement on the other table. No attempt was made to improve triangularity by changing the ordering of blocs. The Tennessee table is perfectly triangular within both the metals and nonmetal blocs, and the present order in the Tennessee table gives perfect triangularity up to the last sector in the energy and services bloc; hence, this order was imposed upon the California table. Thus,

TABLE 6

NUMBERING AND DESCRIPTION OF COMBINED SECTORS

Blocs	*Sector Number for Tables 7 & 8*	*Descriptions*
Metal	1.	Transportation equipment, ordnance and instruments, petroleum, and miscellaneous manufacturing
	2.	Nonelectrical machinery
	3.	Electrical machinery
	4.	Fabricated metals
	5.	Primary metals
Nonmetal	6.	Textile-leather
	7.	Apparel
	8.	Food and beverage
	9.	Rubber
	10.	Chemicals
	11.	Stone, glass, and clay
	12.	Paper
	13.	Printing
	14.	Lumber
	15.	Furniture and fixtures
Energy and services	16.	Transportation, communication, public utilities, and services
	17.	Finance, insurance, and real estate
	18.	Wholesale and retail trade
	19.	Agriculture, forestry, fishing, mining

the order in the Tennessee table completely dictated the order in the California table. (The ordering of the last two sectors, sectors 17 and 16, is actually indeterminant.)

An examination of the Tennessee table reveals that the relationship between metals and nonmetals exhibits bloc-triangularity. Each bloc is perfectly triangular and only two cells indicate connections between the two blocs. Inputs from miscellaneous manufacturing (sector 1) to textiles and leather (sector 6) and inputs from chemicals (sector 10) to fabricated metals (sector 4) are the only connecting links between the two blocs. It is worth noting that the third bloc, energy, services, and miscellaneous, provides an important source of inputs into both the metals and nonmetal blocs, a finding supported by the results of Simpson and Tsukui. In all, applying the Simpson-Tsukui method to data for the Tennessee economy yields results in support of the main hypotheses advanced by Simpson and Tsukui.

The results from applying the Simpson-Tsukui process to the modified California table are somewhat less clear-cut. Imposing the ordering of the Tennessee table upon the California table produces perfect within-bloc triangularity in nonmetals only. Furthermore, direct connections based on input coefficient from metals to nonmetals are more numerous than they were in the Tennessee table. Since sector 1 unavoidably contains both metal and nonmetal sectors and was arbitrarily assigned to the metals bloc, the large input coefficient of 0.1491 reflecting inputs from sector 1 to sector 10 probably includes petroleum inputs and hence should be ignored. The other between-bloc connections consist of inputs from sectors 4 and 5 to sector 15 and from sectors 2 and 5 to sector 9. Regarding between-bloc connections consisting of inputs from nonmetals to metals, one entry of 0.0486 appears in the form of inputs supplied from sector 10 to sector 1. This entry is probably also due to the heterogeneous nature of sector 1.

Inputs from energy and service to both blocs appear to be extensive and relatively important, as was the case in the Tennessee table. In the California table, however, more input appears to be directly supplied from the first two blocs to the energy and services bloc than was the case in Tennessee.

Owing to the vague nature of some of the connections arising from inputs supplied from metals to nonmetals and also due to the lack of triangularity within the metals bloc, the California table seemingly lends somewhat less added support to the main Simpson-Tsukui hypothesis. In general though, the results from both the Tennessee and California tables can be interpreted as supporting the Simpson-Tsukui hypothesis concerning bloc-triangularity for metals and nonmetals. The comparatively advanced technological state of the California economy has neither resulted in significant between-bloc connections nor has it produced extensive variations from the triangular within-bloc pattern.

Because of the classification problem, whether this phenomenon holds for energy or services as separate blocs cannot be answered at present. Obviously, bloc-triangularity does not hold for the combined sector.

While the fundamental structures of production of both economies tend to support the main hypothesis of Simpson and Tsukui, important differences in the two structures can be discerned. Most fundamentally, the sales-flow coefficients in the California table are of a generally larger magnitude than in the Tennessee table. This means that in most cases a smaller amount of employment is directly supported in Tennessee sectors per employee in a given intermediate Tennessee sector. In this sense the structural linkages are not so strong in Tennessee as compared to California; that is, Tennessee is the more open of

TABLE 7

THE FUNDAMENTAL STRUCTURE OF PRODUCTION–TENNESSEE

Columns and Rows Identified by Sector Numbers

	2	3	4	5	1	6	7	11	15	9	14	10	8	12	13	18	19	17	16
2																			
3																			
4		0.014																	
5		0.004	0.007																
1						0.030													
6						0.030													
7																			
11								0.036											
15									0.006										
9																			
14									0.010		0.005								
10			0.007				0.006		0.003	0.014	0.003								
8																			
12								0.012	0.006			0.006		0.019					
13															0.039				0.018
18	0.008	0.004	0.008	0.017	0.044		0.005	0.016	0.002			0.010		0.021		0.008			0.017
19							0.026	0.052				0.016	1.350				0.152		0.020
17	0.028				0.055						0.004	0.012						0.098	
16	0.089	0.039	0.048	0.036	0.330	0.012	0.029	0.090	0.014	0.016	0.025	0.048		0.057	0.059	0.082	0.025	0.099	0.088

TABLE 8

THE FUNDAMENTAL STRUCTURE OF PRODUCTION—CALIFORNIA

Columns and Rows Identified by Sector Numbers

	2	3	4	5	1	6	7	11	15	9	14	10	8	12	13	18	19	17	16
2										0.023									
3		0.045			0.026														
4	0.049		0.125		0.029				0.023									0.007	
5	0.057		0.244	0.033					0.031	0.056									
1		0.031	0.111	0.028	0.131							0.150							0.270
6																			0.126
7																			
11																			
15									0.031										
9									0.031	0.127									
14											0.214						0.028		
10					0.049														
8												0.083				0.057	0.027		
12																			
13						0.024								0.015	0.169			0.007	0.153
18	0.041	0.049	0.042	0.039		0.063	0.058	0.043	0.042	0.056	0.042	0.064	0.099	0.073	0.073	0.157	0.017		0.119
19				0.030	0.050			0.215				0.063	1.360			0.046	0.065		
17						0.016	0.014					0.296					0.011	0.010	0.220
16	0.082	0.083	0.083	0.075	0.077	0.095	0.094	0.084	0.084	0.086	0.084	0.083		0.084	0.086	0.068		0.088	0.961

the two economies. Furthermore, the metal bloc exhibits a more encompassing degree of structural interdependence in the California economy. While the Tennessee economy seems to exhibit more structural interrelatedness within the nonmetal bloc, most of the sales-flow coefficients are quite small; hence the importance of this interdependence in terms of its effect on total employment is called into question. In both economies the energy and services bloc is an important source of local inputs.

It is not suggested, of course, that Tennessee, in planning for development, adopt the California economy as a target model. For example, important resource and locational limitations may stand in the way of developing more interdependence of a fundamental nature in the metal bloc in Tennessee. A comparison between these economies does, nevertheless, reveal certain gaps of a general nature in the structure of the Tennessee economy.

At several points in this chapter, the openness of the Tennessee economy has been alluded to. In each instance, openness was interpreted in terms of the large relative amount of employment directly assigned from intermediate sectors to final demand. Small sales-flow coefficients in general—also an indicator of openness—are a consequence of the direct assignment of a high proportion of employment to final demand. Thus, the assignment of employment to final demand can also be looked upon to compare the extent of openness in the Tennessee economy to that in the California economy. Since the California model does not contain an HC row, the comparisons will be carried out on the basis of model A.

In the California study, some 73.2 per cent of total employment in the manufacturing division is directly assigned to final demand as compared to 93 per cent so assigned in the Tennessee statewide model. This suggests that within the manufacturing division, the Tennessee economy is much more open than is the same division for the California economy. In contrast to this, however, 80 per cent of the total employment in the Tennessee economy is directly assigned to final demand as compared to 77 per cent for the California economy (excluding government employees). The reason for the favorable comparison on a total employment basis can be found in the relative amounts of employment in nonmanufacturing industries directly allocated to final demand. In the nonmanufacturing category in Tennessee, only 72 per cent of the total employment is initially allocated to final demand. For the California economy, 79 per cent is directly assigned to final demand. This suggests that the nonmanufacturing division is a more important supplier of local inputs to other intermediate sectors in Tennessee than in California. This finding, therefore, lends support to the view expressed in a preceding section that the existing sectoral interdependence in the Tennessee economy stems mainly from the relationship of the nonmanufacturing division with manufacturing rather than within the manufacturing division itself.

Summary

In this chapter the Tennessee economy, taken as a single region, was viewed from the vantage point of both intermediate and final-demand sectors and was summarily compared to the California economy. Each of the first two types of analysis was carried out with the household noncapital sector treated endogenously as well as exogenously. The image of the Tennessee economy that emerges is one of general openness and weak interdependence among sectors within the manufacturing division, tempered by a fair degree of interdependence between sectors in the manufacturing and nonmanufacturing divisions.

This picture comes into particularly sharp focus when the Tennessee economy is surveyed from the standpoint of the intermediate sectors. In most cases direct final-demand changes originating with sectors in the manufacturing division produce relatively small changes in total employment in sectors in this same division: the lion's share of the change in employment occurred in sectors outside the manufacturing division. With household spending directed in large part toward the wholesale-retail and service sectors, this tendency is more pronounced in model B than in model A.

The multiplier analysis of intermediate sectors has also brought to light the important industrial sectors in the Tennessee economy. The leading sectors for explaining observed growth of the Tennessee economy are mostly locally oriented nonmanufacturing industries such as services, wholesale-retail, and construction. Although some leading industries are in the manufacturing division, they are light industries such as food-processing and textiles. Thus, if the existing pattern of final demand continues to prevail and if significant structural changes do not occur in the future, the growth in output and employment will heavily depend on industries not strongly connected to the national economy. This does not imply that the growth of the Tennessee economy can be explained solely by the growth of local service industries. They are endogenous in the sense that if the Tennessee economy grows, these industries will also grow and if the Tennessee economy declines, so will these industries. This observation, therefore, calls attention to the need for governmental policies for redistributing final demands on the one hand and for encouraging industrial development in the manufacturing division on the other.

If policy actions can alter the pattern of final demand in the Tennessee economy, the industries to be kept in mind for development are industries such as food-processing, construction, TVA, nonelectrical machinery, and miscellaneous manufacturing including small scientific instruments. On the other hand, it is worth mentioning that for given final-demand changes, a higher degree of interindustry connection within the manufacturing division would exert large employment changes within the manufacturing division and over all sectors. Such interindustry linkages may be attained by bringing in new manufacturing firms and expanding some existing ones. This, however, is not to suggest that the policies should be oriented toward a closed economy or self-sufficiency. In fact, our analysis has indicated that the economic development of Tennessee hinges largely on changes in final demand that are susceptible to external shocks.

The final-demand multipliers portrayed the structure of the Tennessee economy in terms of a given classification of final demand and the employment assigned directly and indirectly to these sectors. The analysis of these multipliers indicates that when the induced effect of household spending is accounted for, business investment is the most important stimulant to Tennessee employment. The expenditures of state and local governments are the next most significant category of final demand as a generator of total employment and the size of its multiplier is very close to that of business investment. Moreover, in a short-run period in which household spending is treated as exogenous, the expenditures of state and local governments yield the largest multiplier effect on total employment. This suggests that discretionary changes in state and local governments' expenditures are effective tools in stimulating the Tennessee economy.

The analysis of final-demand multipliers also indicates that while the employment impact on Tennessee of exports to the foreign countries is low, the impact of exports to the rest of the United States is modestly large. Although it may be difficult to develop closer ties to world trade for geographical and other reasons, policy measures may be taken to encourage the entries of new firms and the expansion of existing ones for the purpose of establishing stronger linkages between the Tennessee economy and the rest of the United States. Finally, the numerical examples of the final-demand analysis clearly show that the correct way to calculate the consumption-induced effect on employment is to create a household row and column in the endogenous part of the model. In this process methodological error in the previous intersectoral analyses is demonstrated.

Comparing the fundamental structure of production in the Tennessee economy with that of California gave additional support to the Simpson-Tsukui hypothesis concerning bloc independence between metals and nonmetals. In addition, the comparatively smaller order of magnitude of the technical coefficients in the Tennessee model indirectly indicated that the Tennessee economy was more open than the California economy. On the basis of this comparison with the California economy, the realization of a greater degree of structural interdependence through industrial development would seemingly be desirable.

While the general conclusions stated above may be illuminating and to some extent useful, the richness and variety of the findings for the Tennessee economy can only be appreciated by a detailed study of the results. Readers interested in such details are invited to consult the relevant tables for further study. Despite the particular application of the intersectoral flow model to the

Tennessee economy, this chapter has demonstrated the usefulness and the flexibility of the intersectoral flow model in general for understanding a variety of problems in interindustry relationships and for development planning.

Notes

1. David Simpson and Jinkichi Tsukui, "The Fundamental Structure of Input-Output Tables, an International Comparison," *Review of Economics and Statistics*, Nov. 1965, 47:434-461.

2. Hansen and Tiebout, "An Intersectoral Flows Analysis."

3. In addition to the two types of multipliers reported in this chapter, the multipliers of each sector for its markets for different final-demand categories were calculated, but they are not reported for the sake of brevity.

4. It should be noted that the HC row of the multiplier matrix was not included in the column sums reported in column 4 of Table 1. HC was omitted in the column sums because the purpose here was to concentrate upon the effect of including HC endogenously upon the various other sectors rather than discerning the impact of its inclusion upon itself. Furthermore, while we have some confidence in the underlying distribution of wages, salaries, and the like for the HC row of the basic-flow table, because of the inaccessibility of data on direct household noncapital employment, the employment figure may be somewhat unreliable. Owing to the nature of the model, however, the impact of HC on the other sectors is determined by the size and distribution of wages, salaries, and the like but not by the employment figure used for HC. This can be easily seen from the iterative method of computation described in ch. 3.

5. For the same reasons stated in the preceding footnote, the effect of household employment on total employment in model B is not included in the calculation of final-demand multipliers. Also, this procedure is partly in keeping with the Hansen-Tiebout method to be discussed later, since the latter does not include household employment as the direct effect. Introducing the correct household employment figure into the model may affect the present results numerically to some extent, but its results will obviously differ from Hansen-Tiebout multipliers not only numerically but also methodologically.

6. Tiebout has recently stated that the iterative procedure employed by Hansen and Tiebout in calculating the multipliers amounts to the same thing as the procedure outlined above. He does not, however, formally demonstrate the equivalence of the two approaches as is done in ch. 3. Furthermore, the two approaches yield the same results only if the intersectoral flow table used is square. See Charles M. Tiebout, "Input-Output and the Firm: A Technique for Using National and Regional Tables," *Review of Economics and Statistics,* May 1967, 49:260-262.

7. In the California statewide model the local consumption ratio is 0.89. One reason why it is considerably higher than the corresponding ratio for Tennessee is that the Tennessee ratio was calculated for HC while, in the California model, it included both HC and HI. Since both intermediate and final-demand sectoring differ between the two models, comparisons are difficult, but the final-demand multipliers with the induced effects included are in general larger for the California model than for the Tennessee model. See Hansen, Robson, and Tiebout, *Markets for California Products,* 62.

8. Simpson and Tsukui, "The Fundamental Structure of Input-Output Tables."

9. Hansen and Tiebout, "An Intersectoral Flows Analysis."

10. Our decision rule differed slightly from this one. We removed all coefficients in a given column that were smaller than 1 divided by the number of sectors times the column total. Hence, many more small coefficients were retained than would have been the case had we adopted the Simpson-Tsukui rule. In this respect the above applications can be regarded as somewhat stronger tests of their hypothesis.

If the Simpson-Tsukui rule were applied, all coefficients smaller than 0.052 would be removed. Due to the openness that characterizes the Tennessee economy almost all the coefficients would be removed (only eleven coefficients would remain and all of these are associated with sectors 16-19). The tendency toward bloc-triangularity would of course be virtually complete in Tennessee and much more pronounced in California. The California table would, for example, exhibit perfect within-bloc triangularity in both metals and nonmetals and the between-bloc connections between these two sectors would become insignificant.

11. The purpose of triangularization in each bloc is to arrange industries so that each bloc is decomposable in such a way that the industries follow a hierarchical order with respect to one another. The procedure for triangularization involves interchanging rows and columns in order to minimize the algebraic sum of the elements above the principal diagonal in each bloc. This is accomplished by interchanging rows and columns in a manner such that: (1) the elements on the principal diagonal remain on that diagonal; (2) the elements symmetric to the principal diagonal remain symmetric. This being the case, only the difference between symmetric elements is important and the elements in the matrix can be restated in terms of differences between symmetric elements.

In moving a sector down in terms of the row it occupies, one may apply the following rule:

$$\sum_{k=1}^{N} a_{i,(j+k)} > \sum_{k=1}^{N} a_{(i+k),j} ,$$

where the first and the second subscripts of the technical coefficient indicate respectively the row and the column of the relevant technical coefficient matrix. Letting k range from 1 to N, we may move the industry downward in terms of row position to that row $(i+N)$ at which the above inequality is first satisfied. If no rearrangement satisfies it, then the order of the row is not changed. The rule for moving industrial sectors upward is similar to that just described for moves downward. It should be noted that movements of groups of industries could still improve the triangularization of the matrix. See Simpson and Tsukui, "The Fundamental Structure of Input-Output Tables," 444-445.

12. Due to the combination of energy and services into one category, the relationship between these sectors could not be determined.

6. The Interregional Model

The Empirical Results

From a conceptual standpoint in interindustry analysis, an interregional intersectoral model is superior to an intersectoral model which deals only with a single region. The interregional model depicts intersectoral relationships not only for each region but also among regions. In other words, the model subdivides the total economic system by region as well as by industry so that both interindustry and interregional linkages may be woven together in the analysis. As was noted in Chapter 2, this model is similar to an interregional model of the Isard type and the interregional feedback effect is captured along with the effect on employment in a particular region of final-demand changes in other regions. Neither of these effects is isolated in a single-region model such as the one presented in the preceding chapter.

This chapter examines the results from an application to Tennessee of the three-region model developed in Chapter 3. As previously shown in the map of the state of Tennessee presented in Chapter 4, the state is subdivided into three regions corresponding roughly to the three grand divisions of the state. Region E consists of the area usually termed East Tennessee, including the Appalachia area and the entire Cumberland plateau to the West. Region M, or Middle Tennessee, extends westward to the Tennessee River, and region W, West Tennessee, includes the remainder of the state, lying between the Tennessee and Mississippi rivers. As in the statewide model, the same twenty-five intermediate sectors are identified but now they are identified for each region of the three-region model. This model contains thirteen final-demand categories: household capital and noncapital expenditures, and business investment from each region to the three regions; and state and local governments, federal government, the rest of the United States, and exports to foreign countries. These last four categories are not broken down on a regional basis. The regional classification of the above final-demand categories makes it possible to measure the effect on a region's economy of changes in final demand of other regions as well as interregional feedback effects.

This type of interregional intersectoral flow model had not been explored before in other studies. Moreover, by making the regional classification of the household noncapital sector, one may bring the household noncapital sector into the endogenous part of the interregional model. Such an extension of an interregional model is not found in prior studies of either the intersectoral flow or input-output type.

The implementation of the interregional flow model described in this chapter is useful in a number of ways. Although the statewide flow model itself indicates the openness of the Tennessee economy, it would be worthwhile to know the varying degree of intraregional connections among industries. It would be also useful for policy-makers to understand both the general nature of interregional relationships and specific interregional links between intermediate and final-demand sectors. For example, instead of using the "butterfly net" approach[1] to seek out new firms for Tennessee, industrial development authorities can concentrate on the intermediate sectors with the largest overall intermediate-sector multipliers while keeping in mind their optimum regional location in terms of the largest multiplier among different regions. Also, in dealing with the problem of "pockets of poverty" where the problem is one of regional structural unemployment, as is the case with Appalachia in East Tennessee, the expansion of those sectors with the highest employment multipliers could be encouraged. At the same time, retraining of the unemployed can be directed not only toward the occupations required in those industries but also for the other industries whose employment is directly and indirectly stimulated by the initial expansion.[2] Moreover, in planning economic development for a subregion of the state, from not only economic but also administrative and political points of view, it is important to know the degree of interregional feedback effects and also the extent of the effect on one region of government expenditures in other regions, no matter whether such effects are large or small. Finally, while this chapter discusses the results of applying the interregional model to the Tennessee economy, the usefulness of applying the same approach to other regions or states can readily be seen from the analysis.

In the first section the intermediate-sector multipliers are taken up, and the analysis is confined to the multipliers for the five largest sectors in each region. The final-demand multipliers are presented in the next section. For the most part only the largest multipliers in each region are discussed. In the third section, the feedback effects as defined by Miller[3] and other region effects are quantified. The main findings of this chapter are summarized in the final section. Each type of the above analyses is conducted with the household noncapital sector, HC, as both exogenous and endogenous. As before, for the sake of convenience, the model with HC exogenous will be termed model A whereas the model with HC endogenous will be called model B. This same terminology would be applied to the various multipliers developed from each model.

Three-Region Intermediate-Sector Employment Multipliers

The intermediate-sector multiplier is defined as a column sum of the relevant interregional multiplier matrix developed in formula (12) of Chapter 3. The multiplier of a given intermediate sector in a particular region measures the employment impact on all industries in all regions of a one-unit change in employment associated with final demand for the given sector. Since each column of the interregional multiplier matrix may be summed according to different regions or sectors, a detailed examination of the multiplier matrix provides knowledge of the impacts of a final-demand change in one industry on the various regions and industries. The multiplier matrix corresponding to model B is given in Table A-3 in Appendix A while that corresponding to model A is omitted to conserve space. Some summary measures of both matrices are reported in Table 9 for discussions in this chapter.

Column 1 of Table 9 gives the numbers identifying the individual intermediate sectors for the region named in the heading of the table. The employment-impact multipliers for model A are presented in columns 2 through 5. Along any given row in the table, the entry in column 2 indicates the total employment change in all sectors in region E resulting from a change of one employee directly assigned to final demand for the sector identified in column 1. The entry in column 3 indicates the total employment impact over all intermediate sectors in region M and the entry in column 4 indicates the same for region W. In the fifth column, the overall employment impact is given by the sum of the entries in columns 2 through 4, as defined by formula (14) given in Chapter 3. By comparing the size of the sector employment multipliers in column 5 over all sectors in the three regions, the rank of each sector as given in column 6 is determined.

As in the statewide model, each sector is also ranked in column 7 by giving the relevant weights of final demand to the intermediate-sector multipliers. For the purpose of this ordering, regional final-demand categories were collapsed into a single final-demand column and the ratio between final demand for a given sector and final demand for all sectors in three regions was multiplied to the unweighted multiplier of the given sector. Symbolically, such a weighted multiplier is defined by formula (15) in Chapter 3.[4] As explained in

TABLE 9

THREE-REGION EMPLOYMENT MULTIPLIERS

REGION E *(East Tennessee)*

(1) Intermediate Sector Name & Number	HC *Exogenous (Model A)* (2) Region E	(3) Region M	(4) Region W	(5) Total	(6) Rank	(7) Weighted Rank	HC *Endogenous (Model B)* (8) Region E	(9) Region M	(10) Region W	(11) Total	(12) Rank	(13) Weighted Rank
1. Retail and wholesale	1.159	0.003	0.003	1.165	33	1	1.336	0.009	0.010	1.355	48	2
2. TVA	1.490	0.004	0.001	1.495	14	33	1.976	0.021	0.020	2.016	7	28
3. Livestock	1.535	0.006	0.009	1.550	11	23	1.706	0.013	0.017	1.736	16	67
4. Crops	1.010	0.004	0.000	1.014	73	32	1.113	0.009	0.004	1.126	74	32
5. Mining	1.111	0.001	0.001	1.114	44	60	1.449	0.013	0.014	1.476	30	56
6. Construction	1.552	0.033	0.060	1.644	6	11	1.823	0.049	0.082	1.954	12	8
7. Food and tobacco	2.703	0.007	0.010	2.720	3	9	3.081	0.022	0.026	3.129	3	11
8. Textiles and apparel	1.063	0.009	0.001	1.074	59	4	1.216	0.016	0.007	1.239	68	3
9. Lumber	1.058	0.020	0.001	1.079	55	40	1.230	0.030	0.009	1.269	60	38
10. Furniture	1.043	0.001	0.001	1.045	67	24	1.261	0.008	0.009	1.278	59	20
11. Paper	1.531	0.013	0.013	1.557	9	42	1.930	0.029	0.031	1.990	10	39
12. Printing and publishing	1.099	0.010	0.001	1.110	47	45	1.293	0.018	0.008	1.319	54	48
13. Ind. inorganic and org. chem.	1.056	0.002	0.001	1.059	65	21	1.416	0.014	0.015	1.445	35	16
14. Plastics and synthetics	1.080	0.002	0.008	1.091	54	15	1.345	0.011	0.020	1.376	43	9
15. Rubber and misc. plastics	1.157	0.002	0.002	1.160	34	69	1.394	0.010	0.011	1.414	40	66
16. Leather	1.064	0.006	0.005	1.075	58	59	1.234	0.013	0.012	1.259	64	57
17. Stone, clay, and glass	1.298	0.007	0.002	1.307	17	39	1.591	0.019	0.013	1.623	19	37
18. Primary metals	1.063	0.005	0.002	1.070	62	23	1.325	0.015	0.012	1.352	50	18
19. Fabricated metals (n.e.c.)	1.110	0.002	0.002	1.113	45	30	1.337	0.010	0.011	1.357	47	23
20. Nonelectrical machinery	1.274	0.007	0.001	1.282	18	51	1.508	0.016	0.010	1.534	26	45
21. Electrical machinery and equip.	1.093	0.014	0.003	1.109	48	27	1.322	0.025	0.012	1.359	46	22
22. Transp., instrument, and misc. mfg.	2.035	0.020	0.024	2.079	5	31	2.387	0.036	0.049	2.472	5	24
23. Transportation and communications	1.103	0.008	0.001	1.111	46	26	1.247	0.014	0.006	1.267	61	25
24. Finance, ins., and real estate	1.468	0.039	0.001	1.508	13	25	1.958	0.064	0.020	2.042	8	44
25. Misc. services	1.171	0.013	0.001	1.185	28	6	1.275	0.018	0.005	1.298	56	15

Note. The sectors are fully defined in Table 1 [illegible]

REGION M *(Middle Tennessee)*

(1) Intermediate Sector Name & Number	HC *Exogenous (Model A)* (2) Region E	(3) Region M	(4) Region W	(5) Total	(6) Rank	(7) Weighted Rank	HC *Endogenous (Model B)* (8) Region E	(9) Region M	(10) Region W	(11) Total	(12) Rank	(13) Weighted Rank
1. Retail and wholesale	0.005	1.189	0.005	1.199	26	3	0.028	1.384	0.024	1.436	38	4
2. TVA	0.099	1.151	0.001	1.251	20	66	0.171	1.565	0.041	1.777	14	64
3. Livestock	0.025	1.480	0.010	1.515	12	29	0.046	1.651	0.028	1.724	17	62
4. Crops	0.001	1.106	0.000	1.107	49	41	0.015	1.235	0.013	1.262	63	43
5. Mining	0.024	1.372	0.013	1.410	16	73	0.058	1.639	0.042	1.738	15	75
6. Construction	0.046	1.453	0.054	1.554	10	15	0.086	1.719	0.093	1.898	13	12
7. Food and tobacco	0.197	3.218	0.019	3.435	1	7	0.290	3.850	0.084	4.224	1	6
8. Textiles and apparel	0.015	1.089	0.001	1.104	51	16	0.029	1.199	0.012	1.240	65	14
9. Lumber	0.003	1.063	0.009	1.075	57	63	0.024	1.241	0.028	1.293	58	60
10. Furniture	0.025	1.078	0.002	1.105	50	57	0.051	1.276	0.021	1.348	52	55
11. Paper	0.013	1.113	0.001	1.127	39	74	0.036	1.298	0.019	1.352	49	73
12. Printing and publishing	0.009	1.231	0.001	1.241	21	46	0.036	1.461	0.023	1.520	27	50
13. Ind. inorganic and org. chem.	0.253	1.291	0.032	1.576	8	54	0.368	1.599	0.074	2.042	9	49
14. Plastics and synthetics	0.008	1.008	0.004	1.020	70	49	0.045	1.320	0.034	1.399	42	41
15. Rubber and misc. plastics	0.006	1.033	0.004	1.043	68	64	0.036	1.295	0.030	1.361	45	59
16. Leather	0.099	1.046	0.011	1.156	36	28	0.141	1.278	0.036	1.455	31	21
17. Stone, clay, and glass	0.079	1.097	0.002	1.179	31	56	0.134	1.422	0.035	1.591	22	51
18. Primary metals	0.094	1.059	0.027	1.180	30	71	0.145	1.251	0.053	1.450	34	71
19. Fabricated metals (n.e.c.)	0.031	1.113	0.004	1.147	37	43	0.064	1.358	0.028	1.451	33	40
20. Nonelectrical machinery	0.043	1.075	0.006	1.125	40	68	0.079	1.306	0.029	1.414	41	65
21. Electrical machinery and equip.	0.030	1.150	0.004	1.183	29	37	0.063	1.386	0.027	1.477	29	34
22. Transp., instrument, and misc. mfg.	0.021	1.151	0.037	1.208	24	36	0.057	1.427	0.070	1.554	24	26
23. Transportation and communications	0.005	1.058	0.002	1.065	63	34	0.022	1.197	0.015	1.235	70	33
24. Finance, ins., and real estate	0.004	1.119	0.001	1.124	42	19	0.033	1.383	0.026	1.443	37	19
25. Misc. services	0.025	1.159	0.003	1.187	27	12	0.043	1.292	0.016	1.352	51	30

TABLE 9 (*cont.*)

REGION W (*West Tennessee*)

(1) *Intermediate Sector Name & Number*	HC *Exogenous (Model A)*						HC *Endogenous (Model B)*					
	(2) *Region* E	(3) *Region* M	(4) *Region* W	(5) *Total*	(6) *Rank*	(7) *Weighted Rank*	(8) *Region* E	(9) *Region* M	(10) *Region* W	(11) *Total*	(12) *Rank*	(13) *Weighted Rank*
1. Retail and wholesale	0.001	0.012	1.058	1.071	61	2	0.031	0.030	1.384	1.445	36	1
2. TVA	0.096	0.001	1.006	1.102	52	70	0.156	0.021	1.376	1.553	25	69
3. Livestock	0.001	0.008	1.468	1.476	15	47	0.015	0.017	1.613	1.645	18	68
4. Crops	0.000	0.004	1.005	1.009	75	18	0.010	0.011	1.108	1.129	73	17
5. Mining	0.004	0.039	1.177	1.219	23	75	0.027	0.058	1.421	1.507	28	74
6. Construction	0.029	0.076	2.222	2.327	4	10	0.075	0.111	2.654	2.840	4	5
7. Food and tobacco	0.292	0.056	2.653	3.001	2	7	0.357	0.083	2.993	3.433	2	7
8. Textiles and apparel	0.013	0.004	1.183	1.200	25	13	0.029	0.012	1.324	1.365	44	10
9. Lumber	0.001	0.006	1.025	1.032	69	38	0.019	0.018	1.225	1.263	62	36
10. Furniture	0.003	0.006	1.039	1.048	66	50	0.019	0.015	1.204	1.239	69	46
11. Paper	0.007	0.003	1.055	1.065	64	52	0.031	0.016	1.294	1.341	53	47
12. Printing and publishing	0.005	0.028	1.051	1.092	53	61	0.034	0.049	1.371	1.454	32	70
13. Ind. inorganic and org. chem.	0.013	0.008	1.257	1.278	19	67	0.042	0.025	1.542	1.609	20	63
14. Plastics and synthetics	0.003	0.007	1.114	1.243	41	57	0.027	0.021	1.371	1.420	39	54
15. Rubber and misc. plastics	0.001	0.000	1.009	1.010	74	53	0.007	0.004	1.082	1.094	75	52
16. Leather	0.001	0.007	1.011	1.019	71	44	0.012	0.015	1.130	1.157	72	42
17. Stone, clay, and glass	0.014	0.148	1.075	1.238	22	72	0.045	0.191	1.341	1.576	23	72
18. Primary metals	0.009	0.008	1.055	1.073	60	65	0.025	0.018	1.197	1.240	66	61
19. Fabricated metals (n.e.c.)	0.037	0.005	1.079	1.120	43	62	0.057	0.014	1.231	1.301	55	58
20. Nonelectrical machinery	0.009	0.003	1.065	1.077	56	48	0.093	0.051	1.973	2.117	6	27
21. Electrical machinery and equip.	0.024	0.021	1.114	1.159	35	55	0.040	0.032	1.222	1.294	57	53
22. Transp., instrument, and misc. mfg.	0.009	0.040	1.574	1.623	7	36	0.037	0.062	1.858	1.957	11	35
23. Transportation and communications	0.001	0.006	1.011	1.018	72	17	0.016	0.016	1.175	1.207	71	13
24. Finance, ins., and real estate	0.017	0.113	1.043	1.173	32	20	0.056	0.153	1.398	1.607	21	29
25. Misc. services	0.005	0.012	1.114	1.131	38	5	0.014	0.019	1.206	1.239	67	31

the preceding chapter, the ranking of the weighted multipliers gives the relative importance of industrial sectors in explaining observed growth of the Tennessee economy on the basis of an existing pattern of final demand, whereas the ranking of the unweighted multipliers provides the relative importance of industrial sectors in Tennessee without focusing on the pattern of final demand in Tennessee. In other words, the former is useful in determining how important various sectors are as they are, while the latter is helpful in finding out which industries in what region to consider first among others when a policy measure takes the form of changing the pattern or level of final demand.

Columns 8 through 12 pertain to model B, and the entries in column 8, indicating the total employment impact on region E, are the counterpart of the entries in column 2 save for the fact that the entries in column 8 are derived from the model which treats HC as endogenous.[5] Entries in columns 9 and 10 give the total employment impact on regions M and W respectively, and the total employment impact over all regions is given in column 11. The multiplier effects on different regions of TVA in East Tennessee under model B, for example, are given in the entries of the second row and the columns 8 through 11 in Table 9 for region E. The figure 2.016 in column 11 for TVA in East Tennessee (which is the sum of 1.976, 0.021, and 0.020 in the second row and the columns 8 through 10 in Table 9) was originally computed by summing all elements of column 2 of Table A-3 in Appendix A. It indicates the overall impact on Tennessee employment as a result of hiring one man by TVA in East Tennessee in order to satisfy TVA's final-demand changes.

Rankings for the total intermediate-sector impact multipliers over three regions under model B are given in column 12. Column 13 is the counterpart of column 7 except that it is related to model B. In column 13, each intermediate-sector employment multiplier of column (11) was weighted by the relative importance of its own final-demand element and the results were ranked. With this presentation format, multipliers for a given sector can be compared as to regional and total impact, and as to the rank of the total impact for a given model. From this table, comparisons can also be made between models A and B.

Although the figures are not presented, the induced effect on employment of moving HC into the endogenous part of the model can readily be calculated by subtracting column 5 from column 11 in Table 9. For most intermediate sectors in three regions, the induced employment effect is quite large relative to the direct plus indirect effect. The significance of the induced employment effect points again, as in the statewide model, to the relative importance of household spending in generating further employment.

In the paragraphs immediately following, each region will be considered in turn and the five largest multipliers in each model will be examined. This detailed look at the major sectors in each region is followed by some general observations as to the nature of both the interregional and intersectoral structure of production in Tennessee.

East Tennessee

Let us examine first the intermediate-sector multipliers for East Tennessee, region E. With model A the direct plus indirect employment effects range from a low of 1.014 for sector 4, crops, to a high of 2.720 for sector 7, food and tobacco products. In descending order of importance the five leading sectors are sectors 7, 22 (transportation, instruments, and miscellaneous manufacturing), 6 (construction), 11 (paper), and 3 (livestock). With model B, the total employment multipliers range again from a low of 1.126 for sector 4 to a high of 3.129 for sector 7. Differences between the model A and B multipliers for sector 3 and sector 7 give some indication of the size of the induced employment generated by household expenditures. In model B the five leading sectors are sectors 7, 22, 2 (TVA), 24 (finance, insurance, and real estate), and 11, in that order of importance.

In model A, the large direct plus indirect employment impact of sector 7 is largely confined to the two agricultural sectors, 3 and 4, in region E. Altogether the total employment generated in these sectors is 1.581. Adding to this figure the change of one employee directly assigned to final demand from sector 7 gives a total of 2.581 and leaves a change of only 0.139 employees as being generated indirectly among all sectors in all regions except sectors 3 and 4 in region E.[6] Most of this change is accounted for by sectors in region E, and the interregional employment impact of final-demand changes in sector 7 is negligible. For this sector, the intersectoral linkages are mainly one-way and direct in nature and involve the connection between agriculture and agribusiness within region E. Under model B, food and tobacco products again lead with a slightly larger multiplier than is the case under model A. The induced employment effects for this sector are fairly large and the main impact of changes in directly assigned final-demand employment in this sector are still confined to the two agricultural sectors in region E.

Sector 22, miscellaneous manufacturing, ranks second in both models. Under model A its size is 2.079, and it increases to 2.472 in model B. In model A almost one-half of the direct plus indirect employment impact generated by final-demand employment changes in this sector is felt by sector 25, miscellaneous services. The remaining employment changes are fairly widely distributed among the rest of the sectors, with the bulk of the total employment impact of final-demand changes in sector 22 (transportation, instruments, and miscellaneous manufacturing) confined to region E. While the size of the induced employment impact is relatively large for this sector, in model B the sectoral incidence of employment changes generated by final-demand employment changes in sector 22 is substantially the same as it was under model A.

Examining the remaining model A multipliers first, one may associate the third-largest multiplier in region E, 1.644, with sector 6, construction. Although the total employment impact on the intermediate sectors in region E of a one-employee final-demand change in sector 6 is fairly widespread, a little more than half of the total impact on employment generated indirectly occurs within sectors 6, 1 (retail and wholesale), and 25 (miscellaneous services). Together, these three sectors account for 0.340 of the total indirect change in employment. As indicated by the size of the employment figures in columns 2 and 3 of row 6 in Table 9, the interregional employment impact of final-demand employment changes for sector 6 is large compared to the remaining sectors in region E. Nevertheless, in absolute terms the size of the interregional impact is still small. Paper and allied products, sector 11, ranks fourth with a multiplier of 1.557, and fifth-ranked is livestock and its products, sector 3, with a multiplier of 1.550. The total impact on employment in region E of direct final-demand employment changes in sector 11 is spread over many sectors, with particularly heavy employment impacts recorded for sector 6, construction, and to a lesser extent for sector 25. The combined employment change in these sectors is 0.335. On the other hand, the large size of the multiplier of sector 3 can be accounted for by a strong connection between sectors 3 and 4 (crops) in the form of the input of feed for livestock. Although the interregional employment impact of final-demand changes in sector 3 is larger than it is for sector 11, for both sectors the interregional component of the total multiplier effect is small in terms of absolute size.

In model B the third-ranked sector is TVA, sector 2, which has a total employment multiplier effect of 2.016, representing a substantial increase over the size of this sector's multiplier under model A. TVA is directly connected with many intermediate sectors both as a supplier of power inputs and as a user of locally produced inputs. A change in directly assigned final-demand employment and the associated change in wages, salaries, and the like touches off relatively widespread induced employment effects, thereby explaining the large size of the TVA employment multiplier under model B. It should be noted that an important part of the total employment change associated with changes in TVA employment in region E directly assigned to final demand is confined to intermediate sectors located in region E, especially sector 1 (wholesale and retail), sector 5 (mining), and sector 25 (miscellaneous services). The combined employment change in these sectors is 0.652. With an interregional employment impact of 0.021 on region M and 0.020 on region W, the interregional impact of TVA in region E is quite small. The fourth- and fifth-ranked sectors in model B are sector 24 (finance, insurance, and real estate), with a total employment multiplier of 2.042, and sector 11 (paper and allied products), where the total employment multiplier is 1.990. Changes of one employee in directly assigned final-demand employment in sector 24 generates a large employment effect in sector 25, services; and the size of this impact is 0.422. For paper and allied products, sector 11, the size of the induced impact is large; for the most part, the sectors most affected by a one-employee change in directly assigned final-demand employment are the same as they were under model A.

In general the five largest multipliers for model B are of fairly impressive size, with the first four being over 2. The long-run employment impact of changes in directly assigned final-demand employment, therefore, is expected to be large compared to the short-run impact given in model A.

For both models, however, it should again be stressed that the incidence of the employment impact of final-demand employment changes is generally intra- rather than interregional in nature and generally affects nonmanufacturing employment more than manufacturing employment. In only a few cases under model A—sector 6, construction, for example—is the interregional employment impact on a given region in the range of 10-99 employees for a change of 1,000 employees directly assigned to final demand. For the majority of the intermediate sectors, the interregional employment impact is on the order of a 1-9 employee change interregionally for a change of 1,000 employees in a given sector of region E directly assigned to final demand. When HC is incorporated in the intermediate sector of the model, this picture improves somewhat, though the order of magnitude of the interregional impact is still quite small. In model B, for most intermediate sectors in region E, the order of magnitude of the interregional employment effect on a given region is 10-99 employees per 1,000 change in directly assigned final-demand employment. While this certainly is an improvement in the size of the interregional employment effects, the size of the impact is still very small and there is little employment impact in general on other regions resulting from final-demand employment changes of sectors in region E.

Looking at columns 7 and 13 in Table 9 for East Tennessee, we recall that these rankings are the result of weighting each sector's total employment multiplier by the relative size of its own final-demand element. As was the case in the statewide model, the rank of many sectors is altered, sometimes dramatically, when their employment multipliers are weighted in this manner. Scanning down column 7 for region E under model A, we see that the leading sectors become sectors 1 (retail and wholesale), 8 (textiles and apparel), 25 (miscellaneous services), 7 (food and tobacco), and 6 (construction), in that order of importance. Only two of these sectors, namely, sectors 7 and 6, were also ranked among those five sectors with the largest total employment multipliers. The move to prominence of sector 1 and sector 25 is due to the fact that total employment in these sectors is large and much of it is assigned to final demand. The relatively large change in final-demand employment in these two sectors more than compensates for the relatively small size of their unweighted employment multipliers. Ranking second in importance in region E, sector 8 also owes its heavy employment impact to the amount of employment in this sector assigned to final demand. Sector 7 and sector 6 have large unweighted multipliers which produce a relatively large change in total employment even when the absolute change in final-demand employment is small in comparison with the other sectors.

For a given percentage change in the final-demand elements of sectors in region E, the five leading sectors together generate 23.9 per cent of the change in total employment over all sectors and regions, and within region E the change in total employment is concentrated in these sectors. Since all sectors in region E generate 42.7 per cent of the total change in employment over all regions, the first five account for slightly over half of the total change in employment generated by all sectors in East Tennessee. Moreover, the change in total employment is largely confined to sectors located in region E.

An examination of the rank of weighted multipliers under model B reveals that the leading sectors in region E are identical to those in model A with one exception, though their rankings differ somewhat. In descending order of importance, the leading sectors are sectors 1, 8, 6, 14 (plastics and synthetics), and 7. As in the statewide model, sector 1, wholesale and retail, maintains its position because the change in final-demand employment is large in comparison to that of the other sectors. Sector 25, miscellaneous services, drops to sixth place because much of the employment of this sector is directly assigned to HC, which is now treated as an intermediate sector. Although the size of the unweighted multiplier for sector 25 increases in model B, this increase is more than offset by the decline in the size of the change in final-demand employment for sector 25. Moving up to the fourth position is sector 14. Its rise to prominence can only be explained by the alteration in the relative importance of the various final-demand elements coupled with the change in the unweighted multipliers.

Under model B, the five leading sectors account for 21.9 per cent of the change in total employment over all sectors and regions. All sectors in region E account for 42.4 per cent of the total change in employment. Hence the leading sectors, while generating a slightly smaller percentage change in employment under model B as compared to model A, still account for approximately half the change in employment due to a given percentage change in final-demand employment in region E.

Even under model B, the interregional employment impact is slight, although for many sectors the size of the impact is significantly larger than for these same sectors in model A. This lends some additional support to the contention that the household sector provides an important interregional link. As one would expect, regardless of which model is used, the total interregional employment impact of final-demand changes in region E is greater on region M than on region W.

It should be recalled that the ranking of weighted multipliers changes considerably from that of unweighted multipliers. This means that the current distribution of final-demand outputs that explains economic growth of this particular region does not necessarily coincide with what may be suggested from a policy point of view. For instance, if final demand for TVA, paper and allied products, and miscellaneous manufacturing in East Tennessee could grow relatively more than other final-demand outputs through direct government expenditures or indirect tax incentives, the total employment impact would be greater than when there are uniform percentage increments in existing final demand.

Middle Tennessee

Turning to a discussion of the employment multipliers for intermediate sectors located in Middle Tennessee, region M, we see that the five leading model A multipliers are for sectors 7 (food and tobacco), 13 (industrial inorganic and organic chemicals), 6 (construction), 3 (livestock), and 5 (mining), listed in order of importance. The most prominent model B multipliers are associated with sectors 7, 13, 6, 2 (TVA), and 5, respectively.

As in region E, in region M sector 7 (food and tobacco products) again leads in both models with a total employment impact multiplier of 3.435 under model A and a model B multiplier of 4.224. Each of these multipliers is the largest recorded over all sectors and regions in either model. As was the case in region E, the impressive size of these multipliers is mainly the result of the total employment created in the two agricultural sectors in region M. In model A, a large interregional impact of 0.197 is recorded for all of the intermediate sectors of region E. Most of this employment is confined, however, to the two agricultural sectors 3 and 4 of region E. Under model B the size of the interregional impact on region E of final-demand employment changes in sector 7 of region M increases to 0.290 employees. This increase is due to the induced employment generated interregionally by including HC in the endogenous part of the model. The major portion of this impact is, however, again restricted to the two agricultural sectors in region E.

Second-ranked in region M in both models is sector 13, chemicals. The model A multiplier for this sector is 1.576 and under model B it increases to 2.042, reflecting the induced employment effects of HC. In both models this sector has a particularly large employment impact on region E. Under model A, a one-employee change in directly assigned final-demand employment in sector 13 (inorganic and organic chemicals) of region M results in a change of 0.253 employees over all sectors in region E. Over half of this employment, 0.163 employees to be precise, is recorded for sector 2, TVA, in region E. The same is the case for sector 13 of region M in model B: a total impact on region E of 0.368 employees is recorded with TVA in region E, accounting for over half of the total.

With a total employment multiplier of 1.554, sector 6, construction, in region M ranks third in model A. The model B multiplier for sector 6 in region M is 1.898 and also ranks third in region M in model B. In both models the employment impacts of final-demand changes in sector 6 of region M are felt to a greater or lesser extent by all sectors in region M but with particularly large impacts recorded for miscellaneous services, sector 25.

In model A, the fourth-ranked sector in region M is sector 3, livestock, with a total employment multiplier of 1.515. As was the case with this sector in region E, the large total employment effect is accounted for by the impressive size of the direct plus indirect employment impact on sector 4, crops. The TVA, sector 2, is fourth-ranked in region M in model B and has a multiplier of 1.777, as compared with a multiplier of 1.251 and a rank of sixth in region M under model A. Final-demand employment changes in TVA in region M result in employment changes of fairly large size in the wholesale-retail and service sectors in region M. The incremental employment impacts in these sectors are 0.119 and 0.270 respectively for a one-employee increase in directly assigned final-demand employment in TVA in region M.

Fifth-ranked in region M in both models is sector 5, mining. Its model A multiplier is 1.410, which increases to 1.898 under model B. In both models, its relatively large size can be accounted for by the size of the total employment effect of final-demand employment changes in this sector upon miscellaneous services, sector 25, in region M.

Returning to the interregional connections of model B, we observe that column 8 of Table 9 for region M shows the model B employment impact on sectors of region E for a one-employee change in directly related final-demand employment for the sectors in region M. The employment figures in this column indicate that for many sectors the interregional employment impact increases over what it is under model A and is of an impressive size. For sectors 2 (TVA), 7 (food and tobacco), 13 (industrial inorganic and organic chemicals), 16 (leather), 17 (stone, clay, and glass), and 18 (primary metals), the total impact on all sectors in region E of a change of 1,000 employees directly assigned to final demand from these intermediate sectors in region M is between 134 and 368. In many other sectors of region M, the interregional employment generated in region E for a change of 1,000 directly related final-demand employment changes in region M is on the order of 50-99 employees. As was the case in region E, the HC sector is an important interregional connecting link not because wages and salaries are paid out by sectors in region M to households residing in other regions, but because intermediate sectors in other regions make sales to household sectors in region M. As in model A, in model B the interregional impact of directly related final-demand employment changes in region M is considerably less on region W than it is on region E.

The sectoral rankings in all regions resulting from weighting the employment multipliers are reported in columns 7 and 13 of Table 9. Except for sectors 7 (food and tobacco) and 6 (construction), the five leading sectors in both models differ from those that lead in terms of the size of their employment multipliers. Under model A for region M, the leading sectors again are sectors 1 (retail and wholesale), 7, 25 (miscellaneous services), 6, and 8 (textiles and apparel), in that order of importance. Thus while the order changes as compared to that in region E, the leading sectors are the same. Together they account for 15.5 per cent of the change in total employment over all sectors and regions. All sectors in region M generate 26.2 per cent of the total change in employment over all sectors and regions. Thus the five leading sectors account for over half of the change in employment generated by all sectors in region M, and the total employment effect as well as that of the leading sectors is smaller relative to the impact generated by their counterparts in region E.

When model B is utilized, the leading sectors for explaining observed economic growth of Middle Tennessee are sectors 1, 7, 6, 8, and 24 (finance, insurance, and real estate), in that order of importance. As was the case for the same model in region E, sector 25, miscellaneous services, drops out of the first five due to the decline in that sector's final-demand employment when HC is treated endogenously, and it is replaced by sector 24. With 14.8 per cent of the total change in employment attributable to the five leading sectors in region M, the relative amount is slightly less than it is for the five leading sectors in region M under model A. Since all sectors in region M account for only 25.9 per cent of the total change in employment, however, again more than half the employment change generated by sectors in region M is concentrated in the five leading sectors. As in region E, the ranking of sectors with unweighted multipliers differs from that with the weighted multipliers, indicating the need of encouraging a particular set of final-demand outputs for policy purposes.

West Tennessee

In West Tennessee, region W, under model A the sectors with the largest total employment multipliers, listed in order of diminishing importance, are sectors 7 (food and tobacco), 6 (construction), 22 (transportation, instruments, and miscellaneous manufacturing), 3 (livestock), and 13 (industrial inorganic and organic chemicals). Listed in descending order, the sectors with the largest multipliers under model B are sectors 7, 6, 20 (nonelectrical machinery), 22, and 3. Thus four of the five leading sectors are the same in both models, though their order of importance differs somewhat.

Regardless of the model, food and tobacco products in region W again has the largest multiplier. The model A multiplier is 3.001, and under model B it increases to 3.433. The explanation of the size of the total employment impact in both cases is the same as that given previously for this sector in the other regions. Under model A a large interregional employment impact of 0.292 on all sectors in region E combined is recorded with 0.267 of the total change in employment occurring in sectors 3 and 4 (crops). The size of this same total impact under model B increases to 0.357 and the impact on sectors

3 and 4 combined is 0.284. The induced impact on sectors other than 3 and 4 is reasonably large and is fairly widespread.

Construction, sector 6, in region W ranks second in both models. Under model A, its multiplier is 2.327 and a particularly large impact of 0.614 employees is registered within wholesale and retail, sector 1, in region W. A smaller but still impressive total employment impact of 0.106 is associated with miscellaneous services, sector 25, in the same region. The model B multiplier for this sector is 2.840 and the total employment impact of a one-employee change in final-demand employment in this sector on wholesale-retail in region W is 0.662 and on services it is 0.349. Under model B, a one-employee change in directly assigned final-demand employment in sector 6 in region W results in change of 0.111 employees over all sectors in region M. Much of this increase is traceable to sector 23, transportation and communications, and to sector 25, miscellaneous services, in region M. The size of the total employment impact on sector 23 is 0.041 and on sector 25 it is 0.020.

Third- and fourth-ranked in region W in model A are sector 22, transportation, instruments, and miscellaneous manufacturing, and sector 3, livestock, with multipliers of 1.623 and 1.476 respectively. A one-employee change in final-demand employment in sector 22 of region W results in a change in total employment in miscellaneous services, sector 25, of 0.129 and a change of 0.197 in wholesale-retail, sector 1, in the same region. Most of the remaining employment impact is on intermediate sectors in region W. As was the case in other regions, the size of the multiplier for sector 3 in region W is largely explained by the employment generated in sector 4, crops, in region W as additional feed inputs are required in the livestock sector.

In model B, sector 20, nonelectrical machinery, ranks third in region W with a multiplier of 2.117; its rise to prominence can be explained by the large size of the induced employment generated in wholesale-retail, sector 1, and miscellaneous services, sector 25, in region W. Together these sectors experience an employment increase of 0.631 for an increase of one employee directly assigned to final demand from sector 20 in region W. Transportation, instruments, and miscellaneous manufacturing, sector 22, ranks fourth in region W with a multiplier of 1.957. The incidence of sector employment changes due to a change of one employee directly assigned to final demand in sector 22 in region W is much the same as it is in model A.

Fifth-ranked in region W in model A is sector 13, industrial inorganic and organic chemicals, with a multiplier of 1.609. While a one-employee change in directly assigned final-demand employment in this sector produces employment changes in most sectors in region W, relatively important total employment effects are recorded for sectors 1 (wholesale-retail), 11 (paper and allied products), and 19 (fabricated metal products).

With a multiplier of 1.645 sector 3, livestock, drops in rank in region W from fourth in model A to fifth in B. Moving the HC sector into the endogenous part of the model results in a relatively small induced employment impact for direct final-demand changes in this sector, and this probably accounts for its decline in importance. As previously was the case, the main impact of directly assigned final-demand employment changes in sector 3 is on sector 4, crops.

The interregional employment impacts of intermediate sectors in region W under model A are generally larger upon region M than on region E, although some obvious exceptions do occur, as an inspection of columns 2 and 3 in Table 9 for region W will show. These interregional effects are, nevertheless, quite small in comparison to the intraregional employment generated by final-demand employment changes for the intermediate sectors in region W.

As was the case for the other regions, the size of the interregional employment changes increases under model B, and in some cases substantially. For a majority of the sectors, fourteen to be exact, the impact is greater on region E than on region M. Generally speaking, it seems that introducing HC into the endogenous part of the model provides an important interregional connecting link between regions W and E. A comparison of the figures in columns 8 and 9 against those in column 10 of Table 9 for region W indicates substantial interregional employment effects for some sectors. For instance, changes of 100 employees in sectors 2 (TVA), 6 (construction), 7 (food and tobacco), 17 (stone, clay, and glass), or 14 (plastics and synthetics) in region W generates changes of about twenty or more employees in regions E and M together. However, for most other sectors, the interregional employment impacts are relatively small.

When the Middle Tennessee intermediate sectors are weighted to explain observed growth, of the five sectors with the largest unweighted multipliers, only sectors 7 and 6 remain ranked within the top five sectors. Thus again, the observed growth of Middle Tennessee is different from an optimally planned growth which could be achieved through changing the composition of final-demand outputs. As in other regions, in region W the five leading sectors under model A listed in order of diminishing importance are sectors 1 (retail-wholesale), 25 (services), 7, 6, and 8 (textiles and apparel) respectively. Altogether the employment generated by a given per cent final-demand change for these sectors amounts to 20.4 per cent of the total change in employment over all sectors and regions. For region W, all of the intermediate sectors account for 31.8 per cent of the change in total employment due to a given percentage change in direct final-demand employment in each sector. A comparison of the two percentages indicates that slightly over 65 per cent of the employment change generated by the sectors in region W is concentrated in the five leading sectors.

With model B, the story is much the same: four of the five leading sectors are the same as they are in model A. Sector 25, miscellaneous services, drops out of the five leading sectors again and is replaced by sector 24, finance, insurance, and real estate. These five sectors account for 20.5 per cent of the total change in employment over all sectors and regions, and all twenty-five sectors in region W generate 31.8 per cent of the change in total employment. In this case also, slightly over 65 per cent of the change in total employment is concentrated in the five leading sectors.

Intraregional and Interregional Interdependence

Viewing the three-region models from a general perspective and in relationship to the statewide model, some observations can be made on the nature of intraregional and interregional interdependence from the standpoint of the intermediate sectors. The general purpose of the comments on interregional interdependence is to offer a tentative rationalization for why interregional employment impacts are for the most part very small and almost insignificant as compared to the intraregional employment impacts. The attempt to rationalize the overall pattern formed by the existing interregional relationships will be pursued further in the last section of this chapter.

In the first place it is apparent that for most intermediate sectors, the size of the intraregional employment impact is much larger than is the interregional impact. This observation holds for both models, although the absolute size of the interregional employment effects is larger for most sectors under model B as compared to model A.

In terms of the intraregional subtotals of the multipliers, several of the largest multipliers are found in region E. This finding holds regardless of which model is used. On this basis it can be said that structural interdependence among the intermediate sectors in this sense is most important in region E. The structural interdependence of region M is also extensive, and the intraregional subtotals of the employment multipliers of sectors in this region rival in size those of region E. One point is fairly clear, though: the intraregional structural interrelations are more extensive in these two regions as compared to their importance in region W. The reasons for this conclusion will become clear in the paragraphs below that deal with the interregional character of the multipliers and the connection between regions.

As in the statewide models, the direct final-demand employment changes in many sectors generate relatively large employment changes in the nonmanufacturing division, with this tendency being more pronounced in model B as compared to model A. Though several exceptions to this tendency can be spotted in each region, it appears to hold in general for all three regions.

It is apparent that the subregions of the Tennessee economy are not strongly connected. The explanation for this can be traced to the location of the major centers of industrial activity in the state. In East Tennessee most industrial activity takes place on a generally north-south axis with the tri-cities area of Bristol, Kingsport, and Johnson City to the north, with Knoxville in the center, and with Chattanooga to the south. Activity in terms of local (region

E) sales and purchases of locally produced inputs tends to run north and south, with the bulk of the output of the majority of the intermediate sectors within the manufacturing division (sectors 7-22) being sold directly to final demand. The fact that much of the activity in East Tennessee is located near the northern and southern borders of the state possibly explains the openness of the manufacturing division. Although these major areas of activity are located some distance from the boundary of region M, some inputs are supplied to Middle Tennessee and to a less important extent to West Tennessee.

In Middle Tennessee most of the activity is generated within or close to the Nashville SMSA, which is located close to the center of the region. As seen above, some of the leading sectors in this region generate fairly large interregional employment impacts on East Tennessee, especially under model B. In general, the interregional employment impacts generated by sectoral final-demand employment changes in Middle Tennessee are the largest generated. Yet, the interregional impact is small relative to the intraregional employment impact. This indicates that, with few exceptions, the bulk of inputs purchased from Tennessee sectors are purchased from those sectors located in Middle Tennessee and that, within the manufacturing sectors, most of the outputs are sold directly to final demand. Sales of the sectors in Middle Tennessee to other regions are directed toward the intermediate sectors in West Tennessee rather than toward East Tennessee.

Economic activity in the West Tennessee is located mainly in the Memphis SMSA in the southwestern corner of the state. With the Mississippi River as a main transportation artery, the output of this region probably flows directly to final demand or outside the state, north, south, and west. This probably accounts in large part for the sparseness of direct connections in the form of inputs supplied from intermediate sectors in West Tennessee to the intermediate sectors in Middle and East Tennessee, thus explaining the low impact of final-demand change in the latter regions upon employment in the former region.

With this pattern of intra- and interregional connections, final-demand changes in regions M and W would generate greater interregional employment responses than would be the case for final-demand changes in region E. Given the existence of such final-demand changes, locating new firms and expanding the old ones in region M and especially region W could increase interregional linkages so as to stimulate intermediate demand for the output of sectors in region E and to a lesser extent region M, leading to industrial expansions in these regions.

In summary, the analysis in this section of interregional intermediate sector multipliers exhibits more detailed information than the analysis with a single-region statewide model. Although the Tennessee economy consists predominantly of agribusiness or of locally oriented industries, some nonagricultural and nonlocal industries appear to have strong impacts on the Tennessee economy but with different effects on different subregions. If the final-demand pattern is assumed to be affected by policy measures, important sectors to be considered for generating employment are chemical and mining industries in Middle Tennessee, nonelectrical machinery in West Tennessee, and paper and allied products in East Tennessee. TVA gives important impetus to regional employment, particularly in the East. Despite the regional characteristics of intermediate sectors in generating employment, regional interdependence is rather weak in the Tennessee economy. This suggests that when dealing with regional development of a poverty area in Tennessee such as the Appalachian region, the planning authorities should conceive of direct investment and expenditures in the area in question. The importance of TVA and the construction industry may also suggest the kind of programs suitable for regional economic advancement. Since an induced effect on employment of household expenditures is by no means negligible, government transfer payments to household sectors would also have an important impact on the local economy. However, the lack of regional interdependence and also the absence to some extent of intersectoral linkages points to the general observation that the ultimate solution to the problem of economic development of a subregion of the state rests on long-term public and private investments that will interconnect the region in question with the rest of the Tennessee economy. For example, TVA has played such a role in the various parts of the Tennessee economy. Our analysis has indicated that TVA as compared to other industries exhibits more extensive sectoral and regional connections.

Interregional Final-Demand Multipliers

The TISG has devised an interregional final-demand multiplier that is somewhat analogous to the single-region final-demand multiplier in its interpretation as a base multiplier. The interregional final-demand multiplier, however, has an important feature that the final-demand multiplier of the statewide model does not have. For each final-demand category, the change in directly assigned employment is restricted to a subregion of the state, and the interregional demand multiplier is designed to capture the impact of this initial change on employment in each subregion separately and also the combined impact over all regions in the state. In other words, the multiplier shows the total employment effect on each region and the effect over all regions per employee directly assigned from a given region to a particular category of final demand. Thus, such a multiplier indicates the effect on a given region of change in another region's final demand. For example, it explains how the employment in East Tennessee would be affected by changes in state and local governmental expenditures in Middle or West Tennessee. A knowledge of this type of interregional link is useful in a policy context, as will be shown later.

As shown in formula (16) in Chapter 3, the multipliers are formed by first

TABLE 10

INTERREGIONAL FINAL-DEMAND MULTIPLIERS

HC EXOGENOUS (MODEL A)

Final Demand Sectors

	(1) HC^E	*(2)* HC^M	*(3)* HC^W	*(4)* HI^E	*(5)* HI^M	*(6)* HI^W	*(7)* BI^E	*(8)* BI^M	*(9)* BI^W	*(10)* GSL	*(11)* GF	*(12)* EUS	*(13)* EW
Region E													
(1) Region E	1.307	1.282	1.718	1.165	1.119	1.133	1.302	1.255	1.106	1.442	1.171	1.204	1.131
(2) Region M	0.010	0.008	0.009	0.004	0.008	0.008	0.012	0.016	0.008	0.027	0.008	0.005	0.005
(3) Region W	0.004	0.002	0.004	0.005	0.002	0.003	0.020	0.022	0.001	0.041	0.005	0.004	0.003
(4) Total	1.320	1.292	1.732	1.174	1.129	1.143	1.334	1.293	1.115	1.509	1.184	1.216	1.139
Region M													
(5) Region E	0.055	0.024	0.033	0.011	0.012	0.008	0.044	0.023	0.015	0.048	0.022	0.039	0.022
(6) Region M	1.443	1.306	1.295	1.152	1.217	1.093	1.425	1.278	1.117	1.467	1.194	1.194	1.180
(7) Region W	0.005	0.005	0.005	0.006	0.011	0.005	0.050	0.019	0.009	0.017	0.009	0.009	0.005
(8) Total	1.506	1.336	1.333	1.169	1.240	1.106	1.519	1.320	1.140	1.532	1.224	1.303	1.206
Region W													
(9) Region E	0.049	0.033	0.019	0.011	0.010	0.003	0.026	0.018	0.028	0.013	0.016	0.023	0.011
(10) Region M	0.055	0.082	0.022	0.009	0.014	0.012	0.069	0.049	0.024	0.063	0.020	0.019	0.007
(11) Region W	1.224	1.157	1.197	1.147	1.157	1.077	2.069	1.720	1.394	1.271	1.227	1.237	1.083
(12) Total	1.323	1.272	1.238	1.168	1.181	1.092	2.164	1.787	1.446	1.348	1.264	1.279	1.101

TABLE 10 (*cont.*)

HC ENDOGENOUS (MODEL B)

Final Demand Sectors

	(1) HC^E	(2) HC^M	(3) HC^W	(4) HI^E	(5) HI^M	(6) HI^W	(7) BI^E	(8) BI^M	(9) BI^W	(10) GSL	(11) GF	(12) EUS	(13) EW
Region E													
(13) Region E				1.350	1.309	1.332	1.522	1.509	1.342	1.681	1.467	1.414	1.321
(14) Region M				0.011	0.016	0.016	0.023	0.028	0.018	0.040	0.020	0.016	0.012
(15) Region W				0.013	0.010	0.011	0.032	0.036	0.011	0.059	0.018	0.013	0.011
(16) Total				1.375	1.335	1.359	1.576	1.574	1.371	1.780	1.505	1.443	1.344
Region M													
(17) Region E				0.036	0.036	0.028	0.082	0.051	0.037	0.082	0.050	0.072	0.046
(18) Region M				1.352	1.421	1.257	1.685	1.495	1.289	1.708	1.407	1.489	1.368
(19) Region W				0.027	0.034	0.021	0.087	0.044	0.027	0.044	0.031	0.034	0.024
(20) Total				1.414	1.491	1.307	1.855	1.590	1.353	1.834	1.488	1.595	1.438
Region W													
(21) Region E				0.027	0.032	0.031	0.069	0.056	0.063	0.046	0.039	0.050	0.027
(22) Region M				0.019	0.027	0.030	0.101	0.076	0.046	0.092	0.035	0.035	0.016
(23) Region W				1.295	1.368	1.383	2.471	2.084	1.724	1.588	1.441	1.486	1.235
(24) Total				1.342	1.427	1.443	2.641	2.216	1.832	1.726	1.515	1.571	1.278

partitioning column-wise the multiplier matrix into three groups corresponding to the three regions and then premultiplying each group of columns to the relevant part of each final-demand column. For example, from Chapter 3, M^{EE}, MME, and M^{WE} indicate the submatrices in the multiplier matrix that are associated with the first group of columns representing region E that is denoted by the second superscript. The first superscript indicates the region in which the change in total employment occurs, whereas the second superscript denotes the region in which initial change in directly assigned final-demand employment occurs. Each of these submatrices is then premultiplied to that portion of a final-demand column containing employment directly assigned from intermediate sectors in region E. The product indicates the total employment traceable from regions E, M, and W to that portion of that particular final-demand column. Dividing each total by the employment directly assigned from region E to that final-demand sector gives the final-demand multipliers for each region.

The interregional final-demand multipliers for model A and B are reported in Table 10. The body of the table is divided into two parts: the first part containing twelve rows gives the multipliers for model A and the second part containing the remaining twelve rows presents the multipliers for model B.[7] The multipliers related to employment directly assigned to final demand from region E are presented in the first four rows. The multipliers in row 1 indicate the employment generated in region E per employee directly assigned from region E to final demand. In rows 2 and 3 the multipliers indicate the employment assignable from regions M and W per employee directly assigned from region E to final demand. Row 4 contains the sum of the partial multipliers in rows 1-3. These multipliers indicate the total employment generated over all sectors and regions per employee directly assigned from intermediate sectors in region E to final demand. The multipliers in rows 5-8 are based on employment assigned to final demand directly from region M and those in rows 9-12 are related to employment directly traceable to final demand from region W. The multipliers given in rows 13-24 have the same interpretation but are based on model B. Thus, looking at the table from the standpoint of the rows, each part of the table consists of three bands or sets of multipliers, one set for each region from which employment is directly assigned to final demand. Each set contains four multipliers; one shows the intraregional employment impact, two indicate the size of the employment effect on the other two regions, and the fourth indicates the impact over all regions.

These multiplier effects originate from different sources of final demand identified by the symbols at the top of thirteen columns of Table 10. Household consumption, HC, household investment, HI, and business investment, BI, are broken down by three regional origins of demand using superscripts. For example, BI^{W} is business investment demand coming from West Tennessee. Final-demand categories that are not classified by the region of origin are state and local governments, GSL, federal government expenditures, GF, exports to the rest of the United States, EUS, and exports to foreign countries, EW. Thus, the total number of sources of final demand is thirteen for our model A. When household consumptions for three regions are treated as intermediate sectors as in Model B, the number of final-demand columns becomes ten.

Looking at the table from the standpoint of the region from which employment is directly assigned to final demand, we can make a comparison between the partial as well as the total multiplier for different categories of final demand. Alternatively, the table can be viewed from the standpoint of the final-demand sectors. For a given final-demand category, the partial and total multipliers can be compared for different regions from which employment is directly assigned to final demand. While all of these comparisons are of interest and potentially useful, the following paragraphs concentrate for the most part on a comparison of the total multipliers given in rows 4, 8, and 12 for model A and rows 16, 20, and 24 for model B.

The multipliers in row 4 again are related to employment directly assigned from region E to final demand. The multipliers in this row range from a low of 1.115 for business investment in region W, BI^W, to a high of 1.732 for household noncapital expenditures in region W, HC^W. Thus, intermediate sectors in East Tennessee sell directly to West Tennessee for household noncapital consumption, and most of the total employment (direct plus indirect) traceable to this portion of the HC^W vector comes, furthermore, from East Tennessee.

Scanning along row 4, we see that the second-largest multiplier, 1.509, is associated with GSL, state and local government expenditures. Since GSL is susceptible to manipulation in the short run, it is somewhat comforting to note that this final-demand sector has a rather large multiplier associated with changes in directly assigned employment to GSL from the intermediate sectors in region E. This multiplier could be used to determine roughly the effect of an increase in state and local government spending on products produced in East Tennessee. For example, suppose a proportional increase in state and local government spending among East Tennessee sectors increased directly assigned final-demand employment by 1,000. An additional increase of 509 employees throughout the state would be produced through the interaction of the indirect effects. By looking at the entries in rows 1 through 3 and in column 10 of Table 10 for model A, one can gauge the regional distribution of this employment change. Of this total an additional 442 employees would be recorded in East Tennessee as compared to only 27 in Middle Tennessee and 41 in West Tennessee. To be sure, this sort of prediction is only approximate and is qualified by a number of simplifying assumptions such as an elastic labor supply. But, while risking oversimplification, these results tend to indicate that increased state and local government spending on outputs produced in East Tennessee may have very little impact on employment in Middle and West Tennessee.

As indicated in Chapter 4, due to difficulty in collecting separate data, state and local governments were merged into one sector. Expenditures by state or local governments separately would have resulted in different multipliers. The implication nevertheless is that perhaps these multipliers would be substantial in comparison with the other final-demand multipliers associated with direct final-demand changes from region E. Other fairly large multipliers are associated with HC^E, household noncapital expenditures in region E, and BI^E, business investment in region E. The size of the multiplier for the former is 1.320 and that for the latter is 1.334.

The total multipliers associated with directly assigned final-demand employment from intermediate sectors in region M are given along row 8. The smallest multiplier in this instance is 1.106 for HI^W and the largest is 1.532 for GSL. The second-largest is 1.519 for business investment in region E, BI^E, and the third-largest is 1.506 for household noncapital sector in region E, HC^E. It is evident, therefore, that final-demand changes in other regions for the output of the intermediate sectors in region M produce relatively large multiplier effects, most of which are confined to employment changes in region M.

Looking across row 12, we see that the largest multiplier associated with employment directly assigned from intermediate sectors in region W to the several final-demand categories is 2.164 for business investment in region E, BI^E. The smallest is 1.092 for household capital sector in region W, HI^W. Apparently a rather strong link exists between the intermediate sectors of region W and business investment by firms in region E, not only in terms of the direct connection but also in terms of the total employment input over all sectors in all regions of changes in directly assigned employment from intermediate sectors in region W to BI^E. The second-largest multiplier for directly assigned employment from region W is 1.787 for BI^M. Seemingly, total employment can be importantly affected by changes in business investment in regions E and M for investment type goods produced in region W. The third-largest multiplier is 1.446 for BI^W and the fourth-largest is 1.348 for GSL.

The results for model B are also given in Table 10. As expected, when the household noncapital sector is moved into the endogenous part of the model, all of the final-demand multipliers become larger than their counterparts under model A. The difference between the two multipliers for any given final-demand sector represents the induced effect on employment produced by the household noncapital expenditures. A comparison of this difference suggests that for most of the final-demand sectors the induced employment effect is large relative to the indirect effect.

Examining row 16 of Table 10, we note that the multipliers therein represent the total (direct plus indirect plus induced) employment effects regionally and interregionally per employee directly assigned from intermediate sectors in region E to the final-demand sectors. In this case the lowest multiplier is 1.335 for household capital expenditures in region M, HI^{M}, and the largest one is 1.780 for the state and local government expenditures, GSL. The second- and third-largest multipliers are 1.576 and 1.574 and are related to business investment in region E, BI^{E}, and business investment in region M, BI^{M}, respectively. It is worth noting that the second-ranked multiplier in model A moves into the first position in model B. With the induced employment effects from household noncapital expenditures coming into play, in the long run the leading final-demand category is no longer HC^{W} but GSL.

Along row 20 in Table 10 are the multipliers of model B pertaining to changes in employment directly assigned from intermediate sectors in region M to the various final-demand sectors. These multipliers range from a low of 1.307 for HI^{W} to a high of 1.855 for BI^{E}. Again, some change in the rankings of the multipliers occurs. In the long run, GSL, which ranked first in model A, ranks second in model B with a multiplier of 1.834 and BI^{E}, which ranked second in model A, now becomes the largest multiplier in model B. Other sizable multipliers related to changes in directly assigned final-demand employment from region M are 1.595 for exports to the rest of the United States, EUS, and 1.590 for business investment in region M, BI^{M}.

The multipliers of model B contained in row 24 of Table 10 indicate the total employment (direct plus indirect plus induced) per employee directly allocated from intermediate sectors in region W to the final-demand sectors. Of these multipliers, the lowest is 1.278 for exports to the outside of the United States, EW, and the highest is 2.641 for business investment in region E, BI^{E}. The four leading final-demand categories ranked in order of importance are BI^{E}, BI^{M}, BI^{W}, and GSL, with a multiplier size ranging from 1.726 to a figure well over 2.

Rows 21 and 22 contain the partial interregional multipliers of model B showing employment assigned from regions E and M per employee directly assigned from region W to final demand. A comparison of these partial multipliers to those in row 23 reveals a modest employment impact on regions E and M of a change in employment of region W associated with all final-demand categories. In four out of ten final-demand categories, however, an increase of 100 employees in region E generates a change of 10 or more employees in the other two regions. Although a more general measure of interregional linkages will be obtained in the next section, this is a measure of the other region effect discussed earlier. This type of interregional linkage becomes considerably weaker when household noncapital expenditures are treated as exogenous. Thus, Tennessee's subregional economic structure does exhibit stronger interregional linkages in the long run, as compared to the short run.

In general, when the long-run impact of induced consumer spending is taken into consideration, business investment in all three regions along with the state and local government expenditures provide important stimuli to Tennessee employment. The employment effect on a given region of final demand from other regions is large, whereas the interregional connections among endogenous sectors themselves appear to be still weak in model B. Business investment in East Tennessee generally stimulates more employment than does the business investment in other parts of the state. Therefore, if an economic development program for the eastern part of the state such as the Federal Appalachian Regional Program or a TVA project holds the promise of bringing in business investment in that area, the overall impact on the Tennessee economy would be sizable. This indeed points to the need for initiating such a regional developmental program not only for that region alone but also for the economy of the entire state.

Interregional Feedback and Other Interregional Linkages

In the preceding sections dealing with sectoral and final-demand multipliers, the weakness of interregional employment effects was noted. Recently, Miller, producing some empirical evidence, has argued that interregional feedback is usually so small that it can be ignored in an interindustry analysis.[8] Whether this is also true in the Tennessee intersectoral analysis will be examined in this section by using the measure of interregional feedback defined by Miller.

As noted in Chapters 2 and 3, however, the interregional feedback is only one kind of interregional effect and the effect of final-demand changes in other regions on employment in a given region should also be included in any measure of the importance of interregional linkages. This procedure appears to be particularly important, since the analysis in the preceding section reveals some effect on a given region of a final demand in other regions. Thus, in this section a new measure of interregional linkages is also estimated and compared with the interregional feedback effect defined by Miller.

Miller measures the interregional feedback effect by defining what he calls the overall percentage error on the basis of Isard's interregional model. Applying Miller's concept to the interregional intersectoral model developed in this monograph, one can define a similar concept as in formula (17) of Chapter 3. Without using symbols, we can state the following: A region increases output and employment due to an increase in its own final demand and, as a result, inputs are required from other regions. As these other regions expand output and employment, inputs are in turn required from the first region. Thus, additional employment is generated in the first region. This increase in employment again generates still more employment in the first region and through the additionally required inputs from other regions sets off another indirect requirement for further inputs from the first region. This type of "feeding back" incremental employment between regions is the interregional feedback effect which is one of the missing links in a single-region interindustry analysis.

Miller's method of measuring the interregional feedback effect amounts to summing all of such incremental employment from each round of feedback and expressing the percentage of this sum to the total employment of the first region attributable to industrial activities in the first region. This is the overall percentage error (hereafter, OPE) expected in the employment estimates of a given region when these estimates do not take the interregional feedback effect into consideration.

As shown in formula (18) of Chapter 3, the effect of final-demand changes in other regions can easily be incorporated into the OPE defined only for the interregional feedback effect. Simply stated it is as follows: First, add to the interregional feedback effect the indirect employment effect generated in the region in question due to the industrial activities in other regions that are initiated by the changes in final demand for other regions. Then, express this total as a percentage of the total employment of the region in question due to changes in final demands in all regions. This percentage is the OPE designed to include the other regions' effect as well as the interregional feedback effect. This modified OPE as such, therefore, measures the quantitative importance of the employment estimates of a given region when the employment estimates do not take all the interregional linkages into consideration.

The OPE's so computed for the three regions in Tennessee are reported in Table 11. In calculating the OPE for each region, we assumed a one-unit change in each final-demand element.[9] The OPE's presented in the first and second columns measure only the effect of feedback. In the first column the OPE's are calculated under model A and in the second column they are computed under model B. The OPE's including the feedback effect and the other regions' effect are given in columns 3 and 4. The results in column 3 are generated from model A and those in column 4 are calculated on the basis of model B.

Judging from the size of the OPE in column 1 for model A, one may deduce that the percentage error for any region is extremely small. The highest OPE is only 0.040 per cent for region M, while the lowest OPE is a negligible 0.023 per cent for region E. Thus, the results in Tennessee appear to confirm Miller's thesis that the interregional feedback effect is in general so small that it can be ignored in an interindustry analysis. But this conclusion is based on model A, which represents the economy from a short-run viewpoint. Since Miller did not investigate the interregional feedback effect from a long-run point of view, it is interesting to see whether Miller's contention still holds true under model B. In column 2 under model B, the size of the OPE's increases for every region, but it is still small. The largest OPE is 0.189 per cent for region M and the lowest OPE is 0.103 for region E. Apparently, the interregional feedback effect is again negligible, even when allowance is made for the effect of induced consumption.

It should be emphasized, however, that the interregional feedback relationship is only one of the two interregional linkages that are incorporated in the

TABLE 11

OVERALL PERCENTAGE ERRORS

	(1)	(2)	(3)	(4)
	Feedback Effect Only		*Feedback Effect Plus Other Regions' Effect*	
	Model A	*Model B*	*Model A*	*Model B*
Region E	0.023	0.103	5.174	8.117
Region M	0.040	0.189	2.735	4.223
Region W	0.036	0.109	1.335	3.628

interregional model. Thus, one cannot argue from the above results that the interregional model is not useful in a regional analysis. The other regions' effect mentioned earlier must be incorporated into the interregional feedback effect in evaluating the usefulness of the interregional model for a regional analysis.

The combined measure of the feedback effect and the other regions' effect for model A reported in column 3 of Table 11 indicates that the combined effects for some regions are by no means negligible. The largest OPE is now 5.174 per cent for region E, while the second-largest OPE is 2.735 per cent for region M. Moreover, when the induced effect of household consumption expenditures is incorporated in calculating the OPE, the combined effect of interregional linkages becomes larger. The OPE for region E in column 4 increases to 8.117 per cent and the OPE's for regions M and W are now 4.223 per cent and 3.628 per cent, respectively. Such increases for all regions and especially for region E indicate that the other regions' effect cannot only be important but also vary—for that matter, the interregional feedback effect can also vary—according to the model selected for measuring the interregional linkages.

Extending the interregional model further by introducing the federal, state, and local government sectors into the endogenous part of the model would further increase the size of the OPE.[10] One must, therefore, conclude that despite some agreement with Miller's contention in a very limited sense, the effects of interregional linkages are important enough to warrant the use of an interregional model. The purpose of the interregional model developed in this monograph is to incorporate such effects into the various multipliers reported in this chapter.

In addition to providing a general quantitative measure of interregional linkages, Table 11 also reveals the nature of interregional connections in the Tennessee economy. In column 4, the absolute sizes of the OPE's for regions

E, M, and W decline in that order. The reduction in the size of the OPE's from the eastern region to the western region indicates a triangular pattern of the submatrices comprising the interregional model of the Tennessee economy. The triangular pattern was also indicated from the analysis in the preceding section. This means that the interregional connections within the state of Tennessee are mainly one-way in nature, running from east to west. In other words, sectors in region E sell to themselves and to sectors in regions M and W. In region M, the sectors sell to themselves and to sectors in region W but not importantly to sectors in region E. Region W trades very little with either regions E or M.

A plausible explanation for this tendency could be framed as follows: The state's industrial development occurred first in the eastern region including the bulk of the TVA's operational territory and then spread to Middle Tennessee and finally to West Tennessee. Firms would have been located in region M for many reasons, one of which is the proximity to the source of the inputs produced by sectors in region E. At the same time, proximity to markets in region E could not have been an important factor in the location decisions of firms settling region M. This same rationalization applies to industrialization in West Tennessee. Proximity to inputs from East and Middle Tennessee would be a locational factor much more so than proximity to the markets of East and Middle Tennessee.

Summary

In this chapter, we have implemented for the Tennessee economy the interregional intersectoral flow model developed in Chapter 3 and analyzed the empirical results. This, as far as we know, is the first attempt to utilize an interregional model of the Isard variety through the use of direct interview survey data. It is also the first time in a regional study that a multiregional model with an endogenous household sector has been constructed. In carrying out this analysis, we have demonstrated both the applicability and the usefulness of the multiregional flow model. The desirability of employing such a model is further shown by presenting a new measure of interregional effects that differs from the traditional definition.

The interregional connections in Tennessee were found to be weak in general, but they nevertheless exist and are found to be important for certain intermediate sectors. The interregional linkage through TVA in particular turned out to be quite important. Although the nonmanufacturing sectors prove to be the more important source of interregional bonds, some manufacturing sectors such as chemicals and plastics and other synthetic materials also demonstrate important interregional impacts.

The degree of interregional interdependence was also seen to be influenced by the extent of openness of the model. Whether viewed from the vantage point of intermediate-sector multipliers, final-demand multipliers, or the OPE, when the model was partially closed by treating the household sector endogenously, the importance of interregional linkages increased. Further closing of the model by introducing the federal, state, and local government sectors as endogenous would have probably produced a higher degree of interregional interdependence. Thus, it may be concluded that even for a relatively small region such as Tennessee, the use of interregional models can be recommended for analyzing the structure of interindustry relationships. Contrary to Miller's assertion, therefore, the above conclusion suggests in general that for an interindustry analysis of the national economy, the interregional models would be very appropriate.

The characteristics of subregions of the Tennessee economy were detailed in the analysis of this chapter. The extent of interregional linkages differs from subregion to subregion. In fact, the interregional connections exhibit the peculiarity of running from east to west. Interindustry inputs produced in different parts of Tennessee are in general shipped westward within the state. As a result, initial employment changes in West Tennessee due to changes in final demand produce noticeable employment impacts on both East and Middle Tennessee. Also, initial employment created in Middle Tennessee affects the employment of East Tennessee for the most part. Finally, the magnitude of interregional impacts of initial employment changes in East Tennessee is the smallest.

From the standpoint of structural analysis, the economic growth of each subregion of Tennessee is mainly accounted for by agribusiness or by locally oriented industries such as construction. An important exception is the contribution of TVA to regional development. As the multiplier analysis indicated, TVA has produced strong impacts on East Tennessee and on the rest of the state through interregional and interindustry linkages.

If policy measures such as the state's expenditures and taxes can alter the existing pattern of final-demand outputs, examples of the important sectors to be counted on are paper and allied products and TVA in East Tennessee, chemical and mining industries in Middle Tennessee, and nonelectrical machinery in West Tennessee. This means that a given magnitude of policy actions for shifting final-demand outputs for different industries and regions would have differential effects on the total employment of Tennessee. It also implies that given a projected growth of final demand in the future, state officials responsible for industrial development might well establish a list of priorities in terms of regions as well as industries when attempts are made to attract new firms and to encourage expansions of the existing business establishments.

The lack of interactions in general among subregions of Tennessee suggests that regional developmental programs such as those of the Appalachian Regional Commission and TVA should be aimed directly at the area in question.

As noted, business investment in East Tennessee relative to other parts of the state stimulates more employment in the entire state as well as in East Tennessee. This observation provides a further rationale for initiating regional projects in the eastern part of the state in the Appalachian area. While business investment cannot be controlled by the state and local governments in the short run, it may be stimulated in the long run by governmental subsidies and tax concessions, by building industrial parks and roads, or even by helping to create the source of power needed for industrial development. The extensive sectoral dependence of other industries on TVA shows that it has indeed played such a role in bringing about private investment and industrial development in this region.

Notes

1. For a further elaboration of this type of argument, see Miernyk, *The Elements of Input-Output Analysis,* 70.

2. See, for example, J. Thomas Romans, *Capital Exports and Growth Among U. S. Regions* (Middletown, Conn.: Wesleyan University Press, 1965), 83-85.

3. Ronald E. Miller, "Interregional Feedback Effects in Input-Output Models."

4. As in the statewide model, it is assumed that each element in the aggregated final-demand vector changes in the same proportion.

5. For the reasons stated in n. 4 of ch. 5, the rows of household noncapital sectors in the three-region multiplier matrix are omitted in calculating column sums for intermediate sector multipliers of model B.

6. We are distinguishing between the one employee directly assigned to final demand and the remaining change in employment.

7. For the same reasons stated in nn. 4 and 5 of ch. 5, the effect of household employment on total employment in model B is not included in calculating interregional final-demand multipliers under model B.

8. Miller, "Interregional Feedback Effects in Input-Output Models."

9. Miller conducts his experiments using several different kinds of changes in final demand. The one adopted here should be sufficient to indicate the importance of feedback and the other regions' effect. See Miller, *ibid.*, p. 115.

10. While the governmental sectors such as the state government are not treated as endogenous sectors because of the difficulty of obtaining the necessary data, they can be so treated when data become available. As an intermediate sector, the government sector should have a row and a column in each subregion of the state. The columns for an intermediate government sector would represent on the basis of subregions goods and services purchased from different industries, including transfer payments and subsidies. The rows for the government sector are tax receipts from households and various industries classified by three regions. While such data cannot be obtained from the rows-only data from sample surveys alone, state and local governments could ultimately compile these types of data.

7. Summary and Conclusions

In this study we have looked in detail at the conceptual basis for a set of regional and interregional interindustry accounts and at the data-collection problems involved in implementing such an accounting structure, and we have attempted to analyze the data emerging from an application of a group of interindustry models to the Tennessee economy. In this summary chapter we will review the whole of this research with a view to pointing up some of the innovations and insights it provides.

It has been suggested, it might be hoped facetiously, that input-output analysis coupled with common sense is at least as useful as common sense alone. Our conviction is that the Tennessee study demonstrates that the use of the basic input-output methodology in the form of intersectoral sales flows can add something to a common-sense understanding of a regional economy and can, moreover, do so at modest cost and without overly heroic assumptions.

Some Contributions to Methodology

For the purpose of regional economic analysis, the rows-only approach is developed in general terms in order to combine both the interregional and intersectoral relationships of industries. It is shown that the model can be used for many of the same types of structural analyses commonly carried out in traditional input-output studies. By way of applying the model to the Tennessee economy, it is further demonstrated that the method is empirically feasible for small-scale regional analysis and that it can yield important implications for regional development programs.

Previously the method of intersectoral flow analysis had been confined to a single-region economy without introducing interregional connections. Moreover, the approach had been limited to an analysis of the base multipliers measuring the impacts of changes in final-demand categories on a given region. Even in this analysis, the base multipliers were not correctly defined. These deficiencies stemmed, primarily, from the fact that the basic properties of the rows-only approach were not fully developed and that the method was not generalized for broader applications.

In an attempt to remedy these shortcomings, in this study we initially tried to clarify the nature of intersectoral flow analysis from a methodological standpoint. From comparatively simple manipulations of the interindustry sales-flow matrix, a number of interesting characteristics and extensions of the method have emerged. First, on a conceptual level the method of intersectoral flow analysis is found to be analogous to that of input-output analysis. They differ, however, on an operational level. While input-output analysis requires information on the absorption of inputs as well as the distribution of sales by industries, intersectoral flow analysis employs information on the latter alone, that is, the rows-only information. The intersectoral flow analysis attempts to estimate input requirements by utilizing the sales flows of industries together with an instrumental variable such as employment or output. Since sales fractions rather than sales volumes are required for the initial sales distribution, the intersectoral flow analysis does not call for an identical unit of measurement for sales distributions of different industries. These features, of course, reduce the data requirement.

Second, the impact of final-demand changes on the economy of a region can be obtained by either the iterative method of computation proposed by Hansen and Tiebout or by the direct inversion of the relevant matrix. Since the identity of the two solution methods is derived strictly by algebra and hence is not related to the conceptual framework of the model, the solution method should not determine the nature of the model. Since the iterative computation is carried out through the rows of the sales matrix and the analysis employs the rows-only information, it is easy to overlook the importance of the necessary one-to-one correspondence between the row and the column of an intermediate sector in interindustry relationships. In previous uses of the intersectoral flow model, this correspondence was indeed ignored and a rectangular matrix for sales flows among intermediate sectors was employed. Similarly, the endogenous treatment of certain final-demand categories was incorrectly undertaken by adding the final-demand columns to the endogenous part of the model but by omitting the corresponding rows. When intersectoral linkages are ignored in this way, such base multipliers do not reflect the response of an economy to changes in final demand through interindustry linkages.

Third, the intersectoral flow model can readily be extended to the types of structural analyses frequently undertaken in input-output studies. In addition to base multipliers, the method yields the intermediate-sector multipliers which measure the impact on a region of the change of one employee or one unit of output produced directly for final demand in a given industry. Moreover, following the method of Simpson and Tsukui, we can adapt the intersectoral flow model to an analysis of the fundamental structure of production. It is also shown that the intersectoral flow model can be modified to incorporate imports as being determined inside the model.

Finally, having identified its basic properties, we extended the single-region intersectoral flow model to the multiregion model. The multiregion model is similar to Isard's interregional input-output model except that the former can be derived from rows-only information. As a result, the present method demands less data but still incorporates the two basic features of Isard's model in connecting regional relationships of industries. The method includes the interregional feedback effects and at the same time captures the effects on a region of a change in the final demand of another region. Such interregional connections are woven together in the model through the matrix of the intersectoral sales-flow relationships.

Empirical Findings and Their Implications

The regional and interregional models developed in this study are applied to the Tennessee economy. On the one hand the application produced interesting findings concerning the structure of the Tennessee economy and yielded some policy implications for the economic development of the state. On the other hand, the empirical analysis provided the opportunity for testing some general hypotheses concerning the structure of the regional economy and the economic interactions among regions.

In Tennessee, business investment as a final-demand category exerts the most important stimulus to employment. The expenditures of the state and local governments follow closely as the next most significant stimulus to employment. While foreign trade appears to have a negligible effect, exports to the rest of the United States show modest impacts on the state's economy. In view of the fact that per capita incomes in Tennessee lag behind those of most other states, it may be desirable that the state economy establish stronger ties with the rest of the United States. One way of accomplishing this is to encourage the establishment of new firms that are strongly export-oriented to the rest of the United States. This, of course, cannot be done in the short run. State and local governments, however, could give tax incentives, provide industrial sites, and engage in other promotional activities such as creation of an agency for helping to finance industrial expansion and relocation.

The analysis of intermediate-sector multipliers indicates that past growth of the Tennessee economy depended very much on agribusiness and also on such locally oriented industries as wholesale and retail trade and services. This finding, however, does not imply that the Tennessee economy is self-sufficient, but instead it indicates the typical pattern of a relatively underdeveloped area which tends to lack economic linkages with outside economies. Since the growth of locally oriented industries relies heavily on the growth of that region's economy, any economic development program for Tennessee should place major emphasis on other manufacturing industries.

In the past one industry which has made a unique contribution to the state's economic growth is the Tennessee Valley Authority. Through its large multiplier effect and its interdependence with other industries, TVA has contributed significantly to the growth of the Tennessee economy. If the state and local governments can alter the existing pattern of final demand through their expenditures, they could exert a greater impact on the Tennessee economy in the future. They could do so, for example, by increasing the expenditures that are directly or indirectly connected with the construction industry, TVA, and a number of other industries such as nonelectrical machinery.

Our analysis, which used an interregional flow model, indicated that while the interregional feedback effects are comparatively weak among subregions of Tennessee, the subregions are connected in an interesting manner. Outputs produced in the eastern part of the state are in general sold to Middle and West Tennessee. This pattern of regional dependence suggests that for a given rate of growth in final demand the eastern part of Tennessee has much to recommend in terms of industrial development. Moreover, it was found that changes in business investment in East Tennessee generate more employment throughout the state than would similar changes in other parts of the state. Thus, if a regional development program holds the promise of encouraging business investment in East Tennessee, its economic impact on the state would be substantial. In this case the program would be attractive not only for that region's economy but also for the rest of the state. It is, therefore, important that development planners evaluate the potential merits of alternative programs in terms of the overall effects on the area in which the proposed program is to be located and on the regions with which the area carries on trade. At the same time, it should be kept in mind that because of the lack of regional interdependence in general within Tennessee, regional development programs such as the Appalachian program must be directly located at their target areas.

The structure of each region mirrors in many respects the characteristics of the structure of the composite statewide model. As was the case in the statewide model, the manufacturing division of each region is extremely open in nature both intraregionally and interregionally. The evidence, therefore, suggests again that in the Tennessee economy the nonmanufacturing division provides important sources of inputs to the manufacturing division and to nonmanufacturing. Combining such a structure with the current distribution of final demand for various products produced in different parts of the state, one can conclude that each region of Tennessee is dominated by locally oriented nonmanufacturing or agriculture and related activities. An important exception is the role of TVA in East Tennessee. The analysis of intermediate sector multipliers from the multiregion model indicates that TVA has had a significant impact on the growth of East Tennessee and to a lesser extent on the growth of other regions of the state through the network of interregional interindustry connections.

If the existing composition of final-demand outputs can be changed through governmental tax and expenditure policies, a higher rate of growth of the Tennessee economy may be attained. Such a growth appears to hinge, to cite a few examples, on increases in the relative shares of final demand for paper and allied products and TVA in East Tennessee, chemicals and mining in Middle Tennessee, and nonelectrical machinery in West Tennessee. Granting that such a shift in the composition of final-demand outputs would occur, this finding suggests that in considering statewide industrial development, development authorities should avoid a "butterfly net" approach in seeking out new business firms. The authorities should instead attempt to attract industries with the large employment multipliers and encourage their development in predetermined regions of the state.

In addition to the specific findings about Tennessee, a general hypothesis was tested concerning the similarity between production structures of seemingly different economies. Simpson and Tsukui have argued that different countries have a similar structure of production. They further assert that the fundamental structure of production tends to show triangularity within each bloc such as metals or nonmetals and exhibits very little connection between blocs. In other words, differences in technology, natural resources, factor endowments, and final demands have not materially changed the substitutability of input uses among broad categories of inputs. Such a hypothesis can be tested on a regional level by making the comparison between seemingly unrelated regional economies. For this purpose, California was chosen for comparison with Tennessee. While the intersectoral flow tables do not strictly describe the technical production function of each industry in detail, they nevertheless provide a rough sketch of the production structure of broad industrial categories. After making a suitable adjustment to flow tables by the method suggested by Simpson and Tsukui, we found that the fundamental structures of production for Tennessee and California are indeed alike. They are also roughly similar to the pattern of production structures for the United States and other countries. This result may, therefore, be taken as some support for the Simpson-Tsukui hypothesis. At the same time it indicates that the intersectoral flow model developed in this monograph captures the basic properties of the production function depicted by traditional input-output analysis.

Finally, to test the general usefulness of multiregional interindustry models, this study measured the overall effects of interregional linkages on a given region. Concerning use of such models, Miller has argued that feedback between regions is usually so small that the interregional relationships of industries can be ignored in the analysis. In support of his argument, Miller has produced experimental results indicating that the feedback effects among regions in the United States are almost negligible. Following this argument, one may similarly assert that the interindustry analysis for a region can be conducted by employing a single-region model without connecting the subregions of the region in question. As shown in this study, the presence of a strong interregional feedback effect is only one reason for choosing a multiregion over a single-region model. The other important reason is that the multiregional model measures the economic effect on a given region of changes in final demand in other regions. Moreover, the sum of the above two effects increased significantly when the household sector was treated endogenously. In addition, if one could specify the state and local governments as an endogenous sector as data become available, the interregional effects would further rise. Since Miller does not consider all these effects in his analysis, his estimate of interregional effects for the United States has a serious downward bias. Therefore, all of these observations indicate that the interregional effects in the United States are by no means negligible, particularly in the long run. They also suggest that multiregional models are useful for analyses of both the national and regional economies.

Pros and Cons of the Rows-Only Approach

Despite the usefulness of regional and interregional flow models of the type described here, several criticisms have been directed at the rows-only approach in general. The most significant and widely aired objection centers on the fact that in the rows-only approach the identity of the purchase of total inputs and the sale of total outputs is not utilized. The discipline required in the balancing of independently derived row and column information is sacrificed, and the magnitude and direction of any resulting errors are unknown. Although this criticism cannot be dismissed lightly, it is tempered somewhat by the fact that, in the practical application of the input-output model at the regional level, reconciliation between row and column estimates for cells is largely based on informed judgment. Furthermore, the additional cost incurred in developing column information must be weighted against the resulting improvements in the accuracy of the estimates for cells in each column.

In this connection, moreover, a very strong case can be made for the suitability of the rows-only approach as a means of implementing an interregional model of the Isard type. The necessity of generating interregional trade flows makes the data requirements of this model especially severe. In this model, column information or the input structure of a given sector would be most difficult to obtain regardless of cost, because most firms have little if any idea of the geographical origin of their inputs, especially if their inputs pass through middlemen. On the other hand, most firms have a much better idea as to who their ultimate customers are and where they are located. Given these considerations, the rows-only approach seems to be uncommonly well suited as a relatively inexpensive and certainly feasible method for generating usable estimates for interregional models.

There are other interregional models developed by Moses and Leontief-Strout that require less data than does the Isard model. These writers have proposed methods of estimating the pattern of interregional trade from secondary data instead of deriving it directly from sample surveys. However, their models still call for information on columns as well as rows for intraregional input-output tables. Although this study estimated the interregional trade pattern directly from the rows-only information, it can also be estimated by using a method suggested by Moses in his multiregion input-output analysis. Thus, from the standpoint of simplifying the data requirement, the interregional flow model developed in this monograph has much to recommend it.

A second criticism of the rows-only approach is directed at the assumed stability of the sales-flow coefficients. This criticism is, however, applicable in varying degree to all interindustry models of this type. While the possibility of instability must be considered in using such models, its presence dictates caution in interpreting the results rather than the abandonment of the approach. Moreover, since the rows-only approach can be carried forward with a relatively small budget on a repeated basis, it is possible to study changes in interindustry structures instead of ruling out such changes by an a priori assumption.

The third criticism is concerned with the use of employment rather than output in dollars as the unit of analysis in the intersectoral flow model. Although this study utilized employment units in empirical application, the nature of the model does not necessarily require the use of these units. If the total output data for each industry is used (as it is available in the years when manufacturing industry surveys or censuses are reported), the intersectoral flow analysis can be carried on in dollar units instead of employment units. In such a case the interregional flow analysis becomes an input-output analysis whose input information is obtained indirectly from the sales distribution by industries. Thus, the flow model per se is not bound to use of employment units. On the other hand, the unit of analysis using employment can be defended on other grounds, as stated in this study.

Finally there are some methodological limitations. The rows-only approach is designed to make the forward link from the endogenous industrial sectors to the exogenous final demands. As a result, while the flow analysis can measure economic impacts on the domestic industries due to final-demand changes, the impact on final-demand markets due to changes in the domestic industries cannot be analyzed. Similarly, the economic effects of changes in the supply of primary factors are not dealt with in the flow analysis. Although input-output models are also based on a forward link similar to that in the flow model, input-output models can be adapted to answer some of these questions. They can even be modified for a linear programming type of model where resource constraints are explicitly considered. The flow analysis does not allow such a flexibility in methodological application.

Concluding Remarks

Although a number of limitations have been noted, the rows-only approach does provide a relatively inexpensive means of implementing regional and interregional interindustry models. Given the pressing need to analyze the structure of regional economies and the limited resources available for such research, some compromise on a conceptual level seems justifiable. The rows-only approach is relatively inexpensive and easy to apply in models dealing with reasonably small regions, and the trade-off between conceptual elegance and "operationalism" does not appear to be too great.

Our study has demonstrated the usefulness of constructing a multiregion model within the boundary of a relatively small region such as the state of Tennessee. Obviously it would be quite useful to connect a regional economy extensively to the national economy. At this writing a Harvard University research project is underway designed to compile a multiregional input-output table for all states of the nation. The multiregional intersectoral flow model of a state may be adapted to fit into such an overall model of the national economy. Indeed, the future research on interindustry analysis of a regional economy should make attempts to connect subregions of a given region and at the same time to link the subregions to the national input-output table.

Appendix A

Tables of Basic Data

In this appendix the basic data underlying the empirical side of the study are presented. Table A-1 gives the statewide flow table in employment units. Tables A-2 and A-3 provide the multiplier matrices for the statewide model and the three-region model respectively. The format and interpretation of each table have been described in Chapters 4, 5, and 6. The definitions of sector numbers can also be found in Tables 1 and 2 (pp. 34-35) and in the questionnaires of Appendix B.

TABLE A-1

STATEWIDE INTERSECTORAL FLOW TABLE FOR TENNESSEE, 1964 (IN EMPLOYMENT UNITS)

Columns and Rows Identified by Sector Number

	1	2	3	4	5	6	7	8
1	1758	1932	241	128	169	10608	471	407
2	158	0	5	6	9	8	62	135
3	0	0	1320	0	0	0	33228	64
4	0	0	18603	0	0	0	12787	2099
5	10	922	0	0	0	1010	0	116
6	72	14	24	0	58	9000	0	130
7	105	0	324	0	0	0	76	0
8	1	0	1	2	2	5	0	250
9	0	0	0	0	0	821	151	0
10	31	0	0	0	0	0	0	0
11	14	0	0	0	82	2	178	245
12	1031	1	0	1	0	7	19	24
13	0	1	96	2	1	78	5	17
14	24	0	161	634	0	85	16	530
15	5	0	1	0	0	25	7	22
16	0	0	24	0	0	0	0	169
17	33	136	0	9	10	4739	107	6
18	0	4	0	0	0	50	0	0
19	2	1	5	0	0	375	530	2
20	0	9	0	0	16	129	37	96
21	0	1	1	0	0	176	0	0
22	192	0	0	0	0	394	0	11
23	1233	259	224	22	112	518	861	718
24	581	422	256	68	71	683	51	59
25	15600	120	1695	632	510	3162	385	1718
26	2842	254	351	447	120	547	482	703

TABLE A-1 (*Cont.*)

Columns and Rows Identified by Sector Number

	9	10	11	12	13	14	15	16
1	31	48	221	41	318	188	1	0
2	13	15	120	11	639	69	17	14
3	0	0	0	0	0	0	0	0
4	0	0	0	0	0	0	0	0
5	0	0	0	0	754	0	0	0
6	0	0	242	17	38	0	0	0
7	0	0	0	0	0	1	0	0
8	1	2	0	38	3	3	0	1
9	88	194	54	0	0	0	0	2
10	0	120	0	0	0	0	0	0
11	27	115	198	40	31	263	5	0
12	1	20	0	634	5	45	0	74
13	2	5	43	0	5	98	5	0
14	45	54	7	0	29	58	105	0
15	2	3	1	1	0	12	1	1
16	0	0	0	0	0	0	0	578
17	0	7	24	0	11	0	0	0
18	20	0	11	0	29	0	4	22
19	0	12	0	0	57	0	0	0
20	1	18	0	29	0	1	0	0
21	0	0	0	36	8	0	0	0
22	0	0	0	0	3	0	0	573
23	213	180	205	271	106	626	55	102
24	69	32	7	19	7	478	0	0
25	205	92	266	670	265	613	56	112
26	193	245	169	212	369	488	70	212

TABLE A-1 (*Cont.*)

	17	18	19	20	21	22	23	24
1	221	278	149	82	87	818	136	22
2	122	364	26	13	95	26	107	70
3	0	0	0	0	0	0	0	0
4	0	0	0	0	0	0	0	0
5	704	0	0	0	0	0	0	0
6	0	34	62	0	0	342	104	1253
7	0	0	0	0	0	0	0	0
8	0	8	6	2	0	36	3	0
9	0	13	23	3	0	180	15	0
10	0	0	0	0	0	1	0	0
11	172	9	37	14	0	171	0	0
12	0	0	60	2	7	276	301	198
13	1	10	43	2	5	34	0	0
14	31	0	84	31	62	139	0	0
15	0	2	10	1	36	221	4	1
16	0	0	0	0	0	62	0	0
17	503	14	26	0	4	19	0	0
18	17	6	139	51	88	107	7	0
19	16	21	45	5	287	59	6	0
20	34	14	63	38	52	183	0	0
21	0	0	0	0	69	40	0	0
22	0	0	0	1	50	156	0	0
23	133	187	208	530	316	1700	851	1413
24	22	0	11	292	34	1039	258	4412
25	1000	43	696	398	404	4464	1431	3454
26	230	236	243	354	249	240	467	903

TABLE A-1 (*Cont.*)

Columns and Rows Identified by Sector Number

	25	26	Final Demand:	Household Capital	Business Investment	State & Local Gov't
1	1589	52414		35604	12273	745
2	280	1788		0	0	34
3	0	17366		0	1216	0
4	3208	2729		0	15	0
5	26	357		0	0	62
6	877	329		2466	11655	3229
7	7	5745		0	385	271
8	3	998		2512	890	1
9	0	52		15	346	15
10	11	0		987	302	0
11	0	145		0	19	0
12	3543	2159		125	120	44
13	17	1		1	29	27
14	236	796		51	141	0
15	1	2		213	10	0
16	0	502		144	442	1
17	10	0		129	150	55
18	43	0		522	423	24
19	14	0		177	1866	0
20	18	0		2	989	73
21	11	0		778	329	0
22	3	485		486	327	182
23	4755	4479		203	70	84
24	203	9386		0	52	950
25	10831	59070		85	47	5875
26	796	54		0	0	1741

TABLE A-1 (*Cont.*)

	Final Demand: Federal Gov't	*Rest of U. S.*	*Exports*	*Total Employment*
1	4761	77688	4773	208200
2	3949	2744	0	10900
3	0	1855	0	55048
4	8570	15500	5560	69072
5	1193	1544	3	6700
6	3947	20708	0	54600
7	373	26627	187	34100
8	5140	76809	1186	87900
9	1202	13332	793	17300
10	54	18495	197	20200
11	44	8241	346	10400
12	41	7515	47	16300
13	4181	13207	186	18100
14	580	25291	1409	30600
15	403	6497	415	7900
16	0	17190	187	19300
17	30	7954	25	14000
18	774	13540	520	16400
19	1060	14550	312	19400
20	1166	7196	436	10600
21	2945	15997	509	20900
22	1074	14600	262	18800
23	3302	28326	338	52600
24	950	24245	244	44900
25	997	33501	55	148450
26	864	0	0	14080

TABLE A-2

STATEWIDE MULTIPLIER MATRIX FOR TENNESSEE WITH HOUSEHOLD NONCAPITAL AS ENDOGENOUS, 1964

Columns and Rows Identified by Sector Number

	1	2	3	4	5	6	7	8
1	1.0756	0.3141	0.0493	0.0325	0.1184	0.3279	0.1442	0.0457
2	0.0034	1.0055	0.0019	0.0013	0.0051	0.0051	0.0070	0.0031
3	0.0291	0.0572	1.0494	0.0132	0.0387	0.0384	1.0597	0.0180
4	0.0196	0.0359	0.3629	1.0083	0.0256	0.0259	0.7520	0.0353
5	0.0009	0.0868	0.0006	0.0003	1.0015	0.0288	0.0018	0.0020
6	0.0028	0.0076	0.0021	0.0009	0.0140	1.2017	0.0046	0.0031
7	0.0077	0.0144	0.0108	0.0033	0.0097	0.0097	1.0215	0.0043
8	0.0012	0.0025	0.0008	0.0006	0.0019	0.0018	0.0023	1.0036
9	0.0002	0.0003	0.0001	0.0001	0.0004	0.0184	0.0048	0.0001
10	0.0002	0.0001	0.0000	0.0000	0.0000	0.0001	0.0000	0.0000
11	0.0004	0.0018	0.0003	0.0002	0.0129	0.0023	0.0060	0.0031
12	0.0126	0.0130	0.0046	0.0028	0.0097	0.0116	0.0123	0.0042
13	0.0001	0.0003	0.0019	0.0001	0.0003	0.0019	0.0022	0.0003
14	0.0016	0.0029	0.0072	0.0099	0.0020	0.0044	0.0128	0.0072
15	0.0001	0.0001	0.0000	0.0000	0.0000	0.0007	0.0003	0.0003
16	0.0006	0.0013	0.0009	0.0003	0.0009	0.0009	0.0017	0.0024
17	0.0005	0.0139	0.0003	0.0002	0.0030	0.1084	0.0040	0.0004
18	0.0001	0.0004	0.0000	0.0000	0.0001	0.0015	0.0002	0.0000
19	0.0002	0.0004	0.0003	0.0000	0.0003	0.0087	0.0160	0.0001
20	0.0001	0.0012	0.0000	0.0000	0.0025	0.0034	0.0012	0.0011
21	0.0001	0.0002	0.0000	0.0000	0.0001	0.0040	0.0000	0.0000
22	0.0016	0.0016	0.0005	0.0003	0.0010	0.0099	0.0013	0.0006
23	0.0189	0.0492	0.0126	0.0054	0.0342	0.0334	0.0514	0.0154
24	0.0168	0.0715	0.0147	0.0074	0.0304	0.0369	0.0332	0.0092
25	0.1682	0.2105	0.0954	0.0499	0.2032	0.2251	0.2170	0.0746
26	0.0170	0.0339	0.0112	0.0079	0.0229	0.0227	0.0316	0.0103

TABLE A-2 (*Cont.*)

	9	10	11	12	13	14	15	16
1	0.0548	0.0603	0.1129	0.0682	0.1295	0.0847	0.0427	0.0565
2	0.0028	0.0030	0.0152	0.0033	0.0394	0.0055	0.0038	0.0029
3	0.0228	0.0249	0.0359	0.0280	0.0449	0.0336	0.0182	0.0237
4	0.0143	0.0154	0.0227	0.0182	0.0280	0.0211	0.0119	0.0149
5	0.0007	0.0007	0.0029	0.0008	0.0459	0.0012	0.0007	0.0007
6	0.0016	0.0017	0.0309	0.0034	0.0060	0.0030	0.0012	0.0022
7	0.0057	0.0062	0.0090	0.0070	0.0112	0.0084	0.0046	0.0059
8	0.0010	0.0012	0.0015	0.0036	0.0021	0.0015	0.0008	0.0011
9	1.0052	0.0099	0.0059	0.0002	0.0003	0.0002	0.0001	0.0006
10	0.0000	1.0060	0.0000	0.0000	0.0000	0.0000	0.0000	0.0000
11	0.0018	0.0061	1.0199	0.0027	0.0028	0.0091	0.0010	0.0005
12	0.0048	0.0059	0.0078	1.0470	0.0094	0.0086	0.0037	0.0094
13	0.0002	0.0003	0.0044	0.0001	1.0004	0.0033	0.0007	0.0001
14	0.0038	0.0039	0.0026	0.0015	0.0039	1.0036	0.0142	0.0014
15	0.0002	0.0001	0.0002	0.0001	0.0000	0.0004	1.0002	0.0004
16	0.0005	0.0006	0.0008	0.0006	0.0010	0.0008	0.0005	1.0315
17	0.0002	0.0006	0.0055	0.0004	0.0018	0.0004	0.0002	0.0003
18	0.0011	0.0000	0.0012	0.0000	0.0017	0.0000	0.0005	0.0014
19	0.0001	0.0007	0.0004	0.0002	0.0034	0.0001	0.0001	0.0002
20	0.0001	0.0009	0.0002	0.0019	0.0002	0.0000	0.0000	0.0004
21	0.0000	0.0000	0.0001	0.0024	0.0005	0.0000	0.0000	0.0001
22	0.0006	0.0006	0.0011	0.0007	0.0013	0.0008	0.0004	0.0314
23	0.0211	0.0182	0.0348	0.0290	0.0241	0.0340	0.0139	0.0172
24	0.0152	0.0136	0.0188	0.0147	0.0237	0.0333	0.0089	0.0131
25	0.0822	0.0807	0.1415	0.1312	0.1573	0.1252	0.0628	0.0862
26	0.0136	0.0148	0.0213	0.0166	0.0266	0.0199	0.0108	0.0141

TABLE A-2 (*Cont.*)

Columns and Rows Identified by Sector Number

	17	18	19	20	21	22	23	24
1	0.1097	0.0920	0.0711	0.1682	0.0642	0.1403	0.0471	0.1178
2	0.0129	0.0249	0.0040	0.0076	0.0070	0.0059	0.0038	0.0061
3	0.0384	0.0305	0.0267	0.0691	0.0254	0.0376	0.0188	0.0470
4	0.0254	0.0188	0.0172	0.0433	0.0160	0.0290	0.0122	0.0309
5	0.0540	0.0028	0.0011	0.0019	0.0011	0.0020	0.0007	0.0022
6	0.0039	0.0044	0.0058	0.0055	0.0019	0.0288	0.0039	0.0406
7	0.0096	0.0076	0.0067	0.0173	0.0063	0.0094	0.0047	0.0118
8	0.0017	0.0018	0.0015	0.0031	0.0011	0.0036	0.0009	0.0020
9	0.0003	0.0010	0.0014	0.0006	0.0002	0.0104	0.0004	0.0008
10	0.0000	0.0000	0.0000	0.0000	0.0000	0.0001	0.0000	0.0000
11	0.0140	0.0009	0.0023	0.0020	0.0003	0.0100	0.0002	0.0005
12	0.0095	0.0060	0.0093	0.0147	0.0059	0.0305	0.0104	0.0165
13	0.0002	0.0007	0.0023	0.0004	0.0004	0.0021	0.0001	0.0002
14	0.0043	0.0015	0.0057	0.0064	0.0044	0.0101	0.0010	0.0025
15	0.0000	0.0001	0.0005	0.0002	0.0018	0.0119	0.0001	0.0001
16	0.0009	0.0007	0.0006	0.0016	0.0006	0.0043	0.0004	0.0011
17	1.0380	0.0016	0.0020	0.0007	0.0005	0.0039	0.0004	0.0038
18	0.0014	1.0004	0.0073	0.0050	0.0044	0.0060	0.0002	0.0001
19	0.0014	0.0015	1.0025	0.0008	0.0140	0.0036	0.0002	0.0005
20	0.0027	0.0009	0.0033	1.0038	0.0026	0.0101	0.0001	0.0002
21	0.0000	0.0000	0.0001	0.0001	1.0033	0.0023	0.0000	0.0002
22	0.0010	0.0008	0.0007	0.0018	0.0030	1.0096	0.0005	0.0014
23	0.0279	0.0230	0.0220	0.0773	0.0257	0.1188	1.0243	0.0553
24	0.0212	0.0154	0.0136	0.0635	0.0143	0.0815	0.0145	1.1320
25	0.2025	0.0970	0.1208	0.2525	0.0994	0.3879	0.0873	0.2378
26	0.0228	0.0181	0.0158	0.0410	0.0151	0.0223	0.0111	0.0279

TABLE A-2 (*Cont.*)

	25	26
1	0.0458	4.5104
2	0.0034	0.1676
3	0.0139	1.9600
4	0.0319	1.2003
5	0.0009	0.0481
6	0.0087	0.1119
7	0.0035	0.4900
8	0.0007	0.0839
9	0.0002	0.0090
10	0.0000	0.0011
11	0.0002	0.0184
12	0.0298	0.3640
13	0.0002	0.0049
14	0.0026	0.0940
15	0.0000	0.0013
16	0.0003	0.0440
17	0.0009	0.0153
18	0.0004	0.0025
19	0.0002	0.0095
20	0.0002	0.0030
21	0.0002	0.0018
22	0.0004	0.0469
23	0.0408	0.6648
24	0.0087	0.9136
25	1.1247	5.8573
26	0.0082	1.1638

TABLE A-3

THREE-REGION MULTIPLIER MATRIX FOR TENNESSEE WITH HOUSEHOLD NON-CAPITAL AS ENDOGENOUS, 1964

By Sector Number with Regional Suffix

	East Tennessee								
	1 E	2 E	3 E	4 E	5 E	6 E	7 E	8 E	9 E
1 E	1.0571	0.3010	0.0481	0.0286	0.1058	0.2071	0.1068	0.0471	0.0512
2 E	0.0027	1.0053	0.0019	0.0011	0.0046	0.0038	0.0061	0.0031	0.0028
3 E	0.0237	0.0646	1.0813	0.0137	0.0450	0.0361	0.9777	0.0206	0.0228
4 E	0.0133	0.0345	0.3970	1.0073	0.0241	0.0195	0.6029	0.0113	0.0123
5 E	0.0008	0.1620	0.0006	0.0003	1.0015	0.0271	0.0017	0.0032	0.0008
6 E	0.0039	0.0092	0.0016	0.0010	0.0098	1.1515	0.0045	0.0121	0.0022
7 E	0.0071	0.0196	0.0402	0.0042	0.0136	0.0110	1.0566	0.0061	0.0069
8 E	0.0015	0.0040	0.0015	0.0009	0.0030	0.0026	0.0032	1.0028	0.0015
9 E	0.0001	0.0002	0.0000	0.0000	0.0003	0.0175	0.0003	0.0002	1.0008
10 E	0.0000	0.0001	0.0000	0.0000	0.0000	0.0000	0.0000	0.0000	0.0000
11 E	0.0001	0.0024	0.0002	0.0000	0.0114	0.0026	0.0038	0.0013	0.0025
12 E	0.0088	0.0093	0.0030	0.0017	0.0060	0.0057	0.0071	0.0044	0.0031
13 E	0.0000	0.0001	0.0000	0.0000	0.0002	0.0047	0.0001	0.0003	0.0010
14 E	0.0004	0.0015	0.0032	0.0074	0.0009	0.0040	0.0054	0.0058	0.0004
15 E	0.0000	0.0000	0.0000	0.0000	0.0000	0.0002	0.0002	0.0006	0.0000
16 E	0.0002	0.0006	0.0010	0.0001	0.0004	0.0004	0.0012	0.0008	0.0002
17 E	0.0005	0.0191	0.0006	0.0007	0.0042	0.0988	0.0054	0.0013	0.0003
18 E	0.0000	0.0005	0.0000	0.0000	0.0001	0.0013	0.0004	0.0001	0.0001
19 E	0.0003	0.0009	0.0017	0.0002	0.0006	0.0043	0.0391	0.0003	0.0003
20 E	0.0000	0.0016	0.0002	0.0000	0.0024	0.0012	0.0045	0.0027	0.0001
21 E	0.0000	0.0000	0.0000	0.0000	0.0000	0.0000	0.0000	0.0000	0.0000
22 E	0.0000	0.0000	0.0000	0.0000	0.0000	0.0013	0.0000	0.0001	0.0000
23 E	0.0218	0.0549	0.0111	0.0052	0.0276	0.0312	0.0446	0.0134	0.0231
24 E	0.0302	0.0950	0.0486	0.0085	0.0438	0.0510	0.0638	0.0141	0.0172
25 E	0.1634	0.1882	0.0636	0.0318	0.1438	0.1398	0.1456	0.0640	0.0803
26 E	0.0129	0.0354	0.0124	0.0075	0.0247	0.0196	0.0276	0.0111	0.0125

Please refer to pages 129 and 138 for the corresponding columns for the other two regions.

TABLE A-3 (*Cont.*)

10 E	11 E	12 E	13 E	14 E	15 E	16 E	17 E	18 E
0.0629	0.1748	0.0591	0.1118	0.0752	0.0668	0.0474	0.1041	0.0862
0.0028	0.0219	0.0023	0.0080	0.0041	0.0049	0.0021	0.0089	0.0200
0.0289	0.0530	0.0257	0.0479	0.0353	0.0315	0.0226	0.0390	0.0348
0.0153	0.0287	0.0139	0.0255	0.0189	0.0169	0.0121	0.0219	0.0185
0.0008	0.0098	0.0008	0.0021	0.0011	0.0013	0.0006	0.0022	0.0040
0.0027	0.2415	0.0065	0.0078	0.0027	0.0029	0.0016	0.0077	0.0063
0.0088	0.0161	0.0078	0.0145	0.0108	0.0095	0.0069	0.0118	0.0105
0.0019	0.0033	0.0078	0.0029	0.0022	0.0019	0.0015	0.0024	0.0026
0.0069	0.0190	0.0002	0.0002	0.0001	0.0001	0.0000	0.0005	0.0001
1.0078	0.0001	0.0000	0.0000	0.0000	0.0000	0.0000	0.0001	0.0000
0.0030	1.0092	0.0036	0.0008	0.0009	0.0030	0.0001	0.0209	0.0006
0.0072	0.0076	1.0067	0.0062	0.0047	0.0042	0.0030	0.0061	0.0045
0.0000	0.0023	0.0000	1.0000	0.0023	0.0002	0.0000	0.0003	0.0000
0.0032	0.0035	0.0005	0.0026	1.0030	0.0917	0.0004	0.0195	0.0007
0.0001	0.0000	0.0000	0.0000	0.0005	1.0001	0.0000	0.0000	0.0001
0.0003	0.0005	0.0003	0.0005	0.0003	0.0003	1.0241	0.0004	0.0003
0.0012	0.0288	0.0007	0.0021	0.0004	0.0005	0.0002	1.0069	0.0025
0.0000	0.0028	0.0000	0.0001	0.0000	0.0008	0.0015	0.0023	1.0006
0.0007	0.0015	0.0003	0.0019	0.0004	0.0004	0.0003	0.0017	0.0004
0.0002	0.0004	0.0001	0.0001	0.0001	0.0001	0.0000	0.0005	0.0003
0.0000	0.0000	0.0000	0.0000	0.0000	0.0000	0.0000	0.0000	0.0000
0.0000	0.0003	0.0000	0.0000	0.0000	0.0000	0.0002	0.0000	0.0000
0.0159	0.0444	0.0306	0.0199	0.0263	0.0286	0.0214	0.0319	0.0214
0.0216	0.0431	0.0205	0.0306	0.0422	0.0217	0.0142	0.0303	0.0226
0.0685	0.2173	0.1050	0.1302	0.1132	0.1065	0.0739	0.2714	0.0875
0.0159	0.0290	0.0141	0.0263	0.0193	0.0173	0.0124	0.0214	0.0191

Please refer to pages 130 and 139 for the corresponding columns for the other two regions.

TABLE A-3 (*Cont.*)

By Sector Number with Regional Suffix

	19 E	20 E	21 E	22 E	23 E	24 E	25 E	26 E
1 E	0.0700	0.0718	0.0654	0.1179	0.0445	0.1398	0.0389	4.3631
2 E	0.0038	0.0044	0.0037	0.0063	0.0036	0.0072	0.0026	0.1502
3 E	0.0302	0.0311	0.0306	0.0470	0.0192	0.0652	0.0140	2.0962
4 E	0.0162	0.0172	0.0165	0.0288	0.0105	0.0364	0.0151	1.1082
5 E	0.0011	0.0012	0.0010	0.0026	0.0009	0.0020	0.0006	0.0506
6 E	0.0033	0.0026	0.0022	0.0441	0.0014	0.0046	0.0010	0.1471
7 E	0.0091	0.0094	0.0093	0.0144	0.0058	0.0198	0.0044	0.6342
8 E	0.0025	0.0023	0.0019	0.0056	0.0013	0.0040	0.0009	0.1268
9 E	0.0046	0.0001	0.0001	0.0033	0.0000	0.0001	0.0000	0.0030
10 E	0.0000	0.0000	0.0000	0.0002	0.0000	0.0001	0.0003	0.0011
11 E	0.0012	0.0017	0.0001	0.0136	0.0001	0.0002	0.0001	0.0061
12 E	0.0189	0.0047	0.0043	0.0253	0.0027	0.0116	0.0081	0.2634
13 E	0.0019	0.0001	0.0001	0.0065	0.0000	0.0000	0.0000	0.0009
14 E	0.0020	0.0189	0.0148	0.0029	0.0003	0.0012	0.0003	0.0369
15 E	0.0002	0.0000	0.0017	0.0028	0.0000	0.0000	0.0000	0.0004
16 E	0.0003	0.0003	0.0003	0.0005	0.0002	0.0007	0.0001	0.0207
17 E	0.0030	0.0005	0.0006	0.0078	0.0003	0.0008	0.0004	0.0209
18 E	0.0091	0.0047	0.0001	0.0008	0.0000	0.0001	0.0002	0.0013
19 E	1.0059	0.0020	0.0084	0.0011	0.0002	0.0008	0.0004	0.0251
20 E	0.0037	1.0002	0.0005	0.0002	0.0000	0.0001	0.0000	0.0035
21 E	0.0000	0.0000	1.0000	0.0394	0.0000	0.0000	0.0000	0.0001
22 E	0.0000	0.0003	0.0005	1.0036	0.0000	0.0001	0.0000	0.0013
23 E	0.0241	0.0856	0.0279	0.2543	1.0376	0.0892	0.0509	0.6616
24 E	0.0207	0.0792	0.0205	0.0888	0.0258	1.1518	0.0182	1.2754
25 E	0.1051	0.1699	0.1121	0.6688	0.0920	0.4224	1.1179	4.7561
26 E	0.0166	0.0171	0.0167	0.0256	0.0105	0.0357	0.0075	1.1497

Please refer to pages 131 and 140 for the corresponding columns for the other two regions.

By Sector Number with Regional Suffix

Middle Tennessee

	1 M	2 M	3 M	4 M	5 M	6 M	7 M	8 M	9 M
1 E	0.0050	0.0186	0.0052	0.0030	0.0081	0.0127	0.0572	0.0035	0.0045
2 E	0.0035	0.0056	0.0023	0.0016	0.0060	0.0049	0.0097	0.0021	0.0029
3 E	0.0019	0.0069	0.0018	0.0011	0.0028	0.0037	0.0874	0.0013	0.0016
4 E	0.0010	0.0037	0.0011	0.0006	0.0015	0.0020	0.0336	0.0007	0.0008
5 E	0.0006	0.0611	0.0004	0.0003	0.0011	0.0010	0.0018	0.0004	0.0005
6 E	0.0001	0.0037	0.0001	0.0000	0.0003	0.0055	0.0008	0.0002	0.0001
7 E	0.0008	0.0026	0.0007	0.0005	0.0012	0.0015	0.0067	0.0005	0.0007
8 E	0.0005	0.0013	0.0005	0.0004	0.0009	0.0009	0.0019	0.0016	0.0005
9 E	0.0000	0.0001	0.0000	0.0000	0.0001	0.0066	0.0001	0.0000	0.0010
10 E	0.0000	0.0001	0.0000	0.0000	0.0000	0.0000	0.0000	0.0000	0.0000
11 E	0.0001	0.0012	0.0000	0.0000	0.0001	0.0013	0.0010	0.0006	0.0000
12 E	0.0006	0.0010	0.0004	0.0002	0.0005	0.0007	0.0015	0.0002	0.0002
13 E	0.0000	0.0001	0.0000	0.0000	0.0005	0.0038	0.0000	0.0002	0.0000
14 E	0.0002	0.0009	0.0002	0.0001	0.0005	0.0013	0.0012	0.0026	0.0002
15 E	0.0000	0.0000	0.0000	0.0000	0.0000	0.0002	0.0003	0.0000	0.0000
16 E	0.0002	0.0004	0.0003	0.0001	0.0003	0.0003	0.0008	0.0067	0.0002
17 E	0.0002	0.0182	0.0001	0.0001	0.0004	0.0119	0.0033	0.0001	0.0001
18 E	0.0000	0.0005	0.0000	0.0000	0.0001	0.0013	0.0001	0.0001	0.0002
19 E	0.0000	0.0002	0.0000	0.0000	0.0001	0.0006	0.0006	0.0000	0.0000
20 E	0.0000	0.0013	0.0000	0.0000	0.0098	0.0015	0.0001	0.0000	0.0001
21 E	0.0000	0.0000	0.0000	0.0000	0.0000	0.0000	0.0000	0.0000	0.0000
22 E	0.0000	0.0001	0.0000	0.0000	0.0001	0.0004	0.0001	0.0003	0.0000
23 E	0.0012	0.0050	0.0018	0.0005	0.0028	0.0025	0.0059	0.0012	0.0009
24 E	0.0008	0.0048	0.0010	0.0004	0.0021	0.0022	0.0076	0.0007	0.0007
25 E	0.0107	0.0333	0.0298	0.0056	0.0183	0.0192	0.0688	0.0063	0.0083
26 E	0.0003	0.0024	0.0004	0.0001	0.0006	0.0010	0.0025	0.0003	0.0002

Please refer to pages 132 and 141 for the corresponding columns for the other two regions.

By Sector Number with Regional Suffix

	10 M	11 M	12 M	13 M	14 M	15 M	16 M	17 M	18 M
1 E	0.0062	0.0055	0.0061	0.0570	0.0085	0.0071	0.0112	0.0164	0.0228
2 E	0.0033	0.0038	0.0041	0.1670	0.0075	0.0064	0.0036	0.0156	0.0621
3 E	0.0022	0.0019	0.0021	0.0135	0.0029	0.0024	0.0042	0.0053	0.0057
4 E	0.0012	0.0010	0.0011	0.0072	0.0015	0.0012	0.0024	0.0028	0.0030
5 E	0.0006	0.0007	0.0008	0.0305	0.0014	0.0012	0.0007	0.0029	0.0114
6 E	0.0004	0.0001	0.0003	0.0019	0.0002	0.0001	0.0021	0.0031	0.0007
7 E	0.0009	0.0008	0.0009	0.0045	0.0012	0.0010	0.0015	0.0020	0.0020
8 E	0.0007	0.0005	0.0031	0.0016	0.0009	0.0007	0.0009	0.0010	0.0020
9 E	0.0021	0.0000	0.0000	0.0001	0.0000	0.0000	0.0002	0.0003	0.0000
10 E	0.0000	0.0000	0.0000	0.0000	0.0000	0.0000	0.0000	0.0000	0.0000
11 E	0.0010	0.0001	0.0009	0.0005	0.0001	0.0001	0.0007	0.0116	0.0002
12 E	0.0147	0.0003	0.0015	0.0019	0.0003	0.0003	0.0057	0.0007	0.0009
13 E	0.0000	0.0039	0.0000	0.0001	0.0002	0.0000	0.0003	0.0002	0.0004
14 E	0.0003	0.0002	0.0003	0.0021	0.0014	0.0003	0.0004	0.0012	0.0007
15 E	0.0002	0.0000	0.0000	0.0000	0.0000	0.0000	0.0001	0.0000	0.0000
16 E	0.0002	0.0002	0.0002	0.0004	0.0003	0.0003	0.0021	0.0003	0.0002
17 E	0.0002	0.0002	0.0002	0.0044	0.0003	0.0002	0.0005	0.0340	0.0016
18 E	0.0001	0.0026	0.0000	0.0002	0.0000	0.0000	0.0001	0.0019	0.0004
19 E	0.0017	0.0001	0.0001	0.0002	0.0001	0.0001	0.0001	0.0001	0.0001
20 E	0.0008	0.0000	0.0000	0.0018	0.0000	0.0000	0.0000	0.0004	0.0001
21 E	0.0000	0.0000	0.0000	0.0000	0.0000	0.0000	0.0018	0.0000	0.0000
22 E	0.0000	0.0000	0.0000	0.0001	0.0001	0.0000	0.0447	0.0001	0.0000
23 E	0.0021	0.0029	0.0016	0.0106	0.0023	0.0013	0.0124	0.0035	0.0041
24 E	0.0012	0.0010	0.0010	0.0169	0.0015	0.0012	0.0049	0.0037	0.0064
25 E	0.0114	0.0102	0.0116	0.0456	0.0140	0.0120	0.0403	0.0274	0.0199
26 E	0.0006	0.0004	0.0004	0.0063	0.0005	0.0004	0.0015	0.0018	0.0024

Please refer to pages 133 and 142 for the corresponding columns for the other two regions.

TABLE A-3 (*Cont.*)

19 M	20 M	21 M	22 M	23 M	24 M	25 M	26 M
0.0080	0.0087	0.0092	0.0086	0.0041	0.0066	0.0048	0.3580
0.0043	0.0044	0.0113	0.0051	0.0042	0.0045	0.0049	0.1751
0.0029	0.0033	0.0030	0.0031	0.0013	0.0023	0.0016	0.1255
0.0015	0.0017	0.0016	0.0016	0.0007	0.0012	0.0010	0.0650
0.0008	0.0008	0.0021	0.0010	0.0008	0.0008	0.0009	0.0323
0.0003	0.0002	0.0002	0.0021	0.0001	0.0001	0.0001	0.0056
0.0012	0.0013	0.0012	0.0013	0.0006	0.0010	0.0007	0.0553
0.0009	0.0009	0.0007	0.0013	0.0005	0.0007	0.0004	0.0414
0.0000	0.0000	0.0000	0.0020	0.0001	0.0000	0.0000	0.0016
0.0000	0.0000	0.0000	0.0000	0.0000	0.0000	0.0000	0.0002
0.0001	0.0001	0.0001	0.0044	0.0001	0.0001	0.0001	0.0038
0.0118	0.0004	0.0006	0.0011	0.0002	0.0003	0.0007	0.0146
0.0018	0.0001	0.0001	0.0030	0.0000	0.0000	0.0000	0.0005
0.0019	0.0317	0.0136	0.0011	0.0002	0.0003	0.0002	0.0163
0.0003	0.0000	0.0005	0.0012	0.0000	0.0000	0.0000	0.0004
0.0002	0.0002	0.0002	0.0003	0.0001	0.0003	0.0001	0.0148
0.0015	0.0002	0.0005	0.0004	0.0002	0.0002	0.0002	0.0081
0.0077	0.0061	0.0002	0.0001	0.0000	0.0000	0.0001	0.0007
0.0003	0.0001	0.0001	0.0001	0.0004	0.0001	0.0001	0.0027
0.0004	0.0002	0.0000	0.0000	0.0000	0.0000	0.0000	0.0009
0.0000	0.0000	0.0000	0.0000	0.0000	0.0000	0.0000	0.0001
0.0000	0.0000	0.0004	0.0004	0.0000	0.0000	0.0000	0.0025
0.0019	0.0019	0.0019	0.0018	0.0009	0.0012	0.0032	0.0590
0.0015	0.0024	0.0022	0.0016	0.0007	0.0011	0.0011	0.0497
0.0147	0.0140	0.0136	0.0150	0.0067	0.0126	0.0227	0.6472
0.0008	0.0010	0.0008	0.0007	0.0003	0.0004	0.0004	0.0167

Please refer to pages 134 and 143 for the corresponding columns for the other two regions.

TABLE A-3 (*Cont.*)

By Sector Number with Regional Suffix

	West Tennessee								
	1 W	**2 W**	**3 W**	**4 W**	**5 W**	**6 W**	**7 W**	**8 W**	**9 W**
1 E	0.0032	0.0124	0.0019	0.0011	0.0031	0.0064	0.0133	0.0024	0.002
2 E	0.0012	0.0015	0.0006	0.0004	0.0023	0.0020	0.0022	0.0011	0.000
3 E	0.0071	0.0114	0.0031	0.0022	0.0054	0.0101	0.2054	0.0034	0.004
4 E	0.0037	0.0060	0.0016	0.0012	0.0028	0.0053	0.0782	0.0018	0.002
5 E	0.0002	0.0604	0.0001	0.0001	0.0004	0.0004	0.0005	0.0002	0.000
6 E	0.0001	0.0036	0.0000	0.0000	0.0002	0.0012	0.0005	0.0001	0.000
7 E	0.0045	0.0062	0.0020	0.0014	0.0034	0.0062	0.0128	0.0021	0.002
8 E	0.0010	0.0014	0.0005	0.0003	0.0011	0.0016	0.0014	0.0012	0.000
9 E	0.0001	0.0001	0.0000	0.0000	0.0002	0.0124	0.0001	0.0000	0.000
10 E	0.0000	0.0001	0.0000	0.0000	0.0000	0.0000	0.0000	0.0000	0.000
11 E	0.0001	0.0011	0.0000	0.0000	0.0001	0.0006	0.0006	0.0000	0.000
12 E	0.0005	0.0008	0.0002	0.0001	0.0003	0.0008	0.0010	0.0002	0.000
13 E	0.0000	0.0001	0.0000	0.0000	0.0001	0.0001	0.0000	0.0001	0.000
14 E	0.0002	0.0006	0.0001	0.0001	0.0002	0.0009	0.0010	0.0099	0.000
15 E	0.0000	0.0000	0.0000	0.0000	0.0000	0.0002	0.0002	0.0004	0.000
16 E	0.0002	0.0003	0.0003	0.0001	0.0002	0.0003	0.0005	0.0002	0.000
17 E	0.0001	0.0182	0.0001	0.0000	0.0004	0.0050	0.0045	0.0001	0.000
18 E	0.0000	0.0005	0.0000	0.0000	0.0000	0.0014	0.0000	0.0000	0.000
19 E	0.0002	0.0003	0.0001	0.0001	0.0001	0.0005	0.0007	0.0001	0.000
20 E	0.0000	0.0013	0.0000	0.0000	0.0001	0.0016	0.0001	0.0000	0.000
21 E	0.0000	0.0000	0.0000	0.0000	0.0000	0.0000	0.0000	0.0000	0.000
22 E	0.0000	0.0001	0.0000	0.0000	0.0000	0.0002	0.0000	0.0000	0.000
23 E	0.0007	0.0039	0.0003	0.0002	0.0006	0.0017	0.0030	0.0009	0.000
24 E	0.0012	0.0047	0.0006	0.0004	0.0011	0.0031	0.0104	0.0010	0.000
25 E	0.0065	0.0209	0.0031	0.0020	0.0053	0.0126	0.0205	0.0041	0.003
26 E	0.0003	0.0022	0.0001	0.0001	0.0003	0.0008	0.0027	0.0003	0.000

Please refer to pages 135 and 144 for the corresponding columns for the other two regions.

TABLE A-3 (*Cont.*)

10 W	11 W	12 W	13 W	14 W	15 W	16 W	17 W	18 W
0.0018	0.0035	0.0035	0.0044	0.0027	0.0008	0.0013	0.0049	0.0030
0.0007	0.0040	0.0011	0.0039	0.0011	0.0006	0.0008	0.0027	0.0054
0.0036	0.0054	0.0068	0.0065	0.0056	0.0016	0.0026	0.0063	0.0034
0.0019	0.0028	0.0036	0.0034	0.0029	0.0008	0.0014	0.0033	0.0018
0.0001	0.0007	0.0002	0.0008	0.0002	0.0001	0.0002	0.0005	0.0010
0.0001	0.0002	0.0004	0.0018	0.0001	0.0000	0.0000	0.0017	0.0001
0.0023	0.0034	0.0043	0.0041	0.0036	0.0010	0.0017	0.0039	0.0021
0.0006	0.0008	0.0010	0.0010	0.0010	0.0002	0.0004	0.0010	0.0012
0.0014	0.0000	0.0001	0.0001	0.0000	0.0000	0.0000	0.0002	0.0000
0.0000	0.0000	0.0000	0.0000	0.0000	0.0000	0.0000	0.0000	0.0000
0.0000	0.0004	0.0013	0.0001	0.0001	0.0000	0.0000	0.0065	0.0000
0.0002	0.0003	0.0021	0.0004	0.0003	0.0001	0.0001	0.0004	0.0002
0.0000	0.0005	0.0000	0.0000	0.0000	0.0000	0.0000	0.0001	0.0002
0.0001	0.0001	0.0002	0.0055	0.0010	0.0000	0.0001	0.0003	0.0002
0.0001	0.0000	0.0000	0.0001	0.0000	0.0000	0.0000	0.0000	0.0006
0.0001	0.0002	0.0002	0.0002	0.0002	0.0000	0.0001	0.0002	0.0001
0.0001	0.0002	0.0002	0.0004	0.0001	0.0000	0.0001	0.0004	0.0002
0.0000	0.0005	0.0000	0.0001	0.0000	0.0000	0.0001	0.0001	0.0001
0.0003	0.0001	0.0002	0.0002	0.0001	0.0000	0.0001	0.0002	0.0001
0.0004	0.0000	0.0000	0.0000	0.0000	0.0000	0.0000	0.0010	0.0000
0.0000	0.0000	0.0000	0.0000	0.0000	0.0000	0.0000	0.0000	0.0000
0.0000	0.0000	0.0000	0.0000	0.0000	0.0000	0.0002	0.0000	0.0000
0.0008	0.0010	0.0012	0.0009	0.0020	0.0002	0.0003	0.0011	0.0006
0.0007	0.0012	0.0012	0.0016	0.0010	0.0003	0.0005	0.0015	0.0010
0.0035	0.0054	0.0068	0.0068	0.0052	0.0015	0.0025	0.0085	0.0038
0.0002	0.0004	0.0003	0.0005	0.0003	0.0001	0.0001	0.0005	0.0003

Please refer to pages 136 and 145 for the corresponding columns for the other two regions.

TABLE A-3 (*Cont.*)

By Sector Number with Regional Suffix

	19 W	20 W	21 W	22 W	23 W	24 W	25 W	26 W
1 E	0.0057	0.0094	0.0031	0.0036	0.0017	0.0056	0.0012	0.1627
2 E	0.0010	0.0030	0.0014	0.0017	0.0010	0.0018	0.0007	0.0485
3 E	0.0042	0.0196	0.0031	0.0064	0.0035	0.0084	0.0021	0.3618
4 E	0.0022	0.0103	0.0016	0.0033	0.0018	0.0044	0.0011	0.1897
5 E	0.0006	0.0006	0.0003	0.0003	0.0002	0.0003	0.0001	0.0093
6 E	0.0189	0.0003	0.0013	0.0003	0.0000	0.0005	0.0001	0.0042
7 E	0.0024	0.0126	0.0017	0.0040	0.0023	0.0051	0.0013	0.2346
8 E	0.0009	0.0030	0.0004	0.0012	0.0006	0.0012	0.0003	0.0540
9 E	0.0003	0.0002	0.0000	0.0005	0.0000	0.0005	0.0001	0.0029
10 E	0.0000	0.0000	0.0000	0.0000	0.0000	0.0000	0.0000	0.0001
11 E	0.0001	0.0002	0.0001	0.0004	0.0000	0.0002	0.0000	0.0035
12 E	0.0003	0.0009	0.0003	0.0013	0.0002	0.0005	0.0010	0.0160
13 E	0.0001	0.0000	0.0001	0.0001	0.0000	0.0002	0.0000	0.0004
14 E	0.0074	0.0064	0.0181	0.0007	0.0001	0.0003	0.0001	0.0090
15 E	0.0005	0.0000	0.0001	0.0016	0.0000	0.0000	0.0000	0.0005
16 E	0.0001	0.0006	0.0001	0.0002	0.0001	0.0002	0.0001	0.0105
17 E	0.0021	0.0004	0.0005	0.0008	0.0001	0.0009	0.0001	0.0070
18 E	0.0008	0.0021	0.0008	0.0001	0.0000	0.0001	0.0000	0.0005
19 E	0.0005	0.0005	0.0002	0.0002	0.0001	0.0002	0.0001	0.0092
20 E	0.0001	0.0002	0.0001	0.0001	0.0000	0.0001	0.0000	0.0019
21 E	0.0000	0.0000	0.0000	0.0000	0.0000	0.0000	0.0000	0.0001
22 E	0.0000	0.0001	0.0000	0.0001	0.0000	0.0001	0.0000	0.0017
23 E	0.0011	0.0019	0.0008	0.0009	0.0003	0.0017	0.0004	0.0314
24 E	0.0018	0.0035	0.0014	0.0019	0.0006	0.0115	0.0005	0.0585
25 E	0.0063	0.0179	0.0048	0.0072	0.0032	0.0125	0.0047	0.3183
26 E	0.0006	0.0009	0.0005	0.0004	0.0002	0.0007	0.0001	0.0141

Please refer to pages 137 and 146 for the corresponding columns for the other two regions.

By Sector Number with Regional Suffix

	East Tennessee								
	1 E	2 E	3 E	4 E	5 E	6 E	7 E	8 E	9 E
1 M	0.0007	0.0016	0.0010	0.0007	0.0010	0.0027	0.0017	0.0010	0.0018
2 M	0.0005	0.0010	0.0004	0.0002	0.0007	0.0008	0.0012	0.0006	0.0006
3 M	0.0008	0.0020	0.0009	0.0006	0.0013	0.0022	0.0018	0.0016	0.0014
4 M	0.0004	0.0009	0.0004	0.0003	0.0006	0.0011	0.0008	0.0006	0.0007
5 M	0.0000	0.0000	0.0000	0.0000	0.0000	0.0020	0.0000	0.0000	0.0000
6 M	0.0004	0.0007	0.0002	0.0001	0.0005	0.0105	0.0005	0.0003	0.0003
7 M	0.0005	0.0011	0.0004	0.0003	0.0008	0.0008	0.0009	0.0004	0.0005
8 M	0.0000	0.0002	0.0001	0.0000	0.0001	0.0001	0.0002	0.0001	0.0001
9 M	0.0000	0.0000	0.0000	0.0000	0.0000	0.0041	0.0000	0.0000	0.0000
0 M	0.0000	0.0000	0.0000	0.0000	0.0000	0.0000	0.0000	0.0000	0.0000
1 M	0.0000	0.0000	0.0000	0.0000	0.0000	0.0000	0.0000	0.0066	0.0000
2 M	0.0005	0.0010	0.0003	0.0001	0.0005	0.0008	0.0007	0.0003	0.0007
3 M	0.0000	0.0000	0.0000	0.0000	0.0000	0.0000	0.0000	0.0000	0.0000
4 M	0.0003	0.0007	0.0045	0.0044	0.0005	0.0005	0.0053	0.0002	0.0003
5 M	0.0000	0.0000	0.0000	0.0000	0.0000	0.0001	0.0001	0.0000	0.0001
6 M	0.0001	0.0004	0.0001	0.0001	0.0002	0.0002	0.0003	0.0001	0.0001
7 M	0.0001	0.0001	0.0000	0.0000	0.0001	0.0044	0.0001	0.0001	0.0000
8 M	0.0000	0.0000	0.0000	0.0000	0.0000	0.0000	0.0000	0.0000	0.0000
9 M	0.0000	0.0000	0.0000	0.0000	0.0000	0.0028	0.0000	0.0000	0.0000
0 M	0.0000	0.0001	0.0000	0.0000	0.0000	0.0002	0.0000	0.0000	0.0000
1 M	0.0000	0.0002	0.0000	0.0000	0.0000	0.0003	0.0000	0.0000	0.0000
2 M	0.0002	0.0001	0.0000	0.0000	0.0001	0.0027	0.0001	0.0001	0.0000
3 M	0.0004	0.0016	0.0007	0.0003	0.0008	0.0023	0.0011	0.0005	0.0008
4 M	0.0017	0.0049	0.0023	0.0008	0.0028	0.0034	0.0036	0.0012	0.0198
5 M	0.0023	0.0038	0.0018	0.0011	0.0026	0.0067	0.0035	0.0023	0.0031
6 M	0.0001	0.0003	0.0002	0.0001	0.0002	0.0006	0.0003	0.0002	0.0004

Please refer to pages 120 and 138 for the corresponding columns for the other two regions

TABLE A-3 (*Cont.*)

By Sector Number with Regional Suffix

	10 E	11 E	12 E	13 E	14 E	15 E	16 E	17 E	18 E
1 M	0.0007	0.0020	0.0011	0.0011	0.0009	0.0008	0.0009	0.0014	0.001
2 M	0.0006	0.0043	0.0005	0.0016	0.0008	0.0010	0.0004	0.0018	0.004
3 M	0.0008	0.0020	0.0010	0.0014	0.0011	0.0010	0.0009	0.0014	0.001
4 M	0.0004	0.0010	0.0005	0.0007	0.0005	0.0005	0.0004	0.0007	0.000
5 M	0.0000	0.0004	0.0000	0.0000	0.0000	0.0000	0.0000	0.0001	0.000
6 M	0.0003	0.0027	0.0003	0.0005	0.0004	0.0003	0.0002	0.0006	0.000
7 M	0.0005	0.0010	0.0005	0.0008	0.0006	0.0005	0.0004	0.0007	0.000
8 M	0.0001	0.0002	0.0001	0.0002	0.0001	0.0001	0.0001	0.0001	0.000
9 M	0.0001	0.0009	0.0000	0.0000	0.0000	0.0000	0.0000	0.0000	0.000
10 M	0.0000	0.0000	0.0000	0.0000	0.0000	0.0000	0.0000	0.0000	0.000
11 M	0.0000	0.0000	0.0001	0.0000	0.0000	0.0000	0.0000	0.0000	0.000
12 M	0.0003	0.0008	0.0082	0.0004	0.0004	0.0004	0.0015	0.0006	0.000
13 M	0.0000	0.0000	0.0000	0.0000	0.0002	0.0000	0.0000	0.0000	0.000
14 M	0.0003	0.0006	0.0003	0.0006	0.0004	0.0004	0.0003	0.0005	0.000
15 M	0.0000	0.0001	0.0001	0.0000	0.0000	0.0003	0.0001	0.0000	0.000
16 M	0.0002	0.0003	0.0001	0.0003	0.0002	0.0002	0.0045	0.0002	0.000
17 M	0.0000	0.0010	0.0000	0.0001	0.0000	0.0000	0.0000	0.0026	0.000
18 M	0.0000	0.0000	0.0000	0.0000	0.0000	0.0000	0.0000	0.0000	0.000
19 M	0.0000	0.0006	0.0000	0.0000	0.0000	0.0000	0.0000	0.0000	0.000
20 M	0.0001	0.0001	0.0002	0.0000	0.0000	0.0000	0.0000	0.0009	0.000
21 M	0.0000	0.0001	0.0000	0.0000	0.0000	0.0000	0.0000	0.0000	0.000
22 M	0.0000	0.0006	0.0000	0.0001	0.0000	0.0000	0.0000	0.0001	0.000
23 M	0.0005	0.0014	0.0005	0.0008	0.0006	0.0005	0.0004	0.0008	0.000
24 M	0.0017	0.0035	0.0015	0.0025	0.0024	0.0017	0.0012	0.0023	0.001
25 M	0.0015	0.0053	0.0028	0.0027	0.0022	0.0020	0.0019	0.0041	0.002
26 M	0.0001	0.0004	0.0002	0.0002	0.0001	0.0001	0.0002	0.0003	0.000

Please refer to pages 121 and 139 for the corresponding columns for the other two regions.

19 E	20 E	21 E	22 E	23 E	24 E	25 E	26 E
0.0007	0.0011	0.0018	0.0022	0.0009	0.0039	0.0009	0.0439
0.0008	0.0009	0.0007	0.0013	0.0007	0.0014	0.0005	0.0298
0.0009	0.0011	0.0013	0.0020	0.0008	0.0033	0.0007	0.0590
0.0004	0.0005	0.0007	0.0011	0.0004	0.0016	0.0006	0.0279
0.0000	0.0000	0.0000	0.0001	0.0000	0.0000	0.0000	0.0008
0.0003	0.0004	0.0004	0.0016	0.0002	0.0016	0.0015	0.0184
0.0005	0.0006	0.0006	0.0009	0.0004	0.0014	0.0003	0.0348
0.0001	0.0001	0.0001	0.0002	0.0001	0.0002	0.0000	0.0066
0.0000	0.0000	0.0000	0.0002	0.0000	0.0000	0.0000	0.0009
0.0000	0.0000	0.0000	0.0000	0.0000	0.0000	0.0000	0.0001
0.0000	0.0000	0.0000	0.0000	0.0000	0.0000	0.0000	0.0010
0.0005	0.0009	0.0005	0.0034	0.0061	0.0028	0.0012	0.0161
0.0000	0.0000	0.0000	0.0000	0.0000	0.0000	0.0000	0.0000
0.0003	0.0004	0.0004	0.0026	0.0002	0.0008	0.0002	0.0240
0.0000	0.0001	0.0001	0.0005	0.0001	0.0000	0.0000	0.0003
0.0002	0.0002	0.0002	0.0003	0.0001	0.0004	0.0001	0.0114
0.0000	0.0000	0.0000	0.0003	0.0000	0.0001	0.0001	0.0017
0.0002	0.0000	0.0019	0.0001	0.0000	0.0000	0.0000	0.0001
0.0000	0.0001	0.0030	0.0023	0.0000	0.0000	0.0000	0.0007
0.0003	0.0023	0.0015	0.0021	0.0000	0.0000	0.0000	0.0002
0.0000	0.0000	0.0033	0.0002	0.0000	0.0000	0.0000	0.0005
0.0000	0.0000	0.0023	0.0003	0.0000	0.0001	0.0000	0.0023
0.0005	0.0007	0.0008	0.0014	0.0004	0.0018	0.0005	0.0314
0.0017	0.0034	0.0017	0.0045	0.0015	0.0362	0.0011	0.1059
0.0019	0.0029	0.0033	0.0088	0.0023	0.0087	0.0100	0.1002
0.0001	0.0002	0.0003	0.0005	0.0002	0.0009	0.0002	0.0066

Please refer to pages 122 and 140 for the corresponding columns for the other two regions.

TABLE A-3 (*Cont.*)

By Sector Number with Regional Suffix

Middle Tennessee

	1 M	2 M	3 M	4 M	5 M	6 M	7 M	8 M	9 M
1 M	1.0774	0.1190	0.1603	0.1160	0.0781	0.0793	0.3432	0.0672	0.051
2 M	0.0007	1.0011	0.0004	0.0003	0.0012	0.0010	0.0019	0.0004	0.000
3 M	0.0324	0.0674	1.0462	0.0210	0.0434	0.0432	1.4656	0.0180	0.029
4 M	0.0189	0.0345	0.3223	1.0099	0.0288	0.0227	0.6310	0.0146	0.014
5 M	0.0001	0.0001	0.0001	0.0000	1.0003	0.0155	0.0003	0.0000	0.000
6 M	0.0019	0.0030	0.0026	0.0010	0.0216	1.1882	0.0067	0.0009	0.001
7 M	0.0070	0.0138	0.0057	0.0043	0.0089	0.0089	1.0211	0.0037	0.005
8 M	0.0002	0.0004	0.0002	0.0001	0.0003	0.0003	0.0006	1.0004	0.000
9 M	0.0001	0.0001	0.0000	0.0000	0.0003	0.0131	0.0023	0.0000	1.007
10 M	0.0014	0.0002	0.0002	0.0002	0.0001	0.0001	0.0005	0.0001	0.000
11 M	0.0000	0.0000	0.0000	0.0000	0.0000	0.0000	0.0000	0.0192	0.000
12 M	0.0076	0.0136	0.0056	0.0042	0.0098	0.0096	0.0231	0.0040	0.006
13 M	0.0000	0.0000	0.0000	0.0000	0.0000	0.0000	0.0000	0.0000	0.000
14 M	0.0006	0.0011	0.0056	0.0126	0.0008	0.0020	0.0109	0.0004	0.000
15 M	0.0000	0.0000	0.0000	0.0000	0.0000	0.0003	0.0001	0.0000	0.000
16 M	0.0004	0.0009	0.0004	0.0003	0.0006	0.0006	0.0014	0.0003	0.000
17 M	0.0005	0.0003	0.0002	0.0001	0.0013	0.0708	0.0005	0.0001	0.000
18 M	0.0000	0.0000	0.0000	0.0000	0.0001	0.0014	0.0001	0.0000	0.000
19 M	0.0001	0.0001	0.0001	0.0000	0.0003	0.0144	0.0001	0.0000	0.000
20 M	0.0000	0.0001	0.0000	0.0000	0.0000	0.0005	0.0000	0.0000	0.000
21 M	0.0001	0.0003	0.0001	0.0000	0.0003	0.0153	0.0003	0.0001	0.000
22 M	0.0004	0.0003	0.0002	0.0001	0.0003	0.0063	0.0006	0.0002	0.000
23 M	0.0110	0.0186	0.0099	0.0046	0.0263	0.0161	0.0433	0.0087	0.018
24 M	0.0131	0.0197	0.0085	0.0064	0.0127	0.0164	0.0307	0.0054	0.010
25 M	0.2099	0.2699	0.0819	0.0535	0.4029	0.1932	0.2654	0.0555	0.094
26 M	0.0145	0.0307	0.0126	0.0096	0.0197	0.0197	0.0468	0.0082	0.013

Please refer to pages 123 and 141 for the corresponding columns for the other two regions.

TABLE A-3 (*Cont.*)

10 M	11 M	12 M	13 M	14 M	15 M	16 M	17 M	18 M
0.0568	0.0532	0.0665	0.0881	0.0890	0.0750	0.0663	0.0927	0.0546
0.0007	0.0007	0.0008	0.0330	0.0015	0.0013	0.0007	0.0031	0.0123
0.0322	0.0300	0.0374	0.0500	0.0507	0.0427	0.0378	0.0528	0.0312
0.0160	0.0161	0.0194	0.0243	0.0230	0.0202	0.0175	0.0243	0.0143
0.0001	0.0001	0.0001	0.1533	0.0002	0.0001	0.0001	0.0321	0.0001
0.0016	0.0018	0.0020	0.0055	0.0023	0.0020	0.0018	0.0031	0.0016
0.0066	0.0061	0.0076	0.0103	0.0104	0.0087	0.0077	0.0108	0.0064
0.0002	0.0002	0.0002	0.0003	0.0003	0.0003	0.0002	0.0003	0.0002
0.0197	0.0000	0.0000	0.0001	0.0001	0.0000	0.0007	0.0001	0.0001
1.0001	0.0001	0.0001	0.0001	0.0001	0.0001	0.0001	0.0001	0.0001
0.0000	1.0000	0.0000	0.0000	0.0000	0.0000	0.0000	0.0000	0.0000
0.0069	0.0063	1.1377	0.0124	0.0097	0.0082	0.0151	0.0101	0.0063
0.0000	0.0000	0.0000	1.0000	0.0007	0.0000	0.0000	0.0000	0.0000
0.0005	0.0005	0.0006	0.0009	1.0008	0.0007	0.0007	0.0008	0.0005
0.0001	0.0004	0.0001	0.0000	0.0003	1.0002	0.0001	0.0000	0.0000
0.0004	0.0004	0.0005	0.0008	0.0007	0.0006	1.0216	0.0007	0.0005
0.0001	0.0001	0.0001	0.0004	0.0002	0.0001	0.0001	1.0421	0.0001
0.0000	0.0000	0.0000	0.0304	0.0000	0.0000	0.0000	0.0000	1.0000
0.0000	0.0000	0.0001	0.0006	0.0001	0.0000	0.0001	0.0001	0.0143
0.0026	0.0000	0.0005	0.0004	0.0000	0.0000	0.0001	0.0035	0.0113
0.0001	0.0001	0.0049	0.0044	0.0001	0.0001	0.0001	0.0001	0.0000
0.0003	0.0005	0.0002	0.0003	0.0002	0.0002	0.0002	0.0003	0.0004
0.0101	0.0256	0.0126	0.0147	0.0125	0.0089	0.0081	0.0122	0.0215
0.0094	0.0087	0.0109	0.0153	0.0147	0.0124	0.0112	0.0155	0.0094
0.1111	0.1463	0.1581	0.1535	0.1022	0.1133	0.0877	0.1167	0.0660
0.0147	0.0137	0.0170	0.0227	0.0231	0.0194	0.0172	0.0241	0.0142

Please refer to pages 124 and 142 for the corresponding columns for the other two regions.

TABLE A-3 (*Cont.*)

By Sector Number with Regional Suffix

	19 M	20 M	21 M	22 M	23 M	24 M	25 M	26 M
1 M	0.0707	0.0658	0.1585	0.0794	0.0399	0.0755	0.0449	4.4431
2 M	0.0008	0.0009	0.0022	0.0010	0.0008	0.0009	0.0010	0.0347
3 M	0.0400	0.0375	0.0386	0.0451	0.0227	0.0430	0.0217	2.5332
4 M	0.0209	0.0171	0.0179	0.0221	0.0109	0.0198	0.0413	1.1501
5 M	0.0001	0.0001	0.0001	0.0001	0.0001	0.0001	0.0001	0.0050
6 M	0.0022	0.0021	0.0019	0.0026	0.0082	0.0040	0.0044	0.1146
7 M	0.0082	0.0077	0.0079	0.0092	0.0046	0.0088	0.0044	0.5170
8 M	0.0002	0.0002	0.0002	0.0003	0.0001	0.0003	0.0001	0.0156
9 M	0.0000	0.0000	0.0001	0.0067	0.0001	0.0001	0.0001	0.0027
10 M	0.0001	0.0001	0.0002	0.0001	0.0001	0.0001	0.0001	0.0059
11 M	0.0000	0.0000	0.0000	0.0000	0.0000	0.0000	0.0000	0.0006
12 M	0.0108	0.0101	0.0090	0.0150	0.0193	0.0216	0.0087	0.4781
13 M	0.0000	0.0000	0.0000	0.0000	0.0000	0.0000	0.0000	0.0001
14 M	0.0007	0.0006	0.0006	0.0064	0.0004	0.0007	0.0007	0.0382
15 M	0.0005	0.0003	0.0025	0.0177	0.0001	0.0000	0.0000	0.0007
16 M	0.0005	0.0005	0.0005	0.0066	0.0003	0.0006	0.0003	0.0343
17 M	0.0002	0.0001	0.0002	0.0002	0.0005	0.0003	0.0003	0.0083
18 M	0.0023	0.0002	0.0044	0.0013	0.0016	0.0000	0.0000	0.0007
19 M	1.0002	0.0014	0.0138	0.0037	0.0001	0.0001	0.0002	0.0023
20 M	0.0001	1.0146	0.0034	0.0125	0.0000	0.0000	0.0000	0.0005
21 M	0.0001	0.0001	1.0022	0.0008	0.0002	0.0002	0.0001	0.0039
22 M	0.0002	0.0003	0.0020	1.0003	0.0002	0.0002	0.0001	0.0118
23 M	0.0127	0.0582	0.0163	0.0347	1.0132	0.0234	0.0270	0.3213
24 M	0.0116	0.0110	0.0116	0.0132	0.0066	1.0877	0.0064	0.7344
25 M	0.1753	0.0769	0.0924	0.1482	0.0671	0.0957	1.1304	5.0881
26 M	0.0182	0.0171	0.0175	0.0205	0.0103	0.0196	0.0099	1.1543

Please refer to pages 125 and 143 for the corresponding columns for the other two regions.

TABLE A-3 (*Cont.*)

By Sector Number with Regional Suffix

West Tennessee								
1 W	2 W	3 W	4 W	5 W	6 W	7 W	8 W	9 W
0.0014	0.0012	0.0010	0.0006	0.0026	0.0048	0.0067	0.0006	0.0009
0.0002	0.0003	0.0001	0.0001	0.0005	0.0004	0.0004	0.0002	0.0001
0.0018	0.0018	0.0010	0.0007	0.0022	0.0040	0.0279	0.0008	0.0011
0.0012	0.0010	0.0005	0.0003	0.0012	0.0023	0.0178	0.0004	0.0006
0.0009	0.0010	0.0004	0.0003	0.0009	0.0063	0.0009	0.0004	0.0005
0.0019	0.0020	0.0012	0.0006	0.0233	0.0053	0.0022	0.0009	0.0017
0.0007	0.0008	0.0003	0.0002	0.0007	0.0013	0.0010	0.0003	0.0004
0.0002	0.0002	0.0001	0.0001	0.0001	0.0003	0.0002	0.0010	0.0001
0.0001	0.0001	0.0000	0.0000	0.0003	0.0062	0.0011	0.0000	0.0033
0.0000	0.0000	0.0000	0.0000	0.0000	0.0000	0.0000	0.0000	0.0000
0.0000	0.0000	0.0000	0.0000	0.0000	0.0000	0.0000	0.0000	0.0000
0.0008	0.0008	0.0004	0.0002	0.0009	0.0020	0.0010	0.0004	0.0004
0.0000	0.0000	0.0000	0.0000	0.0000	0.0000	0.0000	0.0000	0.0000
0.0005	0.0005	0.0040	0.0031	0.0004	0.0009	0.0059	0.0005	0.0003
0.0000	0.0000	0.0000	0.0000	0.0000	0.0003	0.0001	0.0000	0.0001
0.0005	0.0005	0.0002	0.0002	0.0004	0.0007	0.0005	0.0002	0.0003
0.0001	0.0002	0.0001	0.0000	0.0014	0.0014	0.0002	0.0001	0.0001
0.0000	0.0000	0.0000	0.0000	0.0000	0.0002	0.0000	0.0000	0.0000
0.0001	0.0001	0.0000	0.0000	0.0003	0.0039	0.0000	0.0000	0.0000
0.0000	0.0001	0.0000	0.0000	0.0000	0.0003	0.0000	0.0000	0.0000
0.0000	0.0002	0.0001	0.0000	0.0003	0.0012	0.0001	0.0000	0.0000
0.0002	0.0001	0.0000	0.0000	0.0002	0.0035	0.0001	0.0000	0.0000
0.0031	0.0029	0.0018	0.0008	0.0114	0.0414	0.0035	0.0016	0.0016
0.0028	0.0032	0.0032	0.0018	0.0024	0.0047	0.0054	0.0013	0.0032
0.0139	0.0045	0.0029	0.0016	0.0086	0.0202	0.0079	0.0033	0.0029
0.0003	0.0002	0.0002	0.0001	0.0006	0.0012	0.0008	0.0001	0.0002

Please refer to pages 126 and 144 for the corresponding columns for the other two regions.

TABLE A-3 (*Cont.*)

By Sector Number with Regional Suffix

	10 W	11 W	12 W	13 W	14 W	15 W	16 W	17 W	18 W
1 M	0.0007	0.0008	0.0022	0.0012	0.0010	0.0002	0.0007	0.0092	0.0009
2 M	0.0001	0.0008	0.0002	0.0008	0.0002	0.0001	0.0002	0.0005	0.0011
3 M	0.0009	0.0012	0.0021	0.0015	0.0014	0.0003	0.0008	0.0059	0.0010
4 M	0.0005	0.0007	0.0015	0.0008	0.0008	0.0002	0.0004	0.0037	0.0005
5 M	0.0004	0.0006	0.0008	0.0007	0.0008	0.0002	0.0003	0.1037	0.0004
6 M	0.0009	0.0013	0.0017	0.0016	0.0014	0.0004	0.0006	0.0048	0.0008
7 M	0.0004	0.0005	0.0007	0.0006	0.0005	0.0001	0.0003	0.0015	0.0003
8 M	0.0001	0.0001	0.0001	0.0002	0.0001	0.0000	0.0001	0.0002	0.0001
9 M	0.0031	0.0000	0.0000	0.0001	0.0000	0.0000	0.0012	0.0001	0.0000
10 M	0.0000	0.0000	0.0000	0.0000	0.0000	0.0000	0.0000	0.0000	0.0000
11 M	0.0000	0.0000	0.0000	0.0000	0.0000	0.0000	0.0000	0.0000	0.0000
12 M	0.0003	0.0004	0.0135	0.0008	0.0009	0.0002	0.0009	0.0015	0.0004
13 M	0.0000	0.0000	0.0000	0.0000	0.0011	0.0000	0.0000	0.0000	0.0000
14 M	0.0002	0.0003	0.0004	0.0004	0.0003	0.0001	0.0002	0.0004	0.0002
15 M	0.0001	0.0001	0.0001	0.0000	0.0000	0.0001	0.0000	0.0000	0.0000
16 M	0.0002	0.0003	0.0005	0.0004	0.0004	0.0001	0.0034	0.0004	0.0002
17 M	0.0001	0.0001	0.0001	0.0001	0.0001	0.0000	0.0000	0.0003	0.0000
18 M	0.0000	0.0000	0.0000	0.0001	0.0000	0.0000	0.0000	0.0000	0.0000
19 M	0.0000	0.0000	0.0000	0.0000	0.0000	0.0000	0.0000	0.0001	0.0040
20 M	0.0000	0.0000	0.0003	0.0000	0.0000	0.0000	0.0000	0.0042	0.0000
21 M	0.0000	0.0000	0.0001	0.0000	0.0000	0.0000	0.0000	0.0001	0.0000
22 M	0.0000	0.0001	0.0001	0.0001	0.0001	0.0000	0.0000	0.0001	0.0000
23 M	0.0014	0.0019	0.0029	0.0079	0.0056	0.0006	0.0010	0.0055	0.0031
24 M	0.0014	0.0020	0.0028	0.0024	0.0022	0.0006	0.0010	0.0036	0.0013
25 M	0.0043	0.0049	0.0184	0.0049	0.0043	0.0009	0.0035	0.0452	0.0031
26 M	0.0002	0.0002	0.0005	0.0003	0.0002	0.0000	0.0002	0.0023	0.0002

Please refer to pages 127 and 145 for the corresponding columns for the other two regions.

TABLE A-3 (*Cont.*)

19 W	20 W	21 W	22 W	23 W	24 W	25 W	26 W
0.0007	0.0027	0.0022	0.0028	0.0008	0.0074	0.0008	0.0479
0.0002	0.0006	0.0003	0.0003	0.0002	0.0003	0.0001	0.0096
0.0009	0.0043	0.0013	0.0024	0.0009	0.0052	0.0007	0.0786
0.0005	0.0023	0.0006	0.0014	0.0005	0.0027	0.0006	0.0425
0.0004	0.0024	0.0003	0.0010	0.0004	0.0019	0.0003	0.0441
0.0010	0.0049	0.0009	0.0069	0.0011	0.0741	0.0019	0.0887
0.0003	0.0018	0.0004	0.0008	0.0004	0.0014	0.0002	0.0330
0.0001	0.0005	0.0001	0.0002	0.0001	0.0002	0.0001	0.0096
0.0001	0.0001	0.0000	0.0020	0.0000	0.0009	0.0001	0.0026
0.0000	0.0000	0.0000	0.0000	0.0000	0.0000	0.0000	0.0001
0.0000	0.0000	0.0000	0.0000	0.0000	0.0000	0.0000	0.0005
0.0003	0.0015	0.0005	0.0037	0.0054	0.0032	0.0011	0.0251
0.0000	0.0000	0.0000	0.0000	0.0000	0.0000	0.0000	0.0001
0.0002	0.0012	0.0001	0.0004	0.0002	0.0006	0.0002	0.0226
0.0002	0.0001	0.0000	0.0038	0.0001	0.0001	0.0000	0.0010
0.0002	0.0013	0.0002	0.0004	0.0002	0.0006	0.0001	0.0245
0.0001	0.0003	0.0001	0.0005	0.0001	0.0044	0.0001	0.0054
0.0015	0.0000	0.0010	0.0001	0.0000	0.0001	0.0000	0.0003
0.0002	0.0002	0.0092	0.0030	0.0000	0.0009	0.0001	0.0019
0.0002	0.0008	0.0004	0.0000	0.0000	0.0000	0.0000	0.0003
0.0000	0.0001	0.0065	0.0001	0.0000	0.0010	0.0001	0.0016
0.0001	0.0001	0.0012	0.0002	0.0000	0.0004	0.0001	0.0026
0.0027	0.0078	0.0013	0.0146	0.0013	0.0042	0.0022	0.1292
0.0013	0.0075	0.0012	0.0042	0.0015	0.0256	0.0009	0.1393
0.0024	0.0108	0.0039	0.0131	0.0027	0.0180	0.0092	0.1942
0.0002	0.0006	0.0004	0.0007	0.0002	0.0018	0.0002	0.0102

Please refer to pages 128 and 146 for the corresponding columns for the other two regions.

TABLE A-3 (*Cont.*)

By Sector Number with Regional Suffix

East Tennessee

	1 E	2 E	3 E	4 E	5 E	6 E	7 E	8 E	9 E
1 W	0.0017	0.0043	0.0023	0.0009	0.0030	0.0150	0.0042	0.0015	0.0016
2 W	0.0004	0.0008	0.0003	0.0002	0.0006	0.0006	0.0010	0.0005	0.0004
3 W	0.0008	0.0011	0.0005	0.0002	0.0008	0.0016	0.0010	0.0004	0.0004
4 W	0.0011	0.0016	0.0007	0.0003	0.0010	0.0021	0.0014	0.0005	0.0006
5 W	0.0000	0.0000	0.0000	0.0000	0.0000	0.0013	0.0000	0.0000	0.0000
6 W	0.0001	0.0002	0.0001	0.0000	0.0002	0.0216	0.0001	0.0002	0.0001
7 W	0.0010	0.0015	0.0006	0.0003	0.0010	0.0014	0.0012	0.0004	0.0005
8 W	0.0000	0.0000	0.0000	0.0000	0.0000	0.0000	0.0000	0.0001	0.0000
9 W	0.0001	0.0001	0.0001	0.0000	0.0001	0.0040	0.0013	0.0001	0.0004
10 W	0.0000	0.0000	0.0000	0.0000	0.0000	0.0000	0.0000	0.0000	0.0000
11 W	0.0001	0.0001	0.0002	0.0001	0.0001	0.0001	0.0002	0.0001	0.0000
12 W	0.0013	0.0012	0.0004	0.0002	0.0008	0.0013	0.0009	0.0004	0.0004
13 W	0.0002	0.0004	0.0069	0.0001	0.0003	0.0003	0.0063	0.0001	0.0002
14 W	0.0001	0.0003	0.0001	0.0001	0.0002	0.0003	0.0008	0.0001	0.0006
15 W	0.0000	0.0000	0.0000	0.0000	0.0000	0.0000	0.0000	0.0000	0.0000
16 W	0.0000	0.0000	0.0000	0.0000	0.0000	0.0000	0.0000	0.0000	0.0000
17 W	0.0000	0.0001	0.0000	0.0000	0.0001	0.0111	0.0001	0.0001	0.0000
18 W	0.0000	0.0000	0.0000	0.0000	0.0000	0.0001	0.0000	0.0000	0.0002
19 W	0.0000	0.0001	0.0006	0.0000	0.0000	0.0013	0.0006	0.0000	0.0000
20 W	0.0000	0.0000	0.0000	0.0000	0.0000	0.0001	0.0000	0.0000	0.0000
21 W	0.0000	0.0000	0.0000	0.0000	0.0000	0.0000	0.0000	0.0000	0.0000
22 W	0.0002	0.0003	0.0001	0.0001	0.0002	0.0047	0.0002	0.0001	0.0001
23 W	0.0001	0.0003	0.0004	0.0001	0.0002	0.0010	0.0005	0.0001	0.0001
24 W	0.0017	0.0045	0.0017	0.0010	0.0035	0.0040	0.0036	0.0015	0.0018
25 W	0.0013	0.0026	0.0021	0.0006	0.0019	0.0106	0.0033	0.0010	0.0011
26 W	0.0001	0.0003	0.0002	0.0001	0.0002	0.0010	0.0004	0.0001	0.0001

Please refer to pages 120 and 129 for the corresponding columns for the other two regions.

TABLE A-3 (*Cont.*)

10 E	11 E	12 E	13 E	14 E	15 E	16 E	17 E	18 E
0.0019	0.0061	0.0018	0.0032	0.0025	0.0021	0.0016	0.0027	0.0024
0.0005	0.0010	0.0004	0.0013	0.0007	0.0008	0.0003	0.0014	0.0007
0.0005	0.0011	0.0005	0.0008	0.0007	0.0006	0.0004	0.0007	0.0006
0.0007	0.0015	0.0006	0.0011	0.0010	0.0007	0.0006	0.0009	0.0008
0.0000	0.0003	0.0000	0.0000	0.0000	0.0000	0.0000	0.0000	0.0000
0.0001	0.0046	0.0001	0.0002	0.0001	0.0001	0.0001	0.0002	0.0001
0.0006	0.0013	0.0006	0.0010	0.0008	0.0007	0.0005	0.0009	0.0008
0.0000	0.0000	0.0000	0.0000	0.0000	0.0000	0.0000	0.0000	0.0000
0.0004	0.0009	0.0001	0.0001	0.0001	0.0001	0.0000	0.0001	0.0010
0.0000	0.0000	0.0000	0.0000	0.0000	0.0000	0.0000	0.0000	0.0000
0.0001	0.0001	0.0000	0.0001	0.0077	0.0007	0.0000	0.0002	0.0001
0.0005	0.0011	0.0005	0.0008	0.0008	0.0006	0.0004	0.0007	0.0006
0.0002	0.0004	0.0002	0.0003	0.0002	0.0005	0.0002	0.0003	0.0002
0.0001	0.0003	0.0001	0.0002	0.0002	0.0001	0.0001	0.0002	0.0001
0.0000	0.0000	0.0000	0.0000	0.0000	0.0000	0.0000	0.0000	0.0000
0.0000	0.0000	0.0000	0.0000	0.0000	0.0000	0.0046	0.0000	0.0000
0.0000	0.0023	0.0001	0.0001	0.0000	0.0000	0.0000	0.0001	0.0001
0.0000	0.0000	0.0000	0.0000	0.0000	0.0000	0.0000	0.0000	0.0000
0.0000	0.0003	0.0000	0.0002	0.0000	0.0000	0.0000	0.0000	0.0000
0.0000	0.0000	0.0002	0.0000	0.0000	0.0000	0.0000	0.0000	0.0000
0.0000	0.0000	0.0000	0.0000	0.0000	0.0000	0.0000	0.0000	0.0000
0.0001	0.0012	0.0001	0.0003	0.0001	0.0001	0.0001	0.0002	0.0001
0.0001	0.0004	0.0001	0.0002	0.0003	0.0001	0.0001	0.0002	0.0002
0.0020	0.0040	0.0018	0.0033	0.0025	0.0022	0.0016	0.0027	0.0024
0.0012	0.0041	0.0012	0.0021	0.0025	0.0014	0.0012	0.0018	0.0016
0.0001	0.0004	0.0001	0.0002	0.0003	0.0002	0.0001	0.0002	0.0002

Please refer to pages 121 and 130 for the corresponding columns for the other two regions.

TABLE A-3 (*Cont.*)

By Sector Number with Regional Suffix

	19 E	20 E	21 E	22 E	23 E	24 E	25 E	26 E
1 W	0.0021	0.0021	0.0021	0.0062	0.0013	0.0044	0.0010	0.1373
2 W	0.0006	0.0007	0.0006	0.0010	0.0006	0.0012	0.0004	0.0245
3 W	0.0005	0.0005	0.0005	0.0016	0.0003	0.0011	0.0003	0.0349
4 W	0.0007	0.0007	0.0007	0.0021	0.0005	0.0015	0.0004	0.0471
5 W	0.0000	0.0000	0.0000	0.0001	0.0000	0.0000	0.0000	0.0003
6 W	0.0001	0.0001	0.0001	0.0035	0.0000	0.0001	0.0001	0.0041
7 W	0.0007	0.0007	0.0007	0.0015	0.0004	0.0014	0.0003	0.0439
8 W	0.0000	0.0000	0.0000	0.0001	0.0000	0.0000	0.0000	0.0001
9 W	0.0001	0.0001	0.0001	0.0025	0.0003	0.0001	0.0000	0.0035
10 W	0.0000	0.0000	0.0000	0.0000	0.0000	0.0000	0.0000	0.0000
11 W	0.0001	0.0002	0.0002	0.0001	0.0000	0.0001	0.0000	0.0031
12 W	0.0005	0.0005	0.0005	0.0015	0.0003	0.0011	0.0003	0.0349
13 W	0.0002	0.0002	0.0002	0.0003	0.0001	0.0004	0.0001	0.0140
14 W	0.0007	0.0002	0.0001	0.0018	0.0001	0.0004	0.0005	0.0079
15 W	0.0000	0.0000	0.0000	0.0014	0.0000	0.0000	0.0000	0.0000
16 W	0.0000	0.0000	0.0000	0.0000	0.0000	0.0000	0.0000	0.0002
17 W	0.0000	0.0000	0.0000	0.0006	0.0000	0.0001	0.0000	0.0018
18 W	0.0002	0.0005	0.0003	0.0012	0.0000	0.0000	0.0000	0.0001
19 W	0.0000	0.0000	0.0001	0.0003	0.0000	0.0000	0.0000	0.0015
20 W	0.0003	0.0000	0.0000	0.0092	0.0000	0.0000	0.0000	0.0005
21 W	0.0000	0.0000	0.0016	0.0004	0.0000	0.0000	0.0000	0.0002
22 W	0.0001	0.0001	0.0002	0.0004	0.0001	0.0002	0.0001	0.0075
23 W	0.0002	0.0001	0.0002	0.0008	0.0001	0.0003	0.0001	0.0081
24 W	0.0021	0.0022	0.0022	0.0041	0.0014	0.0048	0.0010	0.1415
25 W	0.0015	0.0014	0.0014	0.0085	0.0009	0.0027	0.0007	0.0805
26 W	0.0002	0.0001	0.0002	0.0009	0.0001	0.0003	0.0001	0.0085

Please refer to pages 122 and 131 for the corresponding columns for the other two regions.

TABLE A-3 (*Cont.*)

By Sector Number with Regional Suffix

Middle Tennessee									
	1 M	**2 M**	**3 M**	**4 M**	**5 M**	**6 M**	**7 M**	**8 M**	**9 M**
1 W	0.0027	0.0056	0.0030	0.0017	0.0039	0.0088	0.0097	0.0015	0.0028
2 W	0.0006	0.0009	0.0004	0.0003	0.0010	0.0008	0.0016	0.0003	0.0005
3 W	0.0015	0.0019	0.0009	0.0006	0.0014	0.0022	0.0032	0.0005	0.0009
4 W	0.0020	0.0025	0.0013	0.0008	0.0018	0.0029	0.0044	0.0007	0.0012
5 W	0.0000	0.0000	0.0000	0.0000	0.0000	0.0017	0.0000	0.0000	0.0000
6 W	0.0001	0.0002	0.0001	0.0000	0.0002	0.0053	0.0002	0.0000	0.0001
7 W	0.0018	0.0022	0.0010	0.0007	0.0015	0.0019	0.0036	0.0006	0.0010
8 W	0.0000	0.0000	0.0000	0.0000	0.0000	0.0000	0.0000	0.0003	0.0000
9 W	0.0001	0.0001	0.0000	0.0000	0.0002	0.0049	0.0010	0.0000	0.0036
10 W	0.0000	0.0000	0.0000	0.0000	0.0000	0.0000	0.0000	0.0000	0.0000
11 W	0.0001	0.0002	0.0002	0.0001	0.0001	0.0002	0.0024	0.0002	0.0001
12 W	0.0023	0.0017	0.0009	0.0006	0.0012	0.0016	0.0030	0.0005	0.0009
13 W	0.0002	0.0005	0.0057	0.0001	0.0003	0.0003	0.0097	0.0001	0.0002
14 W	0.0006	0.0008	0.0003	0.0002	0.0008	0.0010	0.0017	0.0002	0.0043
15 W	0.0000	0.0000	0.0000	0.0000	0.0000	0.0000	0.0000	0.0000	0.0000
16 W	0.0000	0.0000	0.0000	0.0000	0.0000	0.0000	0.0000	0.0000	0.0000
17 W	0.0000	0.0001	0.0001	0.0000	0.0005	0.0255	0.0002	0.0000	0.0000
18 W	0.0000	0.0000	0.0000	0.0000	0.0000	0.0001	0.0000	0.0000	0.0005
19 W	0.0000	0.0001	0.0005	0.0000	0.0000	0.0009	0.0009	0.0000	0.0000
20 W	0.0000	0.0000	0.0000	0.0000	0.0001	0.0020	0.0001	0.0000	0.0000
21 W	0.0000	0.0000	0.0000	0.0000	0.0000	0.0000	0.0000	0.0000	0.0000
22 W	0.0003	0.0004	0.0002	0.0001	0.0003	0.0047	0.0006	0.0001	0.0002
23 W	0.0003	0.0006	0.0005	0.0000	0.0099	0.0014	0.0014	0.0002	0.0004
24 W	0.0084	0.0175	0.0073	0.0054	0.0131	0.0147	0.0268	0.0046	0.0076
25 W	0.0034	0.0059	0.0055	0.0018	0.0053	0.0123	0.0138	0.0016	0.0035
26 W	0.0003	0.0006	0.0004	0.0002	0.0006	0.0013	0.0012	0.0002	0.0004

Please refer to pages 123 and 132 for the corresponding columns for the other two regions.

TABLE A-3 (*Cont.*)

By Sector Number with Regional Suffix

	10 M	11 M	12 M	13 M	14 M	15 M	16 M	17 M	18 M
1 W	0.0027	0.0024	0.0030	0.0060	0.0041	0.0037	0.0034	0.0045	0.0035
2 W	0.0005	0.0006	0.0007	0.0272	0.0012	0.0010	0.0006	0.0025	0.0101
3 W	0.0009	0.0008	0.0010	0.0023	0.0014	0.0012	0.0012	0.0015	0.0014
4 W	0.0012	0.0011	0.0014	0.0030	0.0019	0.0016	0.0016	0.0020	0.0019
5 W	0.0000	0.0000	0.0000	0.0000	0.0000	0.0000	0.0000	0.0000	0.0000
6 W	0.0001	0.0001	0.0001	0.0002	0.0001	0.0001	0.0002	0.0001	0.0001
7 W	0.0010	0.0010	0.0012	0.0022	0.0016	0.0014	0.0013	0.0017	0.0013
8 W	0.0000	0.0000	0.0000	0.0000	0.0000	0.0000	0.0000	0.0000	0.0000
9 W	0.0014	0.0001	0.0001	0.0006	0.0001	0.0001	0.0002	0.0001	0.0170
10 W	0.0000	0.0000	0.0000	0.0000	0.0000	0.0000	0.0000	0.0000	0.0000
11 W	0.0002	0.0004	0.0001	0.0002	0.0021	0.0001	0.0001	0.0001	0.0001
12 W	0.0008	0.0008	0.0008	0.0017	0.0021	0.0011	0.0010	0.0014	0.0010
13 W	0.0002	0.0002	0.0002	0.0004	0.0003	0.0027	0.0002	0.0003	0.0002
14 W	0.0004	0.0004	0.0004	0.0006	0.0004	0.0004	0.0004	0.0005	0.0004
15 W	0.0000	0.0000	0.0000	0.0000	0.0000	0.0000	0.0001	0.0000	0.0000
16 W	0.0000	0.0000	0.0000	0.0000	0.0000	0.0000	0.0099	0.0000	0.0000
17 W	0.0000	0.0000	0.0000	0.0001	0.0001	0.0000	0.0001	0.0001	0.0000
18 W	0.0000	0.0000	0.0000	0.0000	0.0000	0.0000	0.0001	0.0000	0.0001
19 W	0.0000	0.0000	0.0000	0.0017	0.0000	0.0002	0.0000	0.0000	0.0000
20 W	0.0000	0.0000	0.0003	0.0001	0.0000	0.0000	0.0004	0.0000	0.0000
21 W	0.0000	0.0000	0.0000	0.0000	0.0000	0.0000	0.0000	0.0000	0.0000
22 W	0.0002	0.0002	0.0002	0.0008	0.0003	0.0002	0.0002	0.0003	0.0002
23 W	0.0003	0.0003	0.0003	0.0022	0.0005	0.0005	0.0004	0.0008	0.0005
24 W	0.0083	0.0077	0.0096	0.0144	0.0130	0.0110	0.0099	0.0138	0.0088
25 W	0.0030	0.0027	0.0034	0.0107	0.0048	0.0041	0.0043	0.0050	0.0067
26 W	0.0003	0.0003	0.0004	0.0012	0.0005	0.0004	0.0005	0.0005	0.0008

Please refer to pages 124 and 133 for the corresponding columns for the other two regions.

19 M	20 M	21 M	22 M	23 M	24 M	25 M	26 M
0.0035	0.0033	0.0033	0.0087	0.0019	0.0035	0.0020	0.2006
0.0007	0.0007	0.0018	0.0008	0.0007	0.0007	0.0008	0.0285
0.0012	0.0011	0.0012	0.0017	0.0006	0.0012	0.0006	0.0674
0.0016	0.0015	0.0016	0.0024	0.0009	0.0016	0.0009	0.0909
0.0000	0.0000	0.0000	0.0001	0.0000	0.0000	0.0000	0.0004
0.0001	0.0001	0.0001	0.0026	0.0001	0.0001	0.0001	0.0037
0.0013	0.0012	0.0013	0.0017	0.0007	0.0014	0.0007	0.0790
0.0000	0.0000	0.0000	0.0001	0.0000	0.0000	0.0000	0.0002
0.0001	0.0001	0.0001	0.0024	0.0008	0.0001	0.0001	0.0029
0.0000	0.0000	0.0000	0.0001	0.0000	0.0000	0.0000	0.0000
0.0002	0.0003	0.0002	0.0001	0.0001	0.0001	0.0001	0.0058
0.0011	0.0010	0.0011	0.0022	0.0006	0.0011	0.0007	0.0624
0.0003	0.0002	0.0003	0.0003	0.0001	0.0003	0.0001	0.0156
0.0015	0.0003	0.0004	0.0016	0.0002	0.0004	0.0018	0.0204
0.0000	0.0000	0.0000	0.0011	0.0000	0.0000	0.0000	0.0000
0.0000	0.0000	0.0000	0.0001	0.0000	0.0000	0.0000	0.0004
0.0001	0.0000	0.0000	0.0002	0.0002	0.0001	0.0001	0.0026
0.0013	0.0052	0.0013	0.0010	0.0000	0.0000	0.0000	0.0002
0.0000	0.0000	0.0000	0.0003	0.0000	0.0000	0.0000	0.0016
0.0006	0.0000	0.0000	0.0008	0.0000	0.0000	0.0000	0.0011
0.0000	0.0000	0.0000	0.0002	0.0000	0.0000	0.0001	0.0003
0.0002	0.0002	0.0003	0.0172	0.0001	0.0002	0.0001	0.0128
0.0004	0.0004	0.0004	0.0013	0.0002	0.0004	0.0002	0.0211
0.0103	0.0097	0.0100	0.0132	0.0059	0.0116	0.0057	0.6472
0.0040	0.0037	0.0038	0.0102	0.0021	0.0038	0.0023	0.2132
0.0004	0.0004	0.0004	0.0009	0.0002	0.0004	0.0002	0.0223

Please refer to pages 125 and 134 for the corresponding columns for the other two regions.

TABLE A-3 (*Cont.*)

By Sector Number with Regional Suffix

West Tennessee

	1 W	2 W	3 W	4 W	5 W	6 W	7 W	8 W	9 W
1 W	1.0419	0.0410	0.0175	0.0115	0.1758	0.6619	0.0389	0.0237	0.0224
2 W	0.0002	1.0002	0.0001	0.0001	0.0004	0.0003	0.0004	0.0002	0.0001
3 W	0.0241	0.0268	1.0306	0.0075	0.0178	0.0316	0.6881	0.0106	0.0145
4 W	0.0322	0.0345	0.3845	1.0098	0.0231	0.0444	0.9367	0.1216	0.0013
5 W	0.0002	0.0002	0.0001	0.0001	1.0002	0.0452	0.0002	0.0001	0.0188
6 W	0.0025	0.0024	0.0016	0.0007	0.0017	1.2994	0.0026	0.0014	0.0001
7 W	0.0141	0.0153	0.0060	0.0043	0.0102	0.0183	1.0141	0.0058	0.0083
8 W	0.0002	0.0002	0.0000	0.0000	0.0001	0.0002	0.0002	1.0005	0.0001
9 W	0.0003	0.0003	0.0001	0.0001	0.0003	0.0073	0.0051	0.0001	1.0047
10 W	0.0000	0.0000	0.0000	0.0000	0.0000	0.0000	0.0000	0.0000	0.0000
11 W	0.0008	0.0007	0.0003	0.0002	0.0005	0.0015	0.0072	0.0036	0.0004
12 W	0.0156	0.0088	0.0035	0.0025	0.0070	0.0155	0.0082	0.0034	0.0048
13 W	0.0001	0.0001	0.0004	0.0000	0.0001	0.0004	0.0017	0.0000	0.0000
14 W	0.0012	0.0010	0.0005	0.0003	0.0007	0.0029	0.0015	0.0005	0.0033
15 W	0.0000	0.0000	0.0000	0.0000	0.0000	0.0014	0.0000	0.0000	0.0000
16 W	0.0000	0.0000	0.0000	0.0000	0.0000	0.0000	0.0000	0.0000	0.0000
17 W	0.0001	0.0002	0.0001	0.0000	0.0006	0.0495	0.0002	0.0001	0.0001
18 W	0.0000	0.0000	0.0000	0.0000	0.0000	0.0012	0.0000	0.0000	0.0002
19 W	0.0001	0.0001	0.0001	0.0000	0.0001	0.0411	0.0002	0.0001	0.0001
20 W	0.0002	0.0002	0.0001	0.0000	0.0002	0.0026	0.0002	0.0001	0.0001
21 W	0.0000	0.0000	0.0000	0.0000	0.0000	0.0016	0.0000	0.0000	0.0000
22 W	0.0046	0.0029	0.0011	0.0008	0.0023	0.0145	0.0026	0.0011	0.0015
23 W	0.0074	0.0095	0.0029	0.0014	0.0202	0.0245	0.0193	0.0139	0.0098
24 W	0.0216	0.0229	0.0131	0.0064	0.0177	0.0399	0.0253	0.0094	0.0208
25 W	0.2162	0.2082	0.1503	0.0627	0.1425	0.3491	0.2400	0.1273	0.1141
26 W	0.0218	0.0247	0.0097	0.0069	0.0163	0.0289	0.0226	0.0094	0.0134

Please refer to pages 126 and 135 for the corresponding columns for the other two regions.

10 W	11 W	12 W	13 W	14 W	15 W	16 W	17 W	18 W
0.0195	0.0265	0.0352	0.1238	0.0874	0.0081	0.0132	0.0374	0.0479
0.0001	0.0007	0.0002	0.0006	0.0002	0.0001	0.0001	0.0004	0.0009
0.0120	0.0174	0.0226	0.0207	0.0187	0.0053	0.0087	0.0192	0.0103
0.0011	0.0015	0.0023	0.0020	0.0242	0.0068	0.0112	0.0247	0.0133
0.0155	0.0224	0.0302	0.0272	0.0001	0.0000	0.0001	0.0539	0.0001
0.0001	0.0001	0.0002	0.0001	0.0017	0.0005	0.0008	0.0017	0.0009
0.0068	0.0099	0.0128	0.0118	0.0107	0.0030	0.0049	0.0110	0.0059
0.0001	0.0001	0.0001	0.0014	0.0001	0.0000	0.0001	0.0001	0.0000
0.0116	0.0002	0.0002	0.0003	0.0002	0.0001	0.0001	0.0002	0.0066
1.0000	0.0000	0.0000	0.0000	0.0000	0.0000	0.0000	0.0000	0.0000
0.0154	1.0416	0.0022	0.0162	0.0009	0.0001	0.0002	0.0005	0.0003
0.0039	0.0057	1.0074	0.0075	0.0295	0.0017	0.0028	0.0064	0.0036
0.0002	0.0001	0.0001	1.0007	0.0001	0.0002	0.0000	0.0001	0.0008
0.0005	0.0009	0.0009	0.0017	1.0014	0.0002	0.0003	0.0008	0.0004
0.0000	0.0000	0.0000	0.0000	0.0000	1.0000	0.0000	0.0000	0.0000
0.0000	0.0000	0.0000	0.0000	0.0000	0.0000	1.0050	0.0000	0.0000
0.0001	0.0001	0.0001	0.0001	0.0001	0.0000	0.0000	1.0002	0.0001
0.0000	0.0000	0.0001	0.0016	0.0000	0.0000	0.0000	0.0000	1.0000
0.0001	0.0001	0.0001	0.0874	0.0001	0.0000	0.0000	0.0001	0.0001
0.0001	0.0001	0.0072	0.0009	0.0003	0.0000	0.0000	0.0001	0.0001
0.0000	0.0000	0.0000	0.0000	0.0000	0.0000	0.0000	0.0000	0.0000
0.0013	0.0018	0.0024	0.0031	0.0021	0.0006	0.0009	0.0021	0.0012
0.0114	0.0155	0.0191	0.0462	0.0292	0.0096	0.0060	0.0153	0.0146
0.0103	0.0148	0.0194	0.0179	0.0160	0.0045	0.0074	0.0177	0.0089
0.0945	0.1349	0.2078	0.1707	0.1486	0.0412	0.0681	0.1487	0.0811
0.0111	0.0160	0.0208	0.0191	0.0172	0.0049	0.0080	0.0176	0.0094

Please refer to pages 127 and 136 for the corresponding columns for the other two regions.

TABLE A-3 (*Cont.*)

By Sector Number with Regional Suffix

	19 W	20 W	21 W	22 W	23 W	24 W	25 W	26 W
1 W	0.0399	0.1141	0.0147	0.2283	0.0181	0.0396	0.0316	1.8802
2 W	0.0002	0.0005	0.0002	0.0003	0.0002	0.0003	0.0001	0.0079
3 W	0.0110	0.0658	0.0079	0.0207	0.0119	0.0257	0.0067	1.2345
4 W	0.0143	0.0849	0.0102	0.0313	0.0153	0.0333	0.0439	1.5894
5 W	0.0001	0.0004	0.0001	0.0017	0.0001	0.0003	0.0009	0.0082
6 W	0.0014	0.0058	0.0007	0.0447	0.0011	0.0026	0.0109	0.1074
7 W	0.0063	0.0374	0.0045	0.0119	0.0067	0.0147	0.0038	0.7022
8 W	0.0001	0.0004	0.0001	0.0018	0.0001	0.0002	0.0000	0.0081
9 W	0.0003	0.0011	0.0002	0.0127	0.0008	0.0006	0.0001	0.0116
10 W	0.0000	0.0000	0.0000	0.0001	0.0000	0.0000	0.0000	0.0000
11 W	0.0085	0.0017	0.0009	0.0038	0.0003	0.0007	0.0002	0.0315
12 W	0.0038	0.0216	0.0026	0.0403	0.0039	0.0085	0.0032	0.4027
13 W	0.0016	0.0003	0.0012	0.0006	0.0000	0.0001	0.0001	0.0038
14 W	0.0024	0.0024	0.0004	0.0031	0.0004	0.0010	0.0022	0.0441
15 W	0.0000	0.0000	0.0000	0.0022	0.0000	0.0000	0.0000	0.0004
16 W	0.0000	0.0000	0.0000	0.0000	0.0000	0.0000	0.0000	0.0003
17 W	0.0002	0.0003	0.0001	0.0019	0.0001	0.0017	0.0005	0.0061
18 W	0.0175	0.0103	0.0168	0.0070	0.0000	0.0000	0.0000	0.0011
19 W	1.0002	0.0002	0.0633	0.0053	0.0000	0.0001	0.0004	0.0043
20 W	0.0085	1.0004	0.0006	0.0094	0.0001	0.0003	0.0004	0.0076
21 W	0.0000	0.0000	1.0005	0.0003	0.0000	0.0000	0.0000	0.0006
22 W	0.0013	0.0070	0.0009	1.0097	0.0013	0.0030	0.0008	0.1309
23 W	0.0127	0.0424	0.0235	0.0430	1.0068	0.0217	0.0148	0.1953
24 W	0.0095	0.0581	0.0102	0.0888	0.0130	1.0377	0.0077	1.0449
25 W	0.0908	0.5172	0.0628	0.2893	0.0943	0.2060	1.0775	0.5963
26 W	0.0101	0.0607	0.0072	0.0190	0.0109	0.0236	0.0062	1.1393

Please refer to pages 128 and 137 for the corresponding columns for the other two regions.

Appendix B

The Form of Interview Questionnaires Used for Manufacturing Firms

Identification Number

The University of Tennessee
Regional Development Program
Tennessee Interindustry Study
March-June 1965

Form M

1965 SURVEY OF TENNESSEE INTERINDUSTRY TRANSACTIONS
(#65-3-6)

1. Date of interview ______________ ______________ ______________
Month Day Year

2. How many manufacturing establishments does your firm operate in Tennessee? ____________________ .

2a. Indicate in Column 2a below the location of manufacturing establishments operated by your firm in Tennessee.

2b. If more than one manufacturing establishment is operated in any locality, indicate the number of establishments at that location in Column 2b.

(PLEASE REFER TO ATTACHED MAP.) NOTE THAT FOR THE PURPOSES OF THIS STUDY WE HAVE DIVIDED THE STATE OF TENNESSEE INTO THREE REGIONS. IF POSSIBLE PLEASE REPORT ON THIS FORM THE ACTIVITIES OF ALL ESTABLISHMENTS OPERATED BY YOUR FIRM IN THE REGION (I, II, OR III*) IN WHICH THIS INTERVIEW IS TAKING PLACE. IF YOU CANNOT REPORT FOR ALL ESTABLISHMENTS OF YOUR FIRM IN THIS REGION, PLEASE REPORT FOR AS MANY AS POSSIBLE. DO NOT REPORT FOR ACTIVITIES OF ESTABLISHMENTS LOCATED IN THE OTHER TWO REGIONS.

2c. Place a check mark in Column 2c to indicate those establishments which are covered in this report.

2a Location (City or Town)	2b Number of Establishments at this Location	2c Check Establishments Reported on in this Form

*E, M, and W have been substituted in the text for I, II, and III.

SCHEDULE A: PRODUCTS SOLD DURING 1964 BY MANUFACTURING ESTABLISHMENTS IN TENNESSEE COVERED BY THIS REPORT

A1. List the major groups of products produced by the establishments for which you are reporting.

____

____

A2. During 1964, did you sell any of these products to wholesalers, other middlemen, or retailers?

( ) Yes. Approximately what percentage of your total calendar year 1964 sales* went into these distribution channels? ______%

( ) No. Go to Question A3.

*FOR THIS AND ALL REMAINING QUESTIONS, PLEASE THINK IN TERMS OF NET SALES (SALES F.O.B. PLANT). IF YOU USE A DELIVERED PRICING SYSTEM, PLEASE THINK IN TERMS OF YOUR SALES NET OF TRANSPORTATION AND DELIVERY CHARGES.

IMPORTANT

IF A PORTION OF YOUR SALES WENT TO WHOLESALERS, OTHER MIDDLEMEN, AND/OR RETAILERS, PLEASE NOTE THE FOLLOWING INSTRUCTION WHICH APPLIES TO THE COMPLETION OF THE REMAINDER OF SCHEDULE A. IF YOU SOLD TO WHOLESALERS, OTHER MIDDLEMEN, AND/OR RETAILERS FOR RESALE, DISREGARD THIS FACT AND INDICATE WHERE THEY RESOLD YOUR PRODUCTS. THUS, IF A PORTION OF YOUR OUTPUT WAS SOLD TO A WHOLESALER WHO THEN RESOLD IT TO A FIRM IN BUILDING CONSTRUCTION, PLEASE INDICATE THAT THIS PORTION OF YOUR SALES WENT TO BUILDING CONSTRUCTION AND IGNORE THE DISTRIBUTION CHANNELS THROUGH WHICH IT PASSED. MAKE A SIMILAR ADJUSTMENT REGARDING THE GEOGRAPHIC DESTINATION OF YOUR PRODUCT. BE SURE TO DISTRIBUTE YOUR *TOTAL NET SALES* AND NOT JUST YOUR SALES TO WHOLESALERS AND RETAILERS.

A3. Thinking of only those establishments covered in this report, please consider the net sales during the calendar year 1964 as going to two types of customers:

(i) Those located INSIDE Tennessee, including sales to TVA in Tennessee, plus sales to state and local governments.

(ii) Those located OUTSIDE Tennessee plus all sales to the federal government, including Oak Ridge National Laboratory (omit sales to TVA in Tennessee).

First, allocate your net sales on a percent basis between these two groups.

(A3a) Percent sold INSIDE Tennessee . . . . ______%

(A3b) Percent sold OUTSIDE plus federal government · ______%

Total Net Sales · · · · · · · · 100 %

A4. Taking the "net sales OUTSIDE Tennessee plus federal government," how would you distribute a typical dollar of such sales among the following groups?

(A4a) sales to federal government . . . . . ____________%

(A4b) sales to the rest of the U. S. . . . . . ____________%

(A4c) sales to foreign countries . . . . . ____________%

Total net sales OUTSIDE Tennessee plus federal government . . . . . ____100____%

A5. On the following page are various industrial groupings. We have indicated the corresponding government standard industrial classifications (SIC) for each of our groups.

(A5a) Consider your "net sales INSIDE Tennessee" only—please distribute a typical dollar of these sales according to the appropriate industrial classifications. If you sell to wholesalers and retailers for *resale,* remember to indicate the sectors to which *they resold* your products. *In other words, please distribute your sales to Tennessee consumers according to their type of business.* Please enter the above information under column heading A5a.

THE PERCENTAGE ENTERED IN THIS COLUMN SHOULD TOTAL 100%.

(A5b) For each entry in Column A5a, what percentage of these sales were of a noncapital* nature? Enter these percentages in Column A5b.

(A5c) We are now concerned with the geographic distribution of these noncapital goods. (REFER TO MAP FOR REGIONAL BOUNDARY LINES.) For each entry in Column A5b please distribute the percentage of *noncapital* goods according to the three geographic regions. These percentages should appear in Column A5c. For each entry in Column A5c, the percentage distribution of *noncapital* goods to the three regions should total 100%.

(A5d) Here we are concerned with the geographic distribution of capital goods. (REFER AGAIN TO MAP FOR REGIONAL BOUNDARY LINES.) For each entry in Column A5b please consider capital goods that are equivalent to (100%—A5b) and distribute the percentage of *capital goods* according to the three geographic regions. These percentages should appear in Column A5d. For each entry in Column A5d, the percentage distribution of *capital goods* to the three regions should total 100%.

NOTE: THE HOUSEHOLD SECTOR (26) CONSISTS OF THOSE INDIVIDUALS AND FAMILIES WHO PURCHASE GOODS AND SERVICES FOR THEIR OWN USE. WHEN INDIVIDUALS AND FAMILIES (e.g., THE SELF-EMPLOYED) MAKE PURCHASES FOR BUSINESS PURPOSES, SUCH SALES SHOULD BE ALLOCATED TO THE APPROPRIATE INDUSTRIAL SECTORS.

*NONCAPITAL GOODS ARE DEFINED AS GOODS WHICH ARE ORDINARILY COMPLETELY USED UP DURING THE YEAR TO PRODUCE OTHER PRODUCTS (BY BUYING FIRMS) OR GOODS COMPLETELY CONSUMED DURING THE YEAR BY HOUSEHOLDS AND STATE AND LOCAL GOVERNMENTS. THE BULK OF AGRICULTURAL COMMODITIES BELONG TO THIS GROUP. HOWEVER, MOTORS SOLD TO THE TRACTOR INDUSTRY, FOR EXAMPLE, ARE NONCAPITAL GOODS ONLY IF THE TRACTOR INDUSTRY USED THE MOTORS AS ENGINES IN THE TRACTORS PRODUCED FOR SALE. THE POSSIBLE USE OF THE PRODUCT BY BUYERS IS MORE IMPORTANT THAN THE NATURE OF THE PRODUCT. SOME ADDITIONAL EXAMPLES SHOULD HELP ILLUSTRATE THIS PRINCIPLE:

(i) A manufacturer of plastic handles and knobs sells these items to stove manufacturers who install these on stoves produced by them for sale. This is a *noncapital* transaction between the manufacturer of plastic handles and the stove manufacturer.

(ii) A marble producer sells marble to a contractor who installs this as sills in a house erected for sale. This is a *noncapital* transaction between the marble producer and the contractor.

(iii) The contractor sells a house (or a stove manufacturer, in example i sells) to households. This is a *capital* transaction between the contractor and the household sector.

(iv) Plastic garbage bags (after passing through distribution channels) are sold to households. This is a *noncapital* transaction between the plastic bag producer and the household sector.

Sector No.	SIC Code		Column A5a Percent of Net Sales Inside Tennessee (Total = 100%)	Column A5b Sales of a Noncapital Nature (Percent of A5a)	Column A5c Allocate 100% of Noncapital (A5b) by Region I	II	III	Column A5d Allocate 100% of Capital (100%–A5b) by Region I	II	III
1	50 thru 59	Retail and wholesale (show only the am't purchased for their own use, e.g. operating supplies. For the am't purchased for resale see the statement following A5)								
FD sec		State and local gov'ts								
2		Tenn. Valley Authority								
26		Household								
3		Livestock and its products								
4		Crops and misc. agri.								
5	10, 12 thru 14	Metal mining; bituminous coal; crude petroleum; natural gas; mining and quarrying of nonmetallic minerals								
6	15 thru 17	Building and other construction, and associated contractors								
7	20 & 21	Food and tobacco products								
8	22 & 23	Textile mill products; apparel and other finished products from fabrics								
9	24	Lumber and other products								
10	25	Furniture and fixtures								
11	26	Paper and allied products								
12	27	Printing and publishing								
13	281	Industrial inorganic and organic chemicals								

Sector No.	SIC Code		Column A5a Percent of Net Sales Inside Tennessee (Total = 100%)	Column A5b Sales of a Noncapital Nature (Percent of A5a)	Column A5c Allocate 100% of Noncapital (A5b) by Region I	II	III	Column A5d Allocate 100% of Capital (100%–A5b) by Region I	II	III
14	282 thru 289	Plastic materials, synthetic resins, synthetic rubber, synthetic man-made fibers								
15	30	Rubber and misc. plastics								
16	31	Leather and its products								
17	32	Stone, clay, and glass								
18	33	Primary metal industries								
19	34	Fabricated metal products								
20	35	Machinery except electrical								
21	36	Electrical machinery								
22	37 thru 39, 29, 19	Transportation equip., professional science and control insts., photographic and optical goods—watches and clocks, misc. manufacturing								
23	40 thru 48	Transportation and communications								
24	60 thru 67	Finance, insurance and real estate								
25	49, 70 thru 89	Agr. services; electric, gas, and sanitary services; business and personal services								
		TOTAL	100%							

SCHEDULE B: INCOME ORIGINATING AND NUMBER OF EMPLOYEES DURING 1964

B1. What is the headquarters location of this firm?

____________________, ______________________________

(City) (State)

(B1a) *For the establishments covered in this report,* what was the total sum of wages,* salaries,* and rent paid to individuals during the calendar year 1964?

$ __________

(B1b) Of this total, what percentage was paid to Tennesseans? (People living or residing in Tennessee.)

**NOTE:* WAGES AND SALARIES INCLUDE BONUS PAYMENTS, COMMISSIONS, SICK PAY, OVERTIME AND VACATION PAY, ETC. FOR *ALL* EMPLOYEES. *DO NOT* DEDUCT EMPLOYEE CONTRIBUTIONS SUCH AS UNION DUES, INSURANCE PAYMENTS, EMPLOYEE SOCIAL SECURITY TAX PAYMENTS, ETC., WHICH WERE WITHHELD FROM YOUR EMPLOYEE'S PAY.

What is the form of organization of this firm?

(B1c) ( ) Corporation. Skip to Question B2.

(B1d) ( ) Other (SPECIFY) ____________________

(B1e) What was the net profit of this *firm* (before federal income taxes) during the calendar year 1964?

$ __________

B2. What was your average employment in 1964 for the establishments covered in this report?

Full time __________ Part time __________

Full-time equivalent __________ (including overtime)

SCHEDULE C: SALES AND ASSETS

C1. What were your total calendar year 1964 sales F.O.B. plant (net sales) for the establishments covered in this report? (If you use a delivered pricing system, please indicate your sales net of transportation and delivery charges.)

$ __________

C2. Are all the establishments operated by your firm in the region in which this interview is taking place covered in this report?

( ) Yes

( ) No. Please estimate the total net sales of all establishments operated by your firm in the region in which this interview is taking place.

$ ____________

C3. Are all establishments operated by your firm in Tennessee covered in this report?

( ) Yes

( ) No. Please estimate the total net sales of *all* establishments operated by your firm in Tennessee.

$ ____________

C4. Again considering only those establishments located in this report—what was the total inventory of finished goods—

(C4a) As of December 31, 1964: $ ____________

(C4b) As of January 1, 1964: $ ____________

(If records are maintained on a fiscal-year basis, please provide estimates from trial balances.)

What was the total depreciation charge for 1964 as reported on your profit and loss statement? (For the establishments covered in this report.)

(C4c) $ ____________

PLEASE REPORT THE FOLLOWING INFORMATION ON A CORPORATION OR COMPANY RATHER THAN ESTABLISHMENT BASIS.

C5. What was the value of total assets and liabilities of your firm as reported on your balance sheet at the end of 1964?

(C5a) Total assets at the end of 1964 . . . . . . $______

(C5b) Total liabilities at the end of 1964 . . . . $______

Respondent ______________________ Title ____________

Company ____

Address ____

Reporter ______________ Office ____________ Date ________

Bibliography

Artle, Roland. *Studies in the Structure of the Stockholm Economy.* Stockholm: Business Research Institute, Stockholm School of Economics, 1959.

Barna, Tibor, ed. *Structural Interdependence and Economic Development.* New York: St. Martin's Press, 1963.

Bramhall, David F. "Markets for California's Products: Analysis of the Sources of Demand." *Journal of Regional Science* 4 (September 1962). 102-104

Carden, John G. D., and F. B. Whittington, Jr. *Studies in the Economic Structure of the State of Mississippi.* Vols. 1 and 2. Jackson: Mississippi Industrial and Technological Research Commission, 1964.

Chenery, Hollis B., Paul G. Clark, and Vera Cao-Pinna. *The Structure and Growth of the Italian Economy.* Rome: United States Mutual Security Agency, 1953.

Dorfman, Robert, Paul A. Samuelson, and Robert M. Solow. *Linear Programming and Economic Analysis.* New York: McGraw-Hill, 1960.

Fishel, W. L., Irving Dubov, D. D. Rohdy, and R. G. Stout. *Hog and Pork Movements in the Southeast.* Southern Cooperative Series Bulletin No. 83. January 1963.

Fuller, C. E., and J. K. Robertson. *The Sources and Disposition of Grain in Tennessee.* Knoxville: University of Tennessee Agricultural Experiment Station, 1964.

Gosh, A. *Experiments with Input-Output Models, An Application to the Economy of the United Kingdom, 1948-1955.* Cambridge: Cambridge University Press, 1964.

Hansen, W. Lee, R. Thayne Robson, and Charles M. Tiebout. *Markets for California Products.* Sacramento: State of California Development Agency, 1961.

Hansen, W. Lee, and Charles M. Tiebout. "An Intersectoral Flows Analysis of the California Economy." *Review of Economics and Statistics* 45 (November 1963): 409-418.

Henderson, James M., and others. *Four Papers on Methodology.* Technical Paper No. 1. Minneapolis: University of Minnesota, 1961.

Hirsch, Werner Z. "Interindustry Relations of a Metropolitan Area." *Review of Economics and Statistics* 41 (August 1959): 360-369.

Isard, Walter. "Interregional and Regional Input-Output Analysis: A Model of Space Economy." *Review of Economics and Statistics* 33 (November 1951): 318-328.

Isard, Walter, and Robert E. Kuenne. "The Impact of Steel Upon the Greater New York-Philadelphia Industrial Region." *Review of Economics and Statistics* 35 (November 1953): 289-301.

Kuenne, Robert E. *The Theory of General Economic Equilibrium.* Princeton, N.J.: Princeton University Press, 1963.

Lee, Tong Hun, David P. Lewis, and John R. Moore. "Multiregion Intersectoral Flow Analysis." *Journal of Regional Science* 11 (April 1971): 49-56.

Leontief, Wassily. *The Structure of the American Economy, 1919-1939.* New York: Oxford University Press, 1951.

Leontief, Wassily, and others. *Studies in the Structure of the American Economy.* New York: Oxford University Press, 1953.

Martin, William E., and Harold O. Carter. *A California Interindustry Analysis Emphasizing Agriculture, Part I: The Input-Output Models and Results.* Giannini Foundation Report No. 250. Davis: California Agricultural Experiment Station, 1962.

Meyer, John R. "Regional Economics: A Survey." *American Economic Review* 53 (March 1963): 19-54.

Miernyk, William H. *The Elements of Input-Output Analysis.* New York: Random House, 1965.

Miller, Ronald E. "The Impact of the Aluminum Industry on the Pacific Northwest: A Regional Input-Output Analysis." *Review of Economics and Statistics* 39 (May 1957): 200-209.

——. "Interregional Feedback Effects in Input-Output Models: Some Preliminary Results." *Papers and Proceedings of the Regional Science Association* 17 (1966): 105-125.

Moore, Frederick T., and James W. Petersen. "Regional Analysis: An Interindustry Model of Utah." *Review of Economics and Statistics* 37 (November 1955): 368-380.

Moses, L. H. "Interregional Input-Output Analysis." *American Economic Review* 45 (December 1955): 803-832.

Peterson, Richard S., and Charles M. Tiebout. "Measuring Regional Defense-Space Expenditures." *Review of Economics and Statistics* 46 (November 1964): 421-428.

Riefler, Roger, and Charles M. Tiebout. "Interregional Input-Output: An Empirical California-Washington Model." *Journal of Regional Science* 10 (August 1970): 135-152.

Romans, J. Thomas. *Capital Exports and Growth among U.S. Regions.* Middletown, Conn.: Wesleyan University Press, 1965.

Simpson, David, and Jinkichi Tsukui. "The Fundamental Structure of Input-Output Tables, an International Comparison." *Review of Economics and Statistics* 47 (November 1965): 434-461.

Smith, Harold T. *The Kalamazoo County Economy.* Kalamazoo, Mich.: W. E. Upjohn Institute for Employment Research, 1960.

State of Tennessee. *Tennessee Code Annotated.* Vol. 2. Indianapolis: Bobbs-Merrill, 1955.

Stone, Richard. *Input-Output and National Accounts.* Paris: Organization for European Economic Co-operation, 1961.

Stout, Roy G., J. C. Purcell, and W. L. Fishel. *Marketing, Slaughter, and Consumption of Livestock and Meats in the South.* Southern Cooperative Series Bulletin No. 66. 1961.

Su, Teddy T. "A Note on Regional Input-Output Models." *Southern Economic Journal* 36 (January 1970): 325-327.

Tennessee Crop Reporting Service. *Annual Report.* Nashville: Tennessee Crop Reporting Service, 1964.

Tiebout, Charles M. "Input-Output and the Firm: A Technique for Using National and Regional Tables." *Review of Economics and Statistics* 49 (May 1967): 260-262.

Index

Agricultural sectors, 32-33, 41-42, 49, 51, 76-77, 80, 82-83, 103. *See also* Crops; Livestock
Apparel. *See* Textiles and apparel
Artle, Roland, 4n, 159

Balance of payments accounts, 1-2
Balanced regional model, 8
Barna, Tibor, 11n, 159
Bloc-triangularity, 59-64, 68n, 104
Bramhall, David F., 26, 29n, 159
Bureau of Labor Statistics, 36
Business investment as final demand, 35, 56-57, 66, 88-93, 102

California, 2, 4, 9-10, 19, 23, 36, 43, 58-64, 66, 67n
Cao-Pinna, Vera, 11n, 159
Carden, John G. D., 4n, 11n, 159
Carter, Harold O., 4n, 5n, 160
Chemicals. *See* Industrial inorganic and organic chemicals
Chenery, Hollis B., 9, 11n, 159
Clark, Paul G., 11n, 159
Clay. *See* Stone, clay, and glass
Coefficients
—input-output, 14
—sales-flow, 14-15, 25-28, 45, 59, 62-64
—technical, 9, 58, 66
—trade, 9, 105-6
Communications. *See* Transportation and communications
Construction, 33, 48, 50, 53-54, 65, 72-74, 77-84, 102
Crops, 32, 48-51, 72-74, 76, 82-83

Dorfman, Robert, 28n, 159
Dubov, Irving, 42n, 159

Economic development, 102-4
Economic planning, 2-4, 22, 55, 64-66, 70, 87, 94, 98-99, 103
Electrical machinery and equipment, 48, 72-74
Employment estimates, 36-37, 44-45, 106
—agricultural sectors, 36
—Bureau of Labor Statistics, 36
—household, 37
—Tennessee Department of Employment Security, 36
Exports to balance of U.S. as final demand, 35-36, 44, 56-57, 66, 89-93, 102
Exports to balance of world as final demand, 35-36, 56-57, 66, 89-93, 102

Fabricated metals, 48, 72-74, 83
Federal government expenditure as final demand, 35-36, 56-57, 66, 89-93, 102
Feedback. *See* Interregional feedback
Final demand sectors, 33, 35-36, 56-58, 66, 69-71, 81, 87-94, 101-5
—business investment, 35, 56-57, 66, 88-93, 102
—exports to balance of U.S., 35-36, 44, 56-57, 66, 89-93, 102

Final demand sectors (*cont.*)
—exports to balance of world, 35-36, 56-57, 66, 89-93, 102
—Federal government expenditures, 35-36, 50-51, 56-57, 89-94
—household capital, 35, 56-57, 88-93
—household noncapital, 35, 37, 39, 56-58, 65-66, 71, 81, 84, 88-93
—state and local government expenditure, 35, 50-51, 56-57, 66, 89-94, 99n, 102-4
Finance, insurance, and real estate, 33, 48, 52, 72-74, 76-77, 82, 84-85
Fishel, W. L., 42n, 159, 161
Food and tobacco products, 32, 44, 48-50, 53-55, 65, 72-74, 76, 78, 80-82, 84
Forward linkages, 3, 27, 55, 106
Fuller, C. E., 42n, 159
Furniture, 48, 72-74

Geographical sectoring, 30-33, 69
Glass. *See* Stone, clay, and glass
Gosh, A., 28n, 159
Gravity flow model, 10

Hansen, W. Lee, 3, 4n, 5n, 10, 11n, 12, 16-19, 23, 28n, 29n, 36, 42n, 43, 56-58, 67n, 159
Hansen-Tiebout model, 3, 13, 16-19, 23, 56-58, 67n
Henderson, James M., 9-10, 11n, 160
Hirsch, Werner Z., 5n, 7, 11n, 160
Household capital as final demand, 35, 56-57, 88-93
Household noncapital as final demand, 35, 37, 39, 56-58, 65-66, 71, 81, 84, 88-93

Imports, 27, 29n, 46-47
Industrial inorganic and organic chemicals, 32, 48, 72-74, 80-83, 104
Industrial sectors. *See* Intermediate sectors
Input-output coefficients, 14
Insurance. *See* Finance, insurance, and real estate
Intermediate sectors, 31-34
—construction, 33, 48, 50, 53-54, 65, 72-74, 77-84, 102
—crops, 32, 48-51, 72-74, 76, 82-83
—electrical machinery and equipment, 48, 72-74
—fabricated metals, 48, 72-74, 83
—finance, insurance, and real estate, 33, 48, 52, 72-74, 76-77, 82, 84-85
—food and tobacco products, 32, 44, 48-50, 53-55, 65, 72-74, 76, 78, 80-82, 84
—furniture, 48, 72-74
—industrial inorganic and organic chemicals, 32, 48, 72-74, 80-83, 104
—leather, 48, 72-74, 81
—livestock, 32, 48-51, 72-74, 76-77, 80-83
—lumber, 48, 72-74
—mining, 33, 48, 52, 72-74, 77, 80-81, 104
—miscellaneous services, 33, 48, 50, 52-54, 65, 72-74, 76-78, 81-82, 84, 102
—nonelectrical machinery, 48, 51-52, 55, 65, 72-74, 82-83, 102

Intermediate sectors (*cont.*)
—paper and allied products, 6-7, 9, 44, 48, 72-74, 76-77, 80, 83, 87, 104
—plastics and synthetics, 32, 48, 72-74, 79, 84
—primary metals, 48, 72-74, 81
—printing and publishing, 44, 48, 72-74
—rubber and miscellaneous plastics, 48, 72-74
—stone, clay, and glass, 44, 48, 72-74, 81, 84
—Tennessee Valley Authority, 7, 13-16, 20-21, 33, 45-46, 48, 51-52, 55, 65, 72-75, 77, 80-81, 84, 87, 97-99, 102-4
—textiles and apparel, 48, 53-54, 65, 72-74, 78-79, 82
—transportation and communications, 33, 39, 48, 52, 72-74
—transportation, instruments, and miscellaneous manufacturing, 32, 48, 51, 55, 65, 72-74, 76, 80, 82-83
—wholesale-retail trade, 13, 33, 48, 50-54, 65, 72-74, 77-79, 81-83, 103
Interregional feedback, 7-8, 23-25, 71, 94-98, 102-3, 105
Interregional models, 2, 4, 6-11, 12, 19-28, 69-99, 101
—feedback, 7-8, 23-25, 71
—Tennessee, 69-99
Isard, Walter, 8-9, 11, 11n, 21, 23-25, 29n, 160
Isard interregional model, 8, 23, 25, 69, 101, 105-6

Kuenne, Robert, 7-9, 11n, 24, 29n, 160

Leather, 48, 72-74, 81
Lee, Tong Hun, 28n, 160
Leontief, Wassily, 1, 4n, 7-11, 26, 28n, 29n, 106, 160
Lewis, David P., 28n, 160
Linear programming model, 107
Linkages, forward, 3, 27, 55, 106
Livestock, 32, 48-51, 72-74, 76-77, 80-83
Lumber, 48, 72-74

Martin, William E., 4n, 5n, 160
Meyer, John R., 30, 42n, 160
Miernyk, William H., 26, 29n, 99n, 160
Miller, Ronald E., 11n, 23-25, 29n, 71, 94-96, 98, 99n, 105, 160
Mining, 33, 48, 52, 72-74, 77, 80-81, 104
Miscellaneous services, 33, 48, 50, 52-54, 65, 72-74, 76-78, 81-82, 84, 102
Money flows accounts, 2
Moore, Frederick T., 4n, 7, 11n, 160
Moore, John R., 28n, 160
Moses, L. H., 5n, 9, 11n, 26, 106, 160
Multipliers
—employment, 15, 20-21, 47-55, 71-87
—final-demand, 16, 23, 55-58, 87-94, 101
—Hansen-Tiebout, 16, 17-19, 23, 56-58, 67n
—intermediate sector, 21, 47-55, 65, 70-87, 98, 102-3

Multipliers (*cont.*)
weighted, 16, 22-23, 48, 53-55, 71-75, 78-80, 84
three region, 71-87
East Tennessee, 72, 76-80
Middle Tennessee, 73, 80-82
West Tennessee, 74, 82-85
—iterative method of calculation, 12, 17-19, 23, 56-58, 67n, 101
—matrix inversion method of calculation, 12, 14, 17-19, 101

National income accounts, 2
Nonelectrical machinery, 48, 51-52, 55, 65, 72-74, 82-83, 102

Overall percentage error, 24, 95-97

Paper and allied products, 6-7, 9, 44, 48, 72-74, 76-77, 80, 83, 87, 100
Petersen, James W., 4n, 7, 11n, 160
Peterson, Richard S., 5n, 19, 29n, 160
Physiocrats, 1
Plastics and synthetics, 32, 48, 72-74, 79, 84
Potential model, 10
Primary metals, 48, 72-74, 81
Printing and publishing, 44, 48, 72-74
Public works programs, 50-51
Purcell, J. C., 42n, 161

Real estate. *See* Finance, insurance, and real estate
Regional models, 2, 4, 6, 8, 11, 12-19, 25-28
Retail. *See* Wholesale-retail trade
Riefler, Roger, 11n, 160
Robertson, J. K., 42n, 159
Robson, R. Thayne, 4n, 5n, 11n, 28n, 29n, 67n, 159
Rohdy, D. D., 42n, 159
Romans, J. Thomas, 99n, 160
Rows-only approach, 3, 5n, 10, 11, 12, 25-28, 99n, 100, 105-7
Rubber and miscellaneous plastics, 48, 72-74

Sales-flow coefficients, 14-15, 25-28
Sales-flow matrix, 13, 26, 28, 37-42, 59, 62-63
—California, triangularized, 63, 104
—Tennessee, triangularized, 62, 104
Sample survey, 37-41
—questionnaire, 149-57
Samuelson, Paul A., 28n, 159
Sectoring
—final demand, 33, 35-36
—geographical, 30-33, 69
—intermediate, 31-34, 69-70
Simpson, David, 43, 58-64, 66, 67n, 102, 104, 160
Smith, Harold T., 5n, 160
Social accounts, 1-2
—balance of payments accounts, 1-2
—interindustry economics, 1
—money flow accounts, 2
—national income accounts, 2
Solow, Robert M., 28n, 159
State and local government expenditures as final demand, 35, 50-51, 56-57, 66, 89-94, 99n, 102-4
Stone, clay, and glass, 44, 48, 72-74, 81, 84
Stone, Richard, 28n, 161
Stout, R. G., 42n, 159, 161
Strout, Alan, 10, 11n, 26, 29n, 106
Su, Teddy T., 11n, 161
Survey questionnaire, 147-57
Synthetics. *See* Plastics

Technical coefficients, 9, 58, 66
Tennessee
—comparison with California, 58-66, 104
—geographical sectoring, 30-33, 69
—interregional model, 2-3, 19-28, 69-99, 101, 106
—statewide flow table, 45, 101, 111-15
—statewide multiplier matrix, 116-19
—statewide regional model, 2-3, 13-19, 25-28, 43-68, 70, 85-87, 101-2
—three region multiplier matrix, 120-46
—triangularized sales-flow matrix, 62
Tennessee Crop Reporting Service, 36-37, 41, 42n
Tennessee Department of Employment Security, 36, 42n
Tennessee Valley Authority, 7, 13-16, 20-21, 33, 45-46, 48, 51-52, 55, 65, 72-75, 77, 80-81, 84, 87, 97-99, 102-4
Textiles and apparel, 48, 53-54, 65, 72-74, 78-79, 82
Tiebout, Charles M., 3, 4n, 5n, 10, 11n, 12, 16-19, 23, 28n, 29n, 36, 42n, 43, 56-58, 67n, 159, 160, 161
Trade coefficients, 9, 105-6
Transportation and communications, 33, 39, 48, 52, 72-74
Transportation, instruments, and miscellaneous manufacturing, 32, 48, 51, 55, 65, 72-74, 76, 80, 82-83
Triangularization, 59-64, 68n
Tsuki, Jinkichi, 43, 58-64, 66, 67n, 68n, 102, 104, 160

Walras, Leon, 1
Weighted employment multiplier, 16, 53-55, 71-75, 78, 84
Whittington, F. B., 4n, 11n, 159
Wholesale-retail trade, 13, 33, 48, 50-54, 65, 72-74, 77-79, 81-83, 103